IN SEARCH OF BLANDINGS

N·T·P·Murphy

INTRODUCTION BY TOM SHARPE

IN SEARCH OF BLANDINGS

IN SEARCH OF
BLANDINGS

N. T. P. MURPHY

With a Preface by
TOM SHARPE

Salem House Publishers
Topsfield, Massachusetts

First published in the United States by Salem House Publishers, 1986
462 Boston Street, Topsfield, MA 01983

Library of Congress Catalog Card Number: 86–60718

ISBN: 0 88162 211 7

Printed in Great Britain

To
CHARLOTTE
TIMOTHY
AND HELEN

CONTENTS

᎐᎐᎐

ILLUSTRATIONS

ACKNOWLEDGEMENTS

THIS book could not have been written without the help, time and patience I was afforded by Mrs Nella Wodehouse, Mrs Sheran Hornby, the late Perceval Graves and Mrs Graves, Mr Charles Westbrook, Mrs Isaac and Mr E. W. Isaac, Lady Winter, Mrs Ruth Chambers, Mrs Viola Meakin and Anthony Lejeune.

My thanks are also due to Benny Green, who encouraged me in the venture, Richard Usborne, David Jasen and other Wodehouse enthusiasts. The staffs of the Westminster Reference Libraries and the Ministry of Defence Library were unfailingly helpful and patient with the demands I made upon them.

To my family and friends, and to the residents of the dozens of houses I called at during the last seven years as I worked my way through this book, I express my apologies for the boredom I imposed upon them and thank them for their consideration, courtesy and encouragement.

Chatto and Windus Ltd have kindly given permission for me to use the illustration at Plate 10.

PREFACE
by Tom Sharpe

꧁꧂

THERE is something mysterious about P. G. Wodehouse.
For a man who, from February 1900 when he first
published a story in the *Public School Magazine* until his death
on St Valentine's Day 1975 with the half-completed *Sunset
Over Blandings* beside him, never wrote an unkind or
offensive word, he has aroused an enormous amount of
controversy. Even now the world still seems divided into those
who consider his work a joy to read and his use of words to be
among the finest penned in English this century, and those
others who find his books trivial and without social content,
and in their ignorance believe that he betrayed his country
during the War. The latter charge has been finally and
irrefutably proven false by Ian Sproat in his book *Wodehouse
at War* but the stigma of having written nothing worth reading
still scars his reputation among earnest and otherwise intelligent people. Even Lady Frances Donaldson, commissioned by
his heirs to write the authorized biography, was puzzled by
Evelyn Waugh's unstinted admiration for him and his use of
the term 'The Master' when speaking of Wodehouse. In her
book *Evelyn Waugh* she wrote '. . . I had never been able to
read his [P.G.W.'s] books. I cannot see the point of them,' and
was admonished by Waugh on the grounds that any writer
who could on average produce two or three unique and
original similes per page, was entitled to be called The Master.
Hugh Walpole too was puzzled when Hilaire Belloc declared
in a broadcast that Wodehouse was the best living writer of
English and 'the head of my profession', praise he repeated in
his introduction to *Week End Wodehouse*. 'It seems such an
extraordinary thing to say. The old man's getting very old,'
Walpole commented with monumental insensitivity to Wode-

house himself. And when, in 1939, Oxford University saw fit to award Wodehouse an honorary doctorate for his services to Literature, F. R. Leavis seemed to find the judgement further proof that Oxford was a sink of trivia. Later on Sean O'Casey attempted to insult him by calling him 'English Literature's performing flea', a title Wodehouse cheerfully took for the collection of his letters to his friend, Bill Townend, published in 1953.

But the mystery does not lie simply in the wildly divided opinions of the critics, his fellow writers and the public, or even in the choice of an authorized biographer who had never been able to read his books: it lies in the gulf that seems to separate Wodehouse the comic novelist from any reality in the world he wrote about. Where on earth did he find Ukridge, the galaxy of Bertie Wooster's aunts, Lord Emsworth and Galahad; or did he create unique and wonderful characters from no other source than his own imagination? Even his greatest defenders have always supposed the latter to be the case, and Evelyn Waugh, in an article on Plum's approaching eightieth birthday, wrote the famous lines, 'Mr Wodehouse's idyllic world can never stale . . . He has made a world for us to live in and delight in,' only to add, 'Mr Wodehouse's characters are not, as has been fatuously suggested, survivals of the Edwardian age. They are creatures of pure fancy.' Again, the world's greatest authority on Wodehouse, Richard Usborne, whose *Wodehouse at Work to the End* is without doubt the best analysis of the novels and stories and of the literary influences in Plum's youth, has never suggested that realism was his forte. Wodehouse himself denied any such thing. In 1935, writing to Townend, he speaks of his writing '. . . musical comedy without music, and ignoring real life altogether' and, in 1938, '. . . I go off the rails unless I stay all the time in a sort of artificial world of my own creation. A real character in one of my books sticks out like a sore thumb.' No statement could be clearer. Plum's characters were creatures of pure fancy and his 'world' was entirely artificial.

But is that the end of the matter? Norman Murphy clearly thinks not and, even if we ignore the evidence he produces in this book, we know enough about Wodehouse to have doubts. If he invented his characters and the world they inhabit, he was not only the genius of the simile and a superb stylist, he was also a writer with an incredibly fertile imagination. Yet the settings of his stories are clearly limited to places and things with which he was familiar: Shropshire, schools, golf clubs, Hollywood, newspaper offices, theatres, New York, banks and, most of all, country houses. We can check all these against his own experience. Never once did he venture into strange territory or set a story against a background he did not know. His characters are similarly limited and form a small familiar cast of types. Hardly surprising in the light of the number of books and stories he wrote, and certainly no criticism – simply a fact, but one that suggests he drew on what he knew. And his knowledge of the world was circumscribed as much by his own nature as by his habit of working prodigiously hard. One had only to meet him, as I did in 1973, to realize that he was a shy, private and thoroughly decent man who, when he wasn't writing, was thinking about it, and liked nothing better than to talk of plots and sub-plots and the whole craft of which he was The Master. It was his wife, Ethel, who hogged the conversation and drove him off to watch television in the afternoon as imperiously as any of the aunts in his books. It was Ethel (Malcolm Muggeridge described her in his autobiography as 'a mixture of Mistress Quickly and Florence Nightingale, with a touch of Lady Macbeth thrown in') who dominated the house, told the interesting stories and managed everything just as she must have done throughout the sixty years of their marriage. For his part, Plum rose early to do his Swedish exercises, to write and let the dogs out, to read and to go for walks (after lunch) with Guy Bolton before writing still more. I came away from the visit in the certain knowledge that I had met one of the kindest and shyest of men and, in Ethel, one of the most extraordinarily assertive and lively old women – a view for sure shared by the Headmaster of Dulwich, who, rumour has it, had his leg pinched by Ethel when she was well into her nineties.

In the biographies there are further indications that Plum

was exceedingly shy and not at all gregarious. He loathed the social life Ethel led between the Wars and disappeared from parties to go to work on the kitchen table. Even with his great friend, Denis Mackail, with whom he took long walks through the streets of London at night, he was in the habit of suddenly flitting across the road without warning leaving Mackail to realize he was on his own, a disappearing trick so customary it became known to his family as 'the Wodehouse glide'. Again, although he wrote with seeming affection about Clubs, he detested nearly every one he joined, called The Garrick 'The Pesthole' and stayed loyal only to the dullest and quietest where he could work in peace. If that weren't enough to prove his love of privacy, there is the testimony of his adored step-daughter Leonora who, writing in *The Strand* magazine in 1929, told of an occasion when Wodehouse suddenly went from New York to Georgia for no better reason than that he had told a reporter he didn't want to meet that he had to go there. Only Lord Emsworth, of all his characters, would have thought of anything so extreme and, if we want an insight into Wodehouse's true nature, we will find it best in his portrait of that delightfully dotty peer of the realm.

But could Lord Emsworth have written the greatest comic novels of the century? Clearly not, unless, of course, he had Gally at his elbow to supply him with names and anecdotes from his own gay, wild youth. This then is the mystery behind Wodehouse and the one Norman Murphy has solved in this book. Having been privileged to be with him when he discovered the Octagon which figures in *Jeeves and the Impending Doom*, I can vouch for the thoroughness with which he has gone about his research. More weirdly, a casual joke of mine, about a hen run looking like a pig sty, inspired him to unearth the origins of the Empress of Blandings. At the time, I must admit, I had my doubts but, since then, Norman Murphy has dug away at the facts and I am convinced. In short, *In Search Of Blandings* has provided us with a mass of new and fascinating material, far beyond the range of any biography yet written. Best of all, he has done nothing to disturb the mystery of Sir Pelham Grenville Wodehouse's genius, and the 'idyllic world' remains intact.

CHAPTER I

INTRODUCTION

WHEN P. G. Wodehouse died in 1975 we saw the end of a career that had lasted for seventy-three years. He earned a great deal of money, he was knighted and Oxford gave him a doctorate. He made people laugh and produced some of the finest and funniest writing in the language.

He gave interviews with great reluctance and hated public appearances. He was admired by men like Balfour, Asquith, Conan Doyle and Hilaire Belloc; he dined with Birkenhead, Galsworthy and Churchill; but little is known of the way he thought, his interests or his hobbies.

Those who knew him all used the same words – unworldly, straightforward, innocent. He was not an intellectual but it didn't bother him in the slightest. He made up for it by working harder at his writing than his fellows and it was this that won his colleagues' respect. They saw what often escaped his readers, that those whimsical phrases and smooth, intricate plots were not accidental. They were the result of hard work, rewriting, revision, more rewriting and more revision till he achieved the final polished result that so many have tried to imitate.

If Wodehouse was, as so many said, a straightforward man, an honest man, then he had to start somewhere. Tucked away in those splendid plots, sub-plots and counter-plots, hidden by the language and imagery must be a starting point that gave him the idea. There are clues scattered throughout the novels. Some are deliberate references to people and places he knew, some seem to be accidental, almost unconscious, memories of a name or an incident of fifty years before. Butlers are a simple example. In *Over Seventy*, one of the three books of semi-autobiography that Wodehouse wrote, he explains that he wrote about butlers because he knew about butlers.

He describes how he met them as a child when his aunts would pay afternoon calls and the butler would take him away to have his tea in the Servants' Hall. He knew them again as a young man when he had to pay calls in tight choker collar, top hat and spats and would be met at the door by butlers of immense dignity and presence ('Any man under thirty who says he is not afraid of butlers is a liar'). He speaks of his sense of relief when he discovers that his own butler is younger than he is.

But where did the safe-breaking butler James Phipps of *The Old Reliable* come from? Or Augustus Robb, the criminal attendant of Stanwood Cobbold in *Spring Fever*? For good Wodehousean reasons both are required to open safes and both have to be made pie-eyed with alcohol by their friends and admirers before they will do it. Did Wodehouse ever know or hear of a drunken or criminal butler? In his letter of 7 May 1937 in *Performing Flea* he wrote: 'Our butler got home last night as tight as a drum and is still sleeping it off. Over here, the help take every Thursday off and he employed his holiday in getting thoroughly pickled.' In an interview with the *Sunday Times* in 1969 he said: 'We once had a black sheep of a butler who was sent to prison for armed robbery.'

That's where James Phipps and Augustus Robb came from.

There's another type of clue – the 'Wodehouse allusion'. I coined the term for those references, some private, some meant for public consumption, which he used in his stories. Always slight, they seem almost accidental, but most were carefully measured. Many now go unnoticed because the allusions were topical and topicality soon dies.

In *Plum Pie* (1966) Freddie Threepwood has the tongue that wins and successfully sells dog-biscuits to owners of English chain stores. We are told some of them. They include Beatle, Beatle and Beatle of Liverpool. An obvious reference to the young men who made the world ring with their songs in the

1960s – but will our children know whom he meant?

In *A Pelican at Blandings* Lady Constance has occasion to telephone Sir Roderick Glossop's office. She is informed that Sir Roderick is in America and all his cases are being turned over to Sir Abercrombie Fitch. Abercrombie and Fitch is one of the most famous shops in New York, a sort of combined Harrods and Fortnum & Mason. In that odd book *Not George Washington*, written jointly with Herbert Westbrook back in 1907, one of the books attributed to one of the characters is 'When It Was Lurid'. This is a clear reference to the novel that had shocked England four years previously, *When It Was Dark* – the book which Lord Montgomery said affected his life more than any other.

Sometimes the allusion is a private one, something that happened to Wodehouse himself. There's a lot of his private life in the novels when one starts to look at them – Miss Starbuck is a case in point. Her alter egos in the novels are Miss Mapleton, Miss Tomlinson, Miss Maitland and Dame Daphne Winkworth. These ladies are headmistresses of girls' schools and have acquired a certain air of authority that Wodehouse describes perfectly:

> The breath-taking exhibit before me was in person a bit on the short side. I mean to say, she didn't tower above one or anything like that. But to compensate for this lack of inches, she possessed to a remarkable degree that sort of quiet air of being unwilling to stand any rannygazoo which females who run schools always have. I had noticed the same thing when *in statu pupillari*, in my old headmaster, one glance from whose eye had invariably been sufficient to make me confess all. Sergeant-majors are like that, too. Also traffic cops and some post office girls. It's something in the way they purse their lips and look through you.
>
> In short, through years of disciplining the young – ticking off Isabel and speaking with quiet severity to Gertrude and that sort of thing – Miss Mapleton had acquired in the process of time rather the air of a female lion-tamer.
>
> (Bertie Wooster in *Very Good, Jeeves*)

Bertie goes in fear of such ladies, and *Carry On, Jeeves* ends with Bertie hiding under the car-rug while Jeeves drives him to safety. Very amusing and to most of us very unreal. In *Portrait of a Master* David Jasen states that when Wodehouse used to meet his stepdaughter Leonora at school, he would hide in the shrubbery from the headmistress, Miss Starbuck, until Leonora was free to see him.

Butlers, topical allusions and headmistresses are only three examples but they indicate the pattern I found in my search for Blandings.

I read and cross-checked everything I could find about Wodehouse himself. I read the novels he wrote and the interviews he gave, and more and more coincidences came to light. *Bring on the Girls*, *Performing Flea* and *Over Seventy*, the three volumes which are as near as we will get to Wodehouse's autobiography, are so amusingly written that the temptation is to regard them as fiction. A truer description is that they are 'doctored' biography, but all that means is that the truth is written in a way to make us laugh.

A surprising amount of information came from *Burke's Peerage*, *Debrett* and Kelly's County Directories. Wodehouse and his relatives seemed to delight in moving around England as though the police were after them, and reference books like these proved invaluable for the information I needed.

There is no secret life of P. G. Wodehouse to be revealed to the world but there are amusing little clues, private jokes that crop up throughout the ninety-seven novels, and this book is an attempt to show how and when he wrote them. There is a Blandings, there was a Bertie Wooster, there was certainly a real Ukridge and Psmith. I do not mean that Wodehouse did not create them – he did. But he had a source, an original to draw on. Miss Mapleton was an ordinary headmistress – yet when Bertie Wooster/Wodehouse describes her, she isn't a headmistress any more. She is *the* headmistress that all of us know but never really recognized till Wodehouse described her for us. Aubrey Upjohn is her male counterpart – and I found him as well.

Wodehouse's literary background is described for ever in

Usborne's *Wodehouse at Work* and its successor, *Wodehouse at Work to the End*. This book attempts to show the other side of the coin, the factual background against which Wodehouse wrote. I owe the germ of the idea to the late Geoffrey Jaggard, whose *Blandings the Blest* and *Wooster's World* are the best concordances to the novels. It was Jaggard who first made me look at the relationship between the Drones Club and the old Pelican and it was the Pelicans who gave me the first clues along the trail to Blandings.

Wodehouse drew heavily on certain authors for both construction and detail and these are well covered in Usborne's books – especially the debt owed to W. S. Gilbert. Wodehouse used many of Gilbert's tricks, quoted from him often and used Gilbert's characters' names. He borrowed the fictional publishers 'Popgood and Grooly' from his first *Punch* editor Sir Francis Burnand's book *Happy Thoughts*. Another favourite was F. Anstey, the creator of Babu Babberjee, whose displaced and transferred metaphors were to become a trademark of Bertie Wooster's as they had been of Mr Babberjee – 'I became once more sotto voce and the silent tomb.' If you want to see where Anatole acquired his splendid English, read Barry Pain's *Confessions of Alphonse*. Wodehouse admired Pain's writing and quotes him often. In *Service With A Smile* (1961) Uncle Fred says:

> 'Did you ever read a book called *The Confessions of Alphonse*, the reminiscences of a French waiter? No, I suppose not, for it was published a number of years ago, long before you were born. At one point in it Alphonse says "Instantly as a man wishes to borrow money off me, I dislike him. It is in the blood. It is more strong than me." '

For many of the twists of Wodehouse's mind I relied on Usborne's *Wodehouse at Work*, and used Jasen's *Portrait of a Master* for the dates and places in his life. I also read and learnt from R. B. D. French's *P. G. Wodehouse* in the Writers and Critics series. Behind the clues these writers gave me were the words of Bob Davis that Wodehouse never forgot. Bob Davis was the editor of *Munsey's Magazine* in New York for whom Wodehouse wrote short stories in 1913/14. He took much of Wodehouse's work and advised him to write about the things he knew. Wodehouse followed his advice, sat down and wrote *Something Fresh*, the first Blandings story, about a castle, an earl, a butler and young lovers.

Where did he get them from? He got them from that period of his life when things are clearer and sharper to our senses, the period that remains with us all although age dims much of the magic. That was a long time ago – Wodehouse was four when Gordon died at Khartoum, he was twenty when Queen Victoria died.

Lord David Cecil states the case in his *Early Victorian Novelists*:

> The novelist's creative achievement is . . . born of the union of his experience and his imagination. But in any one writer there is only a certain proportion of his experience that can be so fertilised, only a certain proportion of what he has seen, felt and heard strikes deep enough into the foundations of his personality to fire his creative energy . . .
>
> . . . the limit of this range is usually determined by the circumstances of an author's life, and especially his youthful life. His imagination is stimulated by what he himself has experienced at the age when he was most susceptible to impression. (p. 31–2)

He has a strong counter to those who categorize Wodehouse's novels as sheer fantasy:

> These [Victorian] writers have been under the cloud that inevitably obscures the heroes of an age just passed. To appreciate the art of another period one must, to a certain extent, enter into its spirit, accept its conventions, adopt a 'willing suspension of disbelief' in its values. For if we have no sympathy for what it is trying to say, we shall not be able to judge if it says it well. But by some mysterious law of human taste it is almost impossible to enter into the spirit of

the age that comes just before one's own . . .

. . . The last age, like a relation, is too close for a man to be able to view it with the detachment necessary for criticism.

Can it have a Freudian explanation, some huge mass Oedipus complex against the father's generation? (p. 3–4)

The enjoyable series of Wodehouse stories shown on television some years ago were all firmly set in the 1920s and 1930s. Wodehouse drew much of his material from that period, but it was a conscious decision. His original settings – and the mental attitudes of his characters through sixty years – were set in an earlier era.

Bingo Little, Bertie Wooster and Freddie Widgeon are correctly described with their Homburgs, whangee canes and grey flannel suits with the quiet red twill. But the first heroes, Psmith and Ukridge, wear what Wodehouse wore as a young man – top-hat, frock-coat and spats. Ukridge only wears such formal clothing when in the company of Aunt Julia, but it was the standard expected.

When we read Wodehouse we are back at the turn of the century, at that time in Wodehouse's life that Lord David Cecil spoke of when the first sharp impressions are made and the attitude of mind starts to set.

Some of the sources of the Arcady that Wodehouse drew are in this book. Some are important characters, some are themes like the idiocy of Hollywood or Wodehouse's propensity for writing about his own trade. Others are little jokes. Sometimes the jokes are deliberate and I have given them the collective title of 'Wodehouse allusions'. Others seem accidental, and are of value since they are a clue to the real source. The plot never relies on them. This is important: the 'allusions' or accidental slips only occur when they have no effect on the plot. The story is going well, the characters are doing what they ought to do, the dialogue is running as smooth as silk – and there is a pause. It may be inserted in the action to allow time for something to happen, or perhaps to balance the dialogue between the characters, but it is never vital. It is a fill-in, a moment when Wodehouse can relax and put in a private joke.

'Big Business', one of the short stories in *A Few Quick Ones*, opens with Reginald Mulliner receiving a letter from a firm of solicitors asking him to call to hear something to his advantage. The firm is Watson, Watson, Watson, Watson and Watson, and the combination allows Wodehouse to proceed with:

> Something to his advantage being always what he was glad to hear of, he took train to London, called at Lincoln's Inn Fields, and you could have knocked him down with a toothpick when Watson – or Watson or Watson, or it may have been Watson – informed him that under the will of a cousin in the Argentine, whom he had not seen for years, he had benefited to the extent of fifty thousand pounds. It is not surprising that on the receipt of the news he reeled and would have fallen, had he not clutched at a passing Watson.

Very easy to miss, but the name of Wodehouse's lawyer at the time happened to be Watson Washburn.

At the back of this book is an appendix of Wodehouse's movements and publications as far as I know them. They are the framework against which this book was written because it is this background that crept so often into the novels Wodehouse wrote. In 1924 he wrote to his friend Bill Townend (see *Performing Flea*) asking specific questions. Wodehouse wanted to describe the arrival of the hero of *Sam the Sudden* in London. The hero had travelled by tramp-steamer and Wodehouse's questions include: what would he be wearing, what would he see, hear and smell as he stood on deck, would he have a cabin to himself, could he be friends with both the captain and the cook or would the etiquette of tramp-steamers prevent this?

Wodehouse liked to get his background right. He was a straightforward man, he never forgot the advice Bob Davis gave him – and there was, at that time in his life that Lord David Cecil speaks of, a group of men and women in London who set a pattern of behaviour that was reflected in his books for sixty years.

~~∽~~

CHAPTER II

PINK 'UNS AND PELICANS

WODEHOUSE had no message for the world, yet a surprisingly large number of cynics admire his novels because they are written of innocents whom the evils of the world do not touch and who live in the true Arcadia of make-believe.

Benny Green, the critic and broadcaster, has written of the outrage expressed by people when the suggestion is made that Wodehouse's stories have some foundation in fact. The reaction appears to be based on various arguments. The first is that life is miserable and anybody who says it isn't must be untrustworthy. The second seems to be that nobody ever enjoyed themselves as much as the characters in Wodehouse's books did – and if they did, they shouldn't have done.

Wodehouse's novels do have a social significance, although it is an unlikely one. There was a time when people behaved as Wodehouse drew them and were as carefree and reckless of social consequences. He knew the people and saw what they did.

Wodehouse went to school at Dulwich from 1894 to 1900. In 1900 he started work in London with the Hong Kong and Shanghai Bank. He left the Bank in 1902 and joined *The Globe* evening newspaper to write the 'By the Way' column of humorous paragraphs and comment on current events. In the next five years he visited New York, started writing lyrics for musical comedies and wrote school stories. He had various aunts and uncles in London to keep an eye on him and he joined, somewhat reluctantly, in the social life of his colleagues and relations.

At the turn of the century Mr Pooter and his fellows were the centre of London society – the clerks, the small businessmen and shopkeepers, the skilled workmen and the upper servants. Above them were the gentry – aristocrats who kept their carriages and mansions in Mayfair, young officers enjoying their leave from India, clergymen, barristers and those who lived on allowances or inherited money and rubbed along as best they could, secure in the knowledge that they were gentry. Below the Pooters were the working classes, porters, hansom cab drivers, navvies and dockers. Three strata of society, clearly defined and definable to those who lived in it. A pound a week was a reasonable wage and families were brought up decently on it while others spent twenty thousand a year and had change left over.

Don't be deceived by stories of the hopelessness of the working classes. One of the greatest attributes of the Victorians was their acceptance of change. A man could rise from a factory bench to become a millionaire in ten years, and a surprising number of them did. Some of the jokes in Victorian copies of *Punch* about the *nouveaux riches* may seem pretty tasteless to us today but there were enough of the new men in society to make the joke run. There were other standards that seem odd to us. In the picture of Piccadilly Circus in the 1890s at Plate 1 everybody is wearing a hat – the flower-sellers, the messenger boys, the bus-drivers. Nobody went bareheaded; to be seen hatless after dark was sufficient grounds for questioning by the police, and this was accepted at all levels of society as being perfectly reasonable. Hats were an almost infallible guide to their wearer's status but varied enormously. The trinity of top-hat, bowler and cloth cap were the main distinguishing marks, but were augmented by dozens of other styles the names of which are difficult even to recognize today.

The importance of clothing and its indication of status was an important factor in London life when Wodehouse was a young man. When he made an article of clothing the cause of arguments between Bertie Wooster and Jeeves he was describing a well-known phenomenon. Bertie speaks of his

10

friends as pirates when they try and steal Jeeves from him but admits that they have good reason. One had a valet who sent him out into Bond Street without spats. This was not at all far-fetched. Wodehouse got the idea from a *Punch* cartoon, and whatever one may say of *Punch* it reflects the current scene. Spend half an hour looking at the cartoons in *Punch* for any year between 1890 and 1910 and then read any of the stories Wodehouse wrote between 1906 and 1926. The 'feel' of the two is remarkably similar.

Victorian manners still prevailed in London at the turn of the century. Gentlemen were definitely gentlemen and the gold sovereign was the staple of the economy. But in one part of London, with its centre in the Strand, there was a small world where dukes mixed with bookmakers, pugilists and actors mingled with journalists and Guardees, and where Wode-house's young men had their origins.

Wodehouse's Ukridge, Bingo Little and Freddie Widgeon exist somehow with the loan of a pound here and a fiver there. They are pursued by duns and bailiffs and spend their spare moments being charming to bookmakers in the hope that their little account can stand over till the next race-meeting. It all seems very unreal, very Wodehousean. But Gally Threep-wood set me on the trail that showed that Wodehouse described his young men accurately.

When we meet Galahad Threepwood, younger brother of Lord Emsworth, he is introduced as:

> A beau sabreur of Romano's. A Pink 'Un. A crony of Hughie Drummond; a brother-in-arms of the Shifter, the Pitcher, Peter Blobbs and the rest of an interesting but not straitlaced circle. Bookmakers had called him by his pet name, barmaids had simpered beneath his gallant chaff.
>
> (*Summer Lightning*)

He is the clue to a group of men and women who set a pattern of behaviour that we find hard to accept today but which Wodehouse used for his characters for sixty years.

One of the elements of the Wodehouse farces are the antics

of members of society acting in direct contrast to their status. Earls behave like con men, baronets behave like fifteen-year-olds, bailiffs behave like dukes. People did behave like that once – especially if they were members of the Pelican Club.

The Pelican Club was started in London in the 1880s. Its members included peers of the realm, Service officers, actors and newspaper men. Their guests included bookmakers, pugilists, Gaiety Girls and anybody else who provided some diversion for the members – including once Buffalo Bill and his entourage of Red Indians. The members, like Wodehouse's Drones Club later, were divided into two categories – those who were always short of money and those who had money to lend. They shared a common determination in pursuing pretty women, in betting on anything that admitted of bets being laid on it, and a firm resolve never to go to bed if there was anyone left in the room wealthy enough to order another drink.

Every Pelican had a nickname. The Marquis of Ailesbury was 'Ducks', the Duke of Beaufort was 'Duke' and Sir John Astley was known as 'the Mate'. The members included Rothschilds, Disraelis and men like Sir Arthur Sullivan. Their carefree attitude to life was recorded in *Pitcher In Paradise* and *A Pink 'Un and Pelican* by Arthur Binstead (1846–1915), 'the Pitcher'. If you could tell a good story, drink till six in the morning, make people laugh, and if you cared nothing for the Victorian attitude to sex, you joined the Pelican Club.

As I read the list of members, it was clear that reminiscences like Gally Threepwood's might indeed cause a stir among the survivors in the 1930s – which is the crux of the plot of *Summer Lightning*. Although, as Gally says, few of the Pelicans lived to old age. Turning night into day on a diet of buttered rums when you were paying, and of champagne and stout when someone else footed the bill, is not conducive to longevity.

The 'Pink 'Un' was the newspaper that reflected the philosophy of the Pelicans. Its official name was *The Sporting Times* and it was a mixture of *Playboy*, *The News of the World* and *Private Eye*. Its editor was John Corlett ('Master'), its most famous member was Arthur Binstead ('Pitcher') and its most eccentric contributor was Willie Goldberg, an Oxford graduate who rejoiced in the nom-de-plume of 'Shifter'. They were all members of the Pelican Club and, except for John Corlett, were perpetually in debt. Their articles were signed with their nicknames and although the 'Pink 'Un' was never seen in respectable homes, it was the most popular newspaper amongst male readers throughout England and the Empire.

Although the Pelican closed its doors in the 1890s, the 'Pink 'Un' carried on till 1914. Its staff were well-known figures in Fleet Street and Wodehouse would certainly have met them during his time on *The Globe* from 1902 to 1910. I sent Wodehouse *Old Pink 'Un Days* by J. B. Booth ('Costs'), to replace a copy he had lost. His letter of thanks included the remark that it completed his set of Pink 'Un books and brought back memories.

Wodehouse's Bingo Little, Freddie Widgeon and Ukridge are always short of money and Wodehouse tells us of their antics to get the fiver they need to pay a bookie, to redeem their aunt's clock or for some other Wodehousean reason. In order to win the fiver, Freddie Widgeon enters a talent contest in the East End, Bingo Little steals Pekinese dogs, gambles with the housekeeping and, on meeting his bookmaker on Wimbledon Common while they are wheeling their babies in their prams, bets him that his (Bingo's) baby is uglier than the bookie's. A policeman is called in to adjudicate and tries to tell them how much uglier his baby is but they cut him short:

> 'Never mind about your baby,' said Charlie Pikelet.
> 'No,' said Bingo. 'Stick closely to the *res.*'
> 'Your baby isn't a runner,' said Charlie Pikelet. 'Only the above have arrived.'

Good Wodehouse but not too unreal. Binstead describes his fellow Pink 'Un, Willie Goldberg ('Shifter') in the refreshment tent at the end of a day's racing at Sandown Park. The rain is pouring down, Shifter has lost on every race and has just spent his last shilling on a plate of cold Irish stew. As Binstead watches, Shifter turns out his empty pockets, looks at his soaked clothes and remarks mournfully: 'And for this, for this

– I pawned my best girl's nickel-plated suspenders!'
Of whom did an irate bookmaker say:

> 'I don't mind him owing me from last Goodwood and I
> don't mind him borrowing a fiver to lay against myself. I
> don't even mind him borrowing five bob for the train home.
> But when he borrows the back page of my betting book to
> write an article on the iniquities of bookmakers – then I do
> draw the line!'

No, it was not Bingo Little, whom Wodehouse made editor
of that moulder of opinion in the nursery *Wee Tots*, although it
so easily could have been. It was 'Shifter' again, Willie
Goldberg, the founder of the Pelican Club.

Ukridge perpetrates the most outrageous exploits in
Wodehouse's novels. None of his friends' clothes are safe from
him, any piece of portable property is susceptible to borrowing
and internment at the nearest pawnbroker's and one of his
finest exploits was to steal his aunt's Pekinese dogs to train as a
performing troupe. The dogs are impounded by his landlord
because the rent has not been paid. When relief arrives (ten
pounds), the landlord finds that the dogs have escaped.
Ukridge launches forth with all the outraged dignity at his
disposal, has the rent cancelled and the landlord promises to
settle 'any other little accounts' that may exist around the
neighbourhood. Ukridge has, of course, stolen the animals
back in the night as a statesmanlike solution to these minor
financial worries, but meets his Waterloo in the shape of Aunt
Julia, who has called to see him and discovered her stolen dogs.

Typical Wodehouse and a delight to read – but by no means
unreal. One member of the Pelican, a doctor who had managed
to secure a temporary Government post and who was universally known as 'the Coroner', used to do his drinking free by
carrying with him a small box containing some black beetles
and a couple of white rats. These were politely introduced for
the edification of the barmaid once the drink had been served.
The ensuing swooning, screaming and confusion was normally
sufficient to enable 'the Coroner' to escape without paying.

This was small-time stuff. 'Shifter' Goldberg, an enthusiastic betting man like all the Pelicans, eventually found himself barred by the Jockey Club. Binstead tells us that every member of the Pink 'Un staff enjoyed that distinction at one time or another. But 'Shifter' surpassed them all when he was struck off for entering a horse in a race without paying the fees. Nothing too outrageous in that; what really annoyed the authorities was that the horse was one that 'Shifter' had never seen, which he had bought for nothing from a man to whom it didn't belong, and that the unfortunate animal was stolen from the paddock just before the race while 'Shifter' and Binstead were trying to persuade a jockey to ride it on a speculative basis, i.e. no win, no fee!

In *Cocktail Time*, Uncle Fred opens the novel by showing the members of the Drones' how to knock off Sir Raymond Bastable's hat at thirty yards with a Brazil nut from a catapult. If he had a single source it must be the Pelican Hughie Drummond. It was Hughie Drummond who decided one night to enter the club by driving a hansom cab up the steps, through the front door and along the corridor into the bar. It was unfortunate that he did so just as the proprietor had finished persuading a group of prospective members that the club was the quiet and respectable institution he had claimed it to be.

When Uncle Fred sold a gold brick to Lord Emsworth's heir, he did so simply as an experiment in psychology. The same spirit of inquiry inspired Hughie Drummond down at Epsom, as he sat with the officers of the Scots Guards awaiting the start of the Derby. Below them was Sir John Bennet, a well-known City Alderman, seated on his brown mare:

'I wonder,' said Hughie, 'how that horse would carry two up?' and promptly launched his twenty-two stone down from the top of the coach on to the back of the horse. The horse went down, as did Hughie and the Alderman. As they got to their feet, the bewildered Sir John asked Hughie if he had any idea what had happened.

'None at all, Sir, none at all. But,' with a quick glance around, 'I rather think it was that fellow there.'

15

'That fellow there' was Hughie's old friend the Marquess of Ailesbury who was sitting on the next coach and, like everyone else, enjoying the situation hugely. Hughie knew what the Alderman did not, that the Marquess possessed the foulest tongue and perpetrated the most inventive form of swearing in the country. As a furious altercation broke out between the livid Sir John and the Marquess, Hughie picked up his hat and went on his way, no doubt thinking, as Uncle Fred did later, that if he could bring a little joy into a life, he was doing a wonderful deed.

My favourite Pelican is Captain Fred Russell. Many soldiers even today tell the joke about the Commander-in-Chief asking a supercilious cavalry officer his views on the role of the cavalry in modern warfare. The famous response is: 'I suppose it's to give tone to what would otherwise be a mere vulgar brawl!' Reginald Cleaver drew the famous cartoon of the infuriated C-in-C and the languid cavalryman which appears as a frontispiece in *Mr Punch on the Warpath* (1907).

Punch did not invent the story. It was the reply Fred Russell gave to the Duke of Cambridge and which ran round England within the week. I don't think Russell was too worried. He was a keen member of the Pelican Club, where he was known by the soubriquet of 'Brer Rabbit' because of his ability to lie low when faced by too many creditors. His most amusing feat came after a period of six months when he seemed to live entirely without sleep, spending his nights in London and the days with his regiment in Colchester. He ran up so many debts that he was forced to take evasive action. This entailed taking extended leave, changing his name and securing employment as writ-server to the solicitors who were suing him. For six months he chased himself around England, eventually returning to say that he had left the country and further action was useless. Having seen the writs against him torn up, he rejoined his unit and carried on as though nothing had happened. Not even Wodehouse dared use that trick – but it happened.

The Pelicans were one of three factors in the social life of the London of the 1890s that Wodehouse used in his books. The other two were the marriages that crossed every one of the social laws of Victorian England.

In the Nineties the upper and lower classes had outside entertainment, clubs for the one, music-halls and pubs for the other. The middle classes, the Pooters, tended to entertain at home. But for the ladies of the upper classes life was very restricted. As a nice young lady you could meet your fiancé at dinner; you could, accompanied by a chaperone, go with him to the opera or the theatre. But you would be unable to lunch or dine with him in public. A lady did not eat in public, for the simple reason that there was nowhere she could go.

In 1885 London still possessed the chop-houses and taverns of Dickens's day. There were a few French restaurants starting to appear but they were restricted to men and their more daring or less respectable female companions.

For this, amongst other reasons, the young blades of the time looked to the theatre for their companions for an evening's entertainment. The stage was nearly the only venue for pretty working-class girls to make money and those who did not earn much on the stage could earn it in other ways. They ate well at the expense of their admirers or accepted jewellery or furs. Sometimes the role was reversed when the admirers fell on hard times. Bessie Bellwood never achieved the fame of her contemporary Marie Lloyd but she was the queen of Romano's restaurant, the centre of the Pink 'Un and Pelican world. Bessie, a labourer's daughter from the East End, became a famous music-hall singer. She attracted many admirers including the Duke of Manchester, a Pelican who had already married American money. The Duke was not a likeable character but Bessie loved him and paid his debts. His wife eventually wrote:

The Duchess of Manchester presents her compliments to Miss Bessie Bellwood and wishes to state that if Miss Bellwood will permit the Duke of Manchester to return to his own home, the Duchess will pay all his debts and will allow him £20 a week.

Bessie's reply read:

> Miss Bessie Bellwood presents her compliments to the Duchess of Manchester, and begs to state that she is now working the Pavilion, the Met., and the South London at £20 a turn so she can allow the Duke £30 a week and he is better off as he is.

But marriage never entered into it – till George Edwardes came along.

In Wodehouse's novels young peers of the realm want to marry chorus-girls and aunts and uncles try to prevent them. It is a standard Wodehouse plot. It is based on the premise that was an article of faith in the late nineteenth century, that actors were vagabonds and actresses were beyond the Pale. We may have difficulty in appreciating this point of view today but it was so and its leading advocates included Wodehouse's aunts.

Their nephew was fully aware of the social obstacles that faced anyone of his background who became too involved with the theatre. As late as 1949 his *The Mating Season* has as its basis an English landowner who wants to marry an actress while the second heroine wants to marry an actor. Even though the actor is Catsmeat Potter-Pirbright, an Oxonian and the vicar's son, being on the stage damns him in the eyes of the landowner's aunts. To go on the stage was something one did not do – until George Edwardes came along.

George Edwardes took over the Gaiety Theatre, which used to stand where the western edge of Bush House now is, in 1885. He was a member of the Pelican Club and decided to give the Gaiety something the other theatres did not have. Today we call it glamour and it took the form of securing the prettiest girls in the country and putting them on the Gaiety stage. As he pulled the Gaiety into the forefront of the musical comedy world, he also pulled up the status of the girls he employed.

The young men flocked to the Gaiety. Tierney, the stage-door keeper, made enough money to build the street in Streatham that bears his name. Edwardes arranged with Romano's restaurant for his girls to dine there at half-price. It was good for the girls and made Romano's the centre of

London's night-life. Edwardes also insisted on his ladies behaving like ladies – which some of them found difficult. He insisted on their dressing well, both on and off the stage, and he had the generous habit of allowing his actors to keep the clothes they wore on stage. The expression 'GB suits' – a derivation from 'God bless George Edwardes' – was a common one amongst those actors fortunate enough to work for him.

Edwardes raised the status of his chorus-girls in a few years to the point where applicants no longer came from one social class. Just as Wodehouse drew them, a large proportion came from vicarages and rectories up and down the country and they enjoyed themselves enormously. In 1892 the dam broke. To the horror of Victorian England the Earl of Orkney married Miss Connie Gilchrist of the Gaiety chorus, and the next twenty years saw a series of similar alliances. Society shuddered but the marriages went on unchecked.

I have been unable to find a full list of noblemen who married chorus girls in the period but the names include the Marquess of Queensbury, the Earl of Euston, Marquis of Headfort, Lord Churston, Lord Victor Paget, the Earl of Drogheda, Lord Poulett, Lord Meux, the Earl of Dudley, the Duke of Leinster and at least twenty more peers between 1895 and 1914. No wonder the wags spoke of the 'actresstocracy' and the papers made it headline news. Wodehouse would have heard of the Orkney marriage when he was a schoolboy and would have known the same thing to cause scandalized comment when he was commissioned to write lyrics for a London musical in 1904. Two years later Wodehouse was employed by Seymour Hicks to provide topical verses for the show *The Beauty of Bath*. It ran at the Aldwych just across the road from the Gaiety, and Seymour Hicks and Grossmith of the Gaiety were *the* young men about town. Wodehouse had close personal experience of the extraordinary social scene of the time and was certainly fully aware of the low opinion of the stage held by his aunts and others like them up and down the country.

At an early stage in his career he was meeting people who were making fairy tales come true. Girls from the lowest ranks of society were marrying peers of the realm or millionaires. Sometimes they managed both, like Jeanne Guinevere, who married the American millionaire Jay Gould and then went on to marry the Earl of Midleton. Both the earl and his wife lived on till the 1970s, the former Gaiety Girl making quite a splash even in her last years when she used to charter her own plane to take her to Switzerland. When Bob Davis told Wodehouse to write about things he knew, Wodehouse took his advice. All those arguments at Blandings over members of the family marrying out of their class and background may seem strange to us but they weren't to Wodehouse. When he wrote of the outraged reaction of Society to such marriages he knew exactly what he was talking about.

A third social phenomenon of the time that Wodehouse used was the marriage of English peers to American heiresses. It is easy to think of this as a phenomenon of the 1920s and the American invasion of Europe, but it started a long time before that. The end of the American Civil War in 1865 saw the emergence of private fortunes unequalled in the world. The Railway King, the Oil King, the Shipping King were titles justly bestowed on men who controlled vast sections of industry in their own hands. In 1874 Lord Randolph Churchill married Miss Jennie Jerome of New York and his example was followed by his kinsman, the Duke of Marlborough, who married a Vanderbilt in 1895, by the Duke of Roxburgh, the Duke of Manchester and dozens of others. One historian has listed 454 American ladies who married into the European aristocracy between 1870 and 1914 and discovered that the going rate for an English duke was about three million dollars. Wodehouse may only have seen these events in the papers in his early years, but in the 1920s he worked closely with Fred and Adele Astaire, and she married the Duke of Devonshire's son in 1932.

Uncle Fred, otherwise known as Frederick Altamont Cornwallis Twistleton, fifth Earl of Ickenham, is one of Wodehouse's best creations. He raises hell in a series of books but has suffered his vicissitudes, as he describes to Sally Painter in *Uncle Dynamite*.

'People see me now the dickens of a fellow with five Christian names and a coronet hanging on a peg in the hats and coats cupboard under the stairs, and they forget that I started at the bottom of the ladder. For years I was a younger son, a mere Honourable.'

'Why have you never told me this?'

'I hadn't the heart to. A worm of an Hon. In Debrett, yes, but only in small print.'

'You're making me cry.'

'I can't help that. Do you know how they treat Hons, Sally? Like dogs. They have to go into dinner behind the Vice-Chancellor of the County Palatinate of Lancaster.'

'Well, it's all over now, darling.'

'The only bit of sunshine in their lives is the privilege of being allowed to stand at the bar of the House of Lords during debates. And I couldn't even do that, my time being earmarked for the cows I was punching in Arizona.'

'I didn't know you had ever punched cows.'

'As a young man, hundreds. I had a beautiful punch in those days, straight and true, like the kick of a mule, and never travelling further than six inches . . . But was I happy? No. Because always at the back of my mind, like some corroding acid, was the thought that I had to go into dinner behind the Vice-Chancellor of the County Palatinate of Lancaster. In the end, by pluck and perseverance, I raised myself from the depths and became what I am today. I'd like to see any Vice-Chancellor of the County Palatinate of Lancaster try and squash in ahead of me now.'

Quite a number of English peers went adventuring in the Americas, and one enjoyed it so much that he brought buffalo and some Indians back with him. His attempt to introduce buffalo herds into Scotland was not successful, but well into this century travellers in the district had to be warned of the landlord and his Redskins as they carried out their annual round-up. Buffalo Bill and his Wild West troupe were the toast of Romano's restaurant when they were in London before they went on as guests of the Pelican Club (that must have been a night to remember) but the 'Roman' was a trifle taken aback when a young man who had unexpectedly come into a title decided to show what he had learnt from his sojourn in America. Like Uncle Fred he had been a cowboy, and after lassoing the waiters, he showed his prowess with the revolver, using the display bottles behind the bar as targets. In anywhere else than Romano's there would have been pandemonium but the habitués took it in their stride, the 'Roman' getting his own back by charging champagne prices for the coloured water the noble marksman had spilt.

Gally Threepwood is never happier than when recounting stories of the Pelican and Romano's and he uses his Pelican training to thwart aunts and provide happy endings for those he holds dear. But he is also a new factor. He is the first middle-aged hero. When Wodehouse introduced him in 1929 he made Gally just a few years older than himself, and Gally was followed by Lord Ickenham, Lord Uffenham, Leila Yorke, Bill Shannon and others, all middle-aged and each the central character of the novel in which they appear. Whether Wodehouse created them deliberately is questionable. Perhaps he simply found it easier to describe people of his own age, since this would fit well with the pattern of 'acceptance' that characterizes his writing. Other writers as they grew older changed or altered their style or wrote more deeply. The years didn't seem to affect Wodehouse this way. His writing certainly improved with time but he never grew introspective. He accepted the habits of the world he saw around him, and those that impressed him most were those he saw at an impressionable age.

Gally Threepwood always related everything – his advice to young lovers or defiance of pig-stealing baronets – to his Pelican training because Wodehouse knew the Pelican anecdotes so well. The point is that not just Gally but *all* Wodehouse's characters behaved as the young men and women in the 1890s behaved because that was the time Wodehouse met them. All Gally did was to show me where to start the search.

Wodehouse's Drones Club reflects the membership of a number of clubs and, chronologically, the Pelicans are the first. The Berties, Pongoes and Freddies may seem typical of the 1920s in their dress, manners and speech but their attitudes to life are those of the young men Wodehouse knew or heard of at the turn of the century.

Like Gussie Mannering-Phipps in *The Man with Two Left Feet*, some of the young-men-about-town went on the stage themselves to be nearer the girl of their choice. Others, like Lord Stockheath in *Something Fresh*, were taken to court in the breach of promise cases that were such a feature of the newspapers of the period. The noble defendant who had to pay the record amount of £50,000 to Miss Daisy Markham in 1913 only died in 1979.

Bailiffs are a common feature in the Wodehouse novels as they were amongst the young men he knew years ago. Arthur Binstead had one in residence for a considerable time and grew so accustomed to him that he only paid him off because his wife could not stand the man's constant whistling about the house. The Pelican Club had bailiffs permanently on the premises. They were set to work as waiters and no one thought more about it. One old man turned out to be a Waterloo veteran and became the club hero. They gave a dinner in his honour at which the old man made an excellent speech, the high spot of which was his recounting the list of famous houses in London in which he had exercised his office!

Like the Drones Club later, the Pelicans were either those who had money to lend or those who borrowed it. They took their tone from the founders of the club, 'Shifter' Goldberg and 'Swears' Wells, whose instructions to the contractors were that the carpets should be nailed to the floor and the pictures similarly affixed to the walls. 'Shifter' in particular specialized in living well at minimum cost and wore the best clothes in London without paying for them. All inquiries on the price were met by the words: 'I don't know. I haven't had the writ yet.'

On a visit to Monte Carlo an urgent telegram to London for more funds only produced an envelope containing an advertisement for the Drury Lane Theatre from his friend and fellow Pelican Augustus Harris. The advertisement was shaped like a banknote – 'I promise to pay fifty laughs etc. etc.' – but 'Shifter' managed to cash it with a Casino clerk and win £2,000 before being ejected by an indignant management.

'Swears' Wells, the co-founder of the Pelican, was equally ingenious at raising cash. A wealthy friend admired a fine bulldog that 'Swears' owned. 'Swears' insisted on his accepting the animal and equally strongly refused to accept any payment. The embarrassed friend persisted. How much was the dog worth? Twenty-five pounds? 'Swears' swept the questions aside. Money – from a friend? Never! Relenting slightly he suggested that between friends a little token might be more appropriate. At 'Swears' suggestion the friend wrote a note to a famous jeweller to the effect that Mr Wells would be calling to choose something from the jeweller's stock. 'Swears' arrived at the jeweller's and inquired if the note had arrived. Indeed it had. What would Mr Wells like? The answer still rings after ninety years:

'Anything you like. But make sure it pawns for two hundred and fifty quid!'

One of the best scenes Wodehouse wrote was the Clothes Stakes in *Uncle Fred in the Springtime*. Pongo Twistleton owes money to his bookmakers and is in the Drones Club when that canniest of bookmakers, Mustard Pott, announces to the members that he has locked someone in the Club telephone booth and will open the Clothes Stakes on the unfortunate individual. Whoever bets correctly on the clothing worn by the prisoner wins. Mustard lays the following odds:

9-4	Blue serge
4-1	Pin-striped grey tweed
10-1	Golf coat and plus-fours
100-6	Gym vest and running shorts
20-1	Court dress
6-1	Herringbone Cheviot Lounge
etc. etc.	

Pongo knows that the man in the booth is Horace Davenport and also knows that Horace has not yet returned home from a fancy dress ball. Horace had announced his intention of going as a Boy Scout and Pongo persuades Oofy Prosser, the wealthiest of the Drones, to stand Pongo in for fifty pounds. Pongo learns the sad lesson Uncle Fred tries to instil:

> 'One of the hard lessons Life will teach you, as you grow to know him better, is that you can't make money out of Mustard. Hundreds have tried it, and hundreds have failed.'

Eventually Mustard closes his book and, followed by a crowd of eager Drones, goes to unlock the door.

Nature hath framed strange fellows in her time, but few stranger than the one that now whizzed out of the telephone booth, whizzed down the corridor, whizzed past the little group at the desk and, bursting through the door of the club, whizzed down the steps and into a passing cab.

The face of this individual, as the hall porter had foreshadowed, was a rich black in colour. Its long body was draped in tights of the same sombre hue, surmounted by a leopard skin. Towering above his head was a head-dress of ostrich feathers and in its right hand it grasped an assegai. It was wearing tortoise-shell-rimmed spectacles.

As Lord Ickenham foretold, Mustard Pott had won again. Horace Davenport had gone to the ball as a Zulu.

Wodehouse could easily have left Pongo owing his bookmaker the fifty pounds or just let him borrow it from Oofy. He didn't – he worked that bit harder and we get the Great Clothes Stakes. It is unlikely, it is funny, it is Wodehouse's version of something that really happened.

Arthur Binstead ('the Pitcher') told the original story about his friend Joe Scott at the turn of the century. Scott and two friends with names that out-Wodehouse Wodehouse, the Punching Machine and the Man Behind the Face, live off their wits and face the prospect of Christmas with gloom. There is no gambling, no roulette, no steeplechasing or boxing matches on which they can raise any money. Joe Scott decides that they must open a book for the Great Hat Stakes. Binstead describes the way they circulate the pubs and bars of the West End spreading the news and taking bets, and speaks admiringly of the skill with which Joe Scott adjusts his prices as the money comes in. Binstead lists some of the runners for the race:

11-10	Black top hat
6-4	Black bowler
9-4	Opera hat
25-10	Brown bowler
3-1	Homburg or trilby (any colour)
4-1	Imperial Yeomanry helmet (the Boer War was in progress)
10-1	Leather motor caps
100-3	White beavers, khaki bowlers or pith helmets

The winner is the first hat through the doors of the American Bar of the Criterion in Piccadilly Circus after 7 o'clock. As the time grows near Scott and his friends take up their positions in the bar, and at two minutes to seven he closes the betting. As the clock over the bar strikes seven, Scott shouts 'They're off!' and quiet falls on the crowded room. There is silence for a minute or so and then they hear the outside door open, a shadow falls on the glass door of the bar and a man comes in. He is the waiter from the restaurant next door with food for the bar. It is an Indian restaurant and the waiter is a Hindu complete with turban! Joe Scott jumps to his feet and embraces the astonished Indian:

'A skinner! By the Great Horned Spoon, a skinner! Hindu Turbans won by a walkover. Twenty-eight and a half quid in the book and not a penny laid on it!'

A splendid anecdote – and a well-known one, if you happened to be a young journalist in London at the time, as Wodehouse was.

On the only occasion I met Guy Bolton, Wodehouse's friend and collaborator for over fifty years, I asked why

Wodehouse used so many Pink 'Un/Pelican stories. He thought that since the American public didn't know the stories, it was worth using them and it transpired that many people in England had not heard of them either. Guy Bolton had also taken Gaiety Girls to Romano's before the First War and agreed that people of an age with Wodehouse and himself liked the plots because they had known people like that. Nowadays he felt that it might be difficult for people to accept that anybody ever behaved the way the Pelicans did.

In the days when the Pelicans flourished, the Strand was *the* street of pleasure in London. Up to 1895 it was a fact that no shop stood any chance of success in the Strand unless it was a foodshop. The Strand had nearly the whole of London's night-life to itself. Shaftesbury Avenue was still being built and sixteen of London's twenty-one theatres stood along the Strand. The rule was that fashion didn't go east of Trafalgar Square nor commerce west of Temple Bar. In between was the Strand, full of restaurants, cafés, theatres and pubs. You could meet the tutor of the Prince of Wales wearing a labourer's smock and smoking a clay pipe, and any man you met without a moustache was either an actor or a barrister, since facial hair was forbidden in these two professions. The whole street was a village of actors, newspapermen, pugilists, bookmakers and young men about town looking for amusement. Even today, it is only in the Strand that I have seen that elderly gentleman who wears a brown or blue bowler hat to match his suit and still sports a pearl tie-pin and a silver-knobbed cane.

Oofy Prosser and Mustard Pott, who appeared in the Great Clothes Stakes from *Uncle Fred in the Springtime*, both got their names from the Pelican period.

In the 1890s a prosser was one who borrowed money or was mean with it. 'Oof' was slang for money and 'an oofy bird' was someone with plenty of it. Oofy Prosser was therefore correctly drawn in the novels as the richest and meanest member of the Drones, who would walk ten miles in tight shoes to save twopence. If you lived in London at the turn of the century you would recognize the term 'mustard pot' for Lord Lonsdale's distinctive yellow barouche which was known everywhere. As the first motor buses appeared, some in bright yellow, the name was transferred to them.

It's all a long time ago, but there are still Gaiety Girls alive and beautiful women they are. C. B. Cochran, the impresario, was a leading Pink 'Un and lived till well into the present era. It was Cochran who brought over Zbysco to England during the wrestling craze of the 1900s – and Zbysco should be known to all Wodehouse enthusiasts as the name like Psmith that does not pronounce its initial letter – so Psmith tells us at his first appearance.

Lord Lonsdale lived till the end of the Second World War after a life of extraordinary incident. He was a leading Pelican and went exploring in Canada. In later years he claimed to have found the North Pole and always insisted that it was bright pink in colour. He spent three thousand pounds a year on cigars alone, owned twenty-eight cars at one time, and rode so well that he could take a horse over any jump and land it in the hoofprints it had made the day before.

He instituted the Lonsdale Belt to bring back control of British boxing, and his monument today is the livery worn by the vans of the Automobile Association. The colours are his and he gave them, with his sponsorship, to the Association in its early days.

The Pink 'Uns and Pelicans were extraordinary men. They were immoral and feckless, often brutal, but never dull. Their philosophy was to enjoy life as best they could, and the cheating and lying of Gally Threepwood and Uncle Fred to smooth the course of true love is exactly how their real-life forebears would have behaved. When we read of Ukridge's escapades, of Bingo Little pawning some treasured possession of his wife's, of Pongo Twistleton's endeavours to get the fiver that is life or death to him, we are reading a translation, in the strict sense, of the men Wodehouse knew when he was young.

To some the 1890s means Sherlock Holmes, the Café Royal, Oscar Wilde and Augustus John. To others it means Doré drawings of appalling poverty or heartless capitalism. To Wodehouse it meant a collection of men and women from every section of society whose headquarters were Romano's restaurant in the Strand and the Pelican Club in Denman Street.

Their epitaph is the final paragraph of *A Pelican at Blandings* (1969). Gally Threepwood has triumphed again. By blackmail and deceit he has once again engineered happy endings for those he holds dear. Evil has been conquered and young lovers made happy. Gally has even worked the miracle of ridding the castle of the sisters who made Lord Emsworth's life a misery. Gally and Lord Emsworth are at dinner, happy and at peace. Gally muses on the events behind them:

'. . . The storm is over, there is sunlight in my heart. I have a glass of wine and sit thinking of what has passed. And now we want something to bring down the curtain. A toast is indicated. Let us drink to the Pelican Club, under whose gentle tuition I learned to keep cool, stiffen the upper lip and always think a shade quicker than the next man. To the Pelican Club,' said Gally raising his glass.

'To the Pelican Club,' said Lord Emsworth, raising his. 'What is the Pelican Club, Galahad?'

'God bless you, Clarence,' said Gally. 'Have some more roly-poly pudding.'

CHAPTER III

THE FAMILY – REVEREND GENTLEMEN AND AUNTS

'When you get to know the family better, you'll realize that there are dozens of aunts you've not heard of yet – far-flung aunts scattered all over England, and each the leading blister of her particular county. It's a sort of family taint.'

Monty Bodkin in *Heavy Weather*

AUNT Agatha, Aunt Julia Ukridge, Aunt Dahlia, Uncle Fred – the names ring down through sixty years. They are the heart of the novels; the occasional mother or father appears but it is the uncles and aunts we remember.

Like many of his class and upbringing, Wodehouse's father was in the Colonial Civil Service. This meant that his children spent most of their childhood separated from him, since home leave was only granted every six years. Before electricity or air-conditioning, the Empire killed thousands of Britons and their families throughout the nineteenth century. The incidence of European children surviving more than three years of the Tropics was low enough to convince even the most loving of mothers that separation from either husband or children was the choice she had to make.

The result was that Wodehouse saw his parents for only six months between the ages of three and fifteen. Together with his older brothers Peveril and Armine, he spent the formative years of his life either at boarding school or with relatives. As one learns about these relatives, they lead more and more to the thought, 'This is why Bertie Wooster got the way he did' – as well as dozens of other young heroes and heroines in the ninety-seven books Wodehouse produced.

If a child doesn't have a mother or father, its emotions or at least its attention will be directed to their surrogates. Whether because of his parents' absence or because of his own nature, Wodehouse observed his uncles and aunts very closely. Closely enough for their influence to last well into his middle age. This was not any mental scar; probably it was simply that no matter how successful we become, there is always some-body who can reduce us to putty. It may be our parents, an elder brother, an old nanny or, in Wodehouse's case, aunts. Who were they?

I knew that:

(a) The Wodehouses are in *Burke's Peerage*.
(b) Wodehouse's mother was the daughter of the Reverend John Bathurst Deane.
(c) He had an Aunt Mary, Aunt Louisa and an Uncle Hugh.
(d) There was a clerical connection in the family somewhere.
(e) There were five children to the Wodehouse grandfather but more on the Deane side.

I started with *Burke's Peerage*. This showed me that one of my assumptions was wrong from the start. Wodehouse's father wasn't one of five boys, he was one of six. Furthermore he had three sisters – and I had three new aunts to look at. *Burke* and *Debrett* provided me with names, births and deaths of members of the Wodehouse family as well as their addresses and professions in some cases.

The Deanes, his mother's family, are not in the standard reference books and I had to find them through Somerset House. From Jasen's *Portrait of a Master* I knew that Wodehouse's maternal grandfather was the Reverend John Bathurst Deane and that he died between 1875 and 1890. From this I was able to find the names and addresses of over fifty Wodehouse cousins and relatives – all through the information available at Somerset House. The system works like this.

If you walk east along the Strand in London, you come to Somerset House on your right. Turn through the gates and walk straight across the quadrangle to the central doorway on the far side. You will find yourself in a hall with waist-high bookshelves all around you. In the bookshelves are the names of all the people in England and Wales who have left wills. They are set out in years and in alphabetical order within each year. The correct year isn't important so long as you know the name. Start at the earliest reasonable date and look up the name under that year, then try the next year and so on. I found the Reverend John Bathurst Deane in the volumes for 1887.

I wanted names, places and dates. The entry in the general register gives:

the name of the person making the will,

his address,

where he died,

the amount he left,

the executors to whom probate was granted.

I paid the 25 pence fee and within ten minutes the will was in front of me. That gave me the names of several children and other relatives; I was then able to look for their wills and their executors and the relatives they left money to. Somerset House gave me everything I wanted and a few bonuses. I found Jeeves's aunt there and the original of the feared McAlister, head gardener of Blandings.

I also came across some of those freak wills one reads about but never really believes. The system of Somerset House is that you are given a will to read bound with others in an enormous volume. The understanding is that you will read the one will – for which you have paid your five bob. But, if the will goes over the page, there is no objection to allowing your eyes to rest on the next. I came across at least five of these freak wills. Two left the sum of £5 out of thousands to sons 'in the hope that he will at last appreciate that, as I promised during my lifetime, my money will not support him in idleness'. There was another where a husband left his estate to a certain lady and a derisory £100 to his wife. She didn't even get that unless she was present when the will was read and had her attention drawn to her husband's reasons: 'the remainder of my estate to Miss – who gave me for forty years the comfort, support and love which should properly have been given to me at home. And in recognition of the fact which my wife often expressed, that she stayed with me only because of my wealth, I leave the sum of £100 only.'

Somerset House now only holds wills. To find birth, marriage and death certificates, you cross the Strand and work your way round Bush House to St Katherine's House at the foot of Kingsway. Somerset House told me when a person died and it was a simple matter to go to St Katharine's House to find from the death certificate the age of the deceased. This subtracted from the year of death gave the year of birth, and the appropriate register added the information of where the birth took place.

For several months I spent my lunchtime filling in the Deane family jigsaw, and the final result was that Monty Bodkin wasn't far out when he spoke those embittered words at the head of the chapter. Wodehouse saddled Gally Threepwood with ten sisters to act as aunts for the younger generation and Esmond Haddock was lucky to get off with his five. Even the aunt-ridden Bertie Wooster gets off lightly compared with his creator. 'Dozens of aunts you've not heard of yet – far-flung aunts scattered all over England,' were the words Monty used. They were an echo of real life. Young Pelham Wodehouse was the reluctant possessor of Aunts Sophia, Augusta, Louisa, Juliette, Marion, Mary, Anne, Edith, Jane, Caroline, Rosamund, Emmeline, another Marion, Jemima, Alice, another Jane, Amy, Lydia, Lucy and Harriet!

He didn't do badly for uncles either. There were Uncles Edward, Hugh, Walter, John, Augustus, William, Clement, Malcolm, Philip, Charles, Frederick, William again, Albert, another Edward and Henry. Twenty aunts and fifteen uncles!

Looking at them closely, another theory starts looking hopeful. All those clergymen in the novels, the vicars of the Mulliner stories and elsewhere, and the 'secondary' uncles, were they based on Wodehouse's family? Not the main characters like Lord Uffenham (Uncle George) or Lord Ickenham (Uncle Fred) but the minor characters who come on for comic relief. Old Tom Travers, Colonel Mant of *Something Fresh*, Colonel Wyvern, Major General Petherick-Soames, Colonel Sir Francis Pashley-Drake are the men I mean. Standard fictional characters, second comedy lead in any drawing-room farce, Wodehouse knew them from his earliest years.

The formal list of Wodehouse uncles and aunts is:

Rev. Philip John Wodehouse, MA (Cantab.). Rector of Bratton Fleming, Devonshire 1875–1913. Married Marion Bryan Wallace, daughter of the Rev. John Wallace.

Colonel Charles Wodehouse, CIE. Indian Army. Of Kolhapur, Bombay. Married Miss Jemima Fawles.

Rev. Frederick Armine Wodehouse. Rector of Gotham, Derbyshire 1882–1915. Married Alice, daughter of the Hon. and Rev. A. L. Powys.

William George Wodehouse of The Shrubs, Powick, Worcestershire. Married Jane Gill.

Henry Ernest Wodehouse, CMG, Hong Kong Civil Service (P.G.'s father).

Colonel Albert Philip Wodehouse of The Royal Inniskillings. Married Amy?? Died Great Malvern 1919.

Miss Lydia Wodehouse. Died Kensington 1914.

Miss Lucy Apollonia Wodehouse. Married Rev. Edward Whitmore Isaac, Vicar of Hanley Castle, Worcs.

Miss Harriet Wodehouse. Married Rev. Henry Bromley Cocks of Leigh Rectory, Worcs.

Wodehouse's mother's family, the Deanes, provide:

Miss Sophia Deane.

Miss Augusta Deane. Married Edward Kynaston Bridger of Berkeley House, Hampton, Middlesex.

Miss Louisa Deane. Died Bourton-on-the-Water, Glos., 1906.

Major Hugh Pollexfen Deane, 31st Regiment of Foot. Of South Kensington. Married Juliette Danielle. Died 1904.

Eleanor Deane. P.G.'s mother.

Walter Meredith Deane, CMG. Hong Kong Civil Service. Married Marian Taverner. Lived Emsworth, Hants 1904–5. Died Bath 1906.

Commander John Deane, Royal Navy. Born 1848, died 1908(?).

Miss Mary Deane. Authoress. Born 1845, died Fairford, Glos., 1940.

Miss Anne Deane. Died Highgate, Middlesex, 1934.

Miss Edith Deane. Married Commander Augustus Bradshaw, RN. Died Folkestone 1910.

Miss Jane Deane. Married William Edgar Matthews. Died either at Florence 1907 or in Devonshire 1917.

Miss Caroline Deane. Married Clement Waldron of The White House, Llandaff. She died Basingstoke, Hants., in 1932.

Miss Rosamund Deane. Married Thompson. Died Worplesdon, Surrey, 1910.

Miss Emmeline Deane. Artist. Died Uxbridge, Middlesex 1944.

There are four clergyman uncles and five uncles in the Navy or Army.

Both families can be properly, if archaically, described as gentlefolk. Wodehouse's own family was headed by the Earl of Kimberley (it's a nice thought that he had his 'own' earl) and they have been the Wodehouses of Norfolk for hundreds of years. The first earl had one of those careers that seem to start at the top and stay there. His curriculum vitae is:

Born 1826, died 1902.
Knight of The Garter, Privy Councillor, Chancellor of the University of London, High Steward Norwich Cathedral.
Under Secretary of State for Foreign Affairs 1852–56.
Minister at St Petersburg 1856–58.
Under Secretary of State Foreign Affairs 1859–61.
Under Secretary of State for India 1864.
Lord Lieutenant of Ireland 1864–68.
Lord Privy Seal 1868–70.

Secretary of State for the Colonies 1870–74 and 80–82.
Chancellor of the Duchy of Lancaster 1882–83.
Secretary of State for India 1883–85 and 92–93.
Secretary of State for Foreign Affairs 1894–95.

A man for his family to be proud of, and one of the sources of the family pride we meet so often in the novels when Bertie Wooster or one of the young ladies from Blandings wants to marry unsuitably. 'How could you think of such a thing? What about the family?'

The Wodehouses have been 'county' since 1402, when John Wodehouse was made Constable of Castle Rising. The family received knighthoods from Henry V, Henry VI and Elizabeth, were raised to a baronetcy in 1611, received a peerage in 1797 and the earldom in 1866.

We know that the family were very conscious of their gentility. Aunt Mary Deane completed the family history started by her father and published it under the title *The Book of Dene, Deane and Adeane*. It lists various illustrious members including an archbishop of Canterbury in the sixteenth century. Wodehouse used to quote his descent from Anne Boleyn on occasion and was perhaps the last man to be able to say that his grandfather fought at Waterloo. This was Colonel Philip Wodehouse (1788–1846), whose widow moved to Powick in Worcestershire with Wodehouse's father and the other eight children.

As I learnt the family history I recalled other comments in the novels. Aunt Dahlia urging Bertie to some task that will turn the moon red with blood, taunting him with the fine record of his ancestors in the Crusades; Monty Bodkin's ancestor unhorsed at the Battle of Joppa and Uncle Fred reproving a terrified nephew when it is clear that all will be discovered and Pongo will suffer the fate worse than death, viz. being looked at by Lady Constance through her lorgnette:

'We must clear out of here at once!'
Lord Ickenham was shocked.
'Clear out? That is no way for a member of a proud family

to talk. Did Twistletons clear out at Agincourt and Crecy? At Malplaquet and Blenheim? When the Old Guard made their last desperate charge up the blood-soaked slopes of Waterloo, do you suppose that Wellington, glancing over his shoulder, saw a Twistleton sneaking off with an air of ill-assumed carelessness in the direction of Brussels? We Twistletons do not clear out, my boy. We stick around, generally long after we have outstayed our welcome.'

(*Uncle Fred in the Springtime*)

Wodehouse took advantage of Aunt Mary's history writing and made it a common pastime of the older gentlemen in his novels. I counted some twelve peers of the realm in the novels who were engaged, willingly or not, in the narration of their family history and I think all these can be set at Aunt Mary's door.

We normally meet aunts in ones or twos in the comedies but one book gives a whole batch. *The Mating Season* was written in 1946–47. Bertie Wooster is compelled by circumstances to pretend to be Gussie Fink-Nottle. For good Wodehousean reasons Gussie then turns up pretending to be Bertie. The action takes place at Deverill Hall, King's Deverill, Hampshire, where the local landowner is the young Esmond Haddock who lives at the Hall with his five aunts.

'*Five?*'
'Yes, sir. The Misses Charlotte, Emmeline, Harriet and Myrtle Deverill and Dame Daphne Winkworth, relict of the late P. B. Winkworth, the historian. Dame Daphne's daughter, Miss Gertrude Winkworth, is, I understand, also in residence.'
On the cue 'five aunts' I had given at the knees a trifle, for the thought of being confronted with such a solid gaggle of aunts, even if those of another, was an unnerving one.

This is a strong echo of the ménage at Cheney Court, Box in Wiltshire. Wodehouse's maternal grandfather died in 1887 at Sion Hill, Bath. His widow Mrs Louise Deane and the four unmarried daughters Louisa, Mary, Anne and Emmeline all moved to Cheney Court where Wodehouse spent much of his childhood. The description in *The Mating Season* of Deverill Hall and of four strong-minded ladies together with one, far older than the others, who muttered to herself in corners, would fit very well with Cheney Court and the five ladies as Wodehouse knew them.

The Mating Season is written around Bertie, Jeeves, Gussie Fink-Nottle and their friends. The aunts are secondary characters and it is normally in the secondary characters of the novels that we shall find the coincidences of fact and fiction. Wodehouse's last aunt died in 1944 and I find it no surprise that a novel that has five aunts dominating a young man should be written two years after the last of Wodehouse's own aunts had died. No matter how the world applauds you there is always somebody shaking their head and saying what a pity it all is. In Wodehouse's case it was his aunts.

What is clearly not a coincidence are the clergymen. There are thirty or so in the novels and it is a fair assumption that they are based on Uncle Philip of Bratton Fleming, Uncle Frederick of Gotham, Uncle Edward of Hanley Castle and Uncle Henry of Leigh. The Isaac family confirm that Wodehouse used to spend holidays with them at Hanley Castle and we know from *Portrait of a Master* that he looked forward to his summer holidays down in Devon with Uncle Philip. The world owes a debt to these gentlemen.

Wodehouse's stories of the Anglican clergy are an excellent example of laughing at and with something at the same time. The bishops are dignified and respected (unless under the influence of Mulliner's Buck-U-Uppo), the vicars are hard-working and conscientious, the curates are upstanding Christians with Blues for boxing or rowing, whose only weakness is a tendency to fall in love with spirited young ladies whose ideas of right and wrong are diametrically opposed to those of their fiancés.

We learn from the wills of the clergymen uncles that they had curates as well. A comparison of *Crockford's Clerical Directory* and the marriage certificates in St Katherine's House shows that, like their fictional successors, the real uncles tended not to marry till they had their own vicarage or rectory. This was the root of half the problems of Wodehouse's young reverend gentlemen and their complicated love affairs.

Wodehouse learnt a great deal from his uncles. It sounds very dated now, carrying bowls of soup to the deserving poor ('Amazing the way these bimbos soak up soup. Like sponges . . .'), but look at a volume of *Punch* between 1885 and 1905 and the picture solidifies. He knew exactly the scene he was drawing, the problems with the church roof, heresy or loose thinking amongst the Bible Class, episcopal visitations – he saw them all and drew them for us with affection.

Two aunts stand out in the long list – Aunt Mary and Aunt Louisa Deane. They were in the group who moved to Cheney Court after their father had died and, in 1892, his widow followed him. Her will left the house jointly to the four daughters on the condition that if any one left, her share would revert to the other three. Within eighteen months the four daughters joined together to break the conditions, sold Cheney Court and went their separate ways.

Aunt Louisa was Wodehouse's favourite. She was the eldest and had the task of helping her mother to bring up the large family. She moved to Bourton-on-the-Water and died there in 1906. Jasen mentions that Wodehouse had her in mind when he created Bertie's Aunt Dahlia. Later in *Portrait of a Master* Jasen says that Wodehouse based Aunt Dahlia on Lady Ilchester, whom he met in 1923. He quotes Wodehouse as saying: 'I always thought of her when I was doing Aunt Dahlia.'

Lady Helen Mary Theresa Vane-Tempest-Stewart, daughter of the sixth Marquess of Londonderry, married Lord Ilchester and died in 1956. She hunted, and her obituary speaks of her deep voice and great sense of humour. To her and Miss Louisa Deane our thanks are due.

Wodehouse used his immediate family rarely. This is not to imply that he put uncles and aunts rather than fathers or mothers into his novels deliberately. Probably it was just that since aunts and clergymen uncles formed such a large part of his life, he assumed that they did so in everybody else's. Although his favourite brother Armine joined the Theosophists when he was teaching in India, Wodehouse mentions theosophy only three or four times. It is what heroines at Blandings read when they are scorning their fiancés; it is what Bertie thinks of when Jeeves shimmers and vanishes from sight only to reappear as if by magic when the young master needs him.

His eldest brother, Philip Peveril, appears only once. He followed his father and went out to Hong Kong in 1897, was awarded the CIE in 1919 and retired in 1932. George Emerson is the second hero in the first Blandings story, *Something Fresh*. He is in love with Aline Peters and she realizes she loves him when he is recalled to Hong Kong. At the time when Wodehouse wrote that his brother was, as George Emerson was, an officer in the Hong Kong Police and he retired twenty years later as its deputy commander.

Like all the Deane ladies, Wodehouse's mother seems to have been strong-willed, and I think we meet her only once when we suffer with Frederick Mulliner at the hands of his old nanny down at Bingley-on-Sea in *Meet Mr Mulliner*. Bingley-on-Sea became Bramley-on-Sea later, and I spent some time wondering which South Coast resort could claim to be the original. I think Bexhill-on-Sea will fit very well since Wodehouse often used the initial letter of a real source and he certainly visited Bexhill often to see his parents, who moved there from Cheltenham.

In one of his later books, *Do Butlers Burgle Banks?*, Wodehouse showed surprising knowledge of the workings of a small private bank. There are none left now: the amalgamations of the Big Five clearing banks swept them all away in the 1920s. The background of such an organization puzzled me till I started down the side-paths of the wills in Somerset House. Aunt Lucy Wodehouse married the Reverend Edward Isaac of Hanley Castle, and while looking through his background, I kept coming across relations who were bankers or were mentioned as vicars in Shropshire. The upshot was that my Mr Isaac had a brother who owned or was partner in a small bank in Worcester a few miles from Hanley Castle. It was known at various times as the 'Worcester Old Bank', the 'Lechmere and Isaac Bank' and as the 'Berwick, Lechmere, Isaac, Martin Bank'. Quite sufficient for Wodehouse to have known of it and also to have made the acquaintance of the Lechmeres of Severn End, one of Worcestershire's oldest families. The present Mr Isaac confirms that his father had known the Lechmeres well and that Wodehouse met them in his childhood.

Both the Deane and Wodehouse families numbered authors amongst their members. Lord Kimberley wrote of his days in Government, Uncle Walter Deane wrote a book on Whist, Wodehouse's grandfather (Rev. Mr Deane) wrote the life of an ancestor who had been one of Cromwell's generals, and Aunt Mary Deane has a dozen titles to her name in the British Museum catalogue.

One of Aunt Mary's books is dedicated to a cousin, the Rt Hon. Robert Wodehouse, who was MP for Bath from 1880 till 1906. I do not know how well she knew the Rt Hon. but I suspect that her friendship with him might be a forerunner of the attempts by Bertie Wooster's Aunt Agatha to persuade the Rt Hon. A. B. Fillmer MP to take Bertie as his private secretary in *Very Good, Jeeves*. The address of the Rt Hon. Robert Wodehouse was Woolmers, Hertfordshire, which has always struck me as being very similar to Aunt Agatha's house where we meet Mr Fillmer – 'Woollam Chersey, Hertfordshire'. Did Aunt Mary plan a political career for Wodehouse? With one cousin as Foreign Secretary and two more as MPs it could well have been possible.

Wodehouse always drew his main characters very carefully. When he wrote his secondary characters he might take certain liberties (cf. the aunts at Cheney Court/Deverill Hall) but when somebody refers to a fact superfluous to the plot, then in comes the 'Wodehouse allusion' – the private joke. In 'All's Well with Bingo', a story from *Eggs, Beans and Crumpets*, Bingo Little is sent by Mrs Bingo to Monte Carlo to collect local colour for the book she is writing. It is completely immaterial to Wodehouse's story but he tells us that the character Mrs Bingo wants to write about is 'Lord Peter Shipbourne'. At the time he wrote it, Wodehouse's son-in-law was Peter Cazalet, who lived at Shipbourne in Kent. Nothing dramatic, just a private family joke. Something to make Wodehouse and the rest of the family smile.

In *Galahad at Blandings* there's another one. The hero is Sam Bagshot and he is trying to get enough money to sell his house to Oofy Prosser. The house needs repairs and Sam Bagshot, a young barrister (like Wodehouse's grandson), tells Gally that it is called 'Great Swifts'. The only house in England by that name belonged to Victor Cazalet, Peter Cazalet's brother. His obituary speaks of his generosity in allowing youth organizations to camp regularly in the grounds. Was this the origin of Lord Emsworth's problem with the Church Lads at Blandings?

Most of us remember McAlister, the dreaded gardener of Blandings. But in *Something Fresh*, the first Blandings novel in 1915, the gardener is Thorne, not McAlister. I found the real Thorne in the will of Wodehouse's grandmother. He was the gardener at Cheney Court!

Thorne the gardener in 1915, 'Lord Peter Shipbourne' in 1937, 'Great Swifts' in 1965. Only three examples but they are an indication that we are on the right lines. But I wish I knew more about those clergymen uncles from whom Wodehouse learnt so much. Did any of them have their boxing Blues? How do you address a bishop who was at school with you? And how many orphreys should there be on a chasuble?

CHAPTER IV

UKRIDGE

STANLEY Featherstonhaugh Ukridge was born in *Love among the Chickens* in 1906. He was still with us unchanged in *Plum Pie* in 1966. He was the first Wodehouse humorous character, the first anti-hero, the rogue who wins our affection while we deplore his unscrupulous successes.

Ukridge is unforgettable. The pince-nez, the yellow mackintosh worn like Napoleon's cloak, Walter Raleigh's doublet or Caesar's toga depending on its owner's mood of defiance, gallantry or reproach, the collar-stud unable to do its work – all are the outward symbols of the bold spirit Wodehouse drew for us. He is an Old Wrykynian, the black sheep of a respectable family, he addresses everyone from bishops to bookmakers as 'Old horse', he is the supreme optimist. In search of easy money he runs a chicken farm (with the chickens on tick), a gambling joint (in his aunt's house), a hotel (again in his aunt's house), organizes a flag day (in favour of himself), starts a school for performing dogs (with dogs stolen from his aunt) and manages a heavyweight boxer.

In *Love among the Chickens* he is married, but Wodehouse realized that he is one of Nature's bachelors and a bachelor is how he appears thereafter. Bertie Wooster is another who can never marry, and the comparison of the two leads directly to the two worlds they represent. With Bertie we are with the Drones, the Pongoes and Freddies, Old Etonians all – 'Dracula? Never met him. Must be a Harrow man . . ' – of the high farces. With Ukridge we are in an earlier period and a different world. We can read a story about Bertie and Jeeves,

43

turn the page and plunge into another of Ukridge's adventures, but a story with both men in it wouldn't work. Wodehouse's integrity in maintaining the worlds he created won't allow such miscegenation. Ukridge and his Alma Mater Wrykyn are part of the world of young Corcoran, of Sam Shotter and George Tupper, young men with their names to make. It is far removed from the world of Blandings Castle and the Drones.

Why did Wodehouse keep Ukridge going for so long? From the first novel through the high farces of Jeeves, Uncle Fred and Blandings, he appears every few years, always the same and always against the same background. R. B. D. French suggests that Ukridge gave Wodehouse a means of escape into a little wholesome vulgarity and that he used Ukridge to touch society at all levels. French describes the care with which Wodehouse defines precisely the attitude of young Corcoran, based on Wodehouse himself, to the docks of the East End at one end of the scale and to Belgravia and the moneyed respectability of Wimbledon at the other.

To do it when one was of the same age and background of Corcoran is one thing. To be able to reproduce the same emotions and attitudes sixty years later is quite another. This is the reason for Ukridge's survival in the Wodehouse canon. He is part of the time when there was anxiety over whether one could pay the landlady, when four courses in an Italian restaurant at one and sixpence was the weekly treat.

When life was so straitened and uncertain, Ukridge's grandiose schemes for riches all flowing from the big, broad, flexible outlook arouse wonderment and admiration from his less confident fellows. French makes an important point – that Wodehouse was a very shy man and must have been deeply impressed by the boldness and self-assurance that are Ukridge's hallmark. Bookmakers and bishops, dukes and dustmen, Ukridge treats them all exactly the same way. To the shy young Wodehouse, Ukridge was a phenomenon and his impact was never forgotten. Bertie Wooster and Blandings may be timeless but Ukridge is fixed for ever in one period of Wodehouse's life, that interval of freedom and excitement after school or university when our careers are still a matter of choice rather than necessity. Pick out any Ukridge story and try and date it. Occasionally the clothes provide a clue but without some indication like this it is difficult to tell whether it was written in 1922 or 1962. The memory of Stanley Feather-stonhaugh Ukridge is as fresh in Wodehouse's memory as the day he sat down eighty years ago to record Jeremy Garnet's alarm in *Love among the Chickens* when he learnt that Ukridge intended to pay him a visit.

The identity of the real Ukridge was befogged for years by rumours circulating about the wrong man. I had therefore to find the real Ukridge and prove the error of the other attribution. In recent years Wodehouse and Jasen have given us more clues but the name has never been confirmed beyond doubt. But there was a real Ukridge and this chapter tells how I found him.

We know from the dedication of *Love among the Chickens* that William Townend wrote to Wodehouse in 1905 describing the adventures of a friend of his on a chicken farm and Wodehouse used the letter to write his first Ukridge story. But one letter is clearly insufficient to provide the basis for all the Ukridge stories of later years. There must have been somebody else, somebody in Wodehouse's life who could be adapted to follow on the original idea.

One of the most famous autobiographies of this century is Robert Graves' *Goodbye to All That*. In the early chapters Graves describes his childhood at Red Branch House in Lauriston Road, Wimbledon. He says that Wodehouse was a friend of Robert's elder brother Perceval, and because Wode-house once gave him twopence to buy marshmallows, Robert felt he could not criticize Wodehouse's novels.

If your copy says that it is one of the later editions. If you have a first or second edition it will say something about Perceval Graves sharing a flat with Wodehouse, and Wode-house's many references to Wimbledon made Robert think that Perceval and his aunt Grace Pontifex had both figured in the Ukridge stories. Another brother, Charles Graves, the first of the present-day gossip columnists, says the same thing in his *The Bad Old Days*.

The Graves family may not be unique but they are certainly unusual. Their pedigree goes back to the Conquest and they have provided bishops, soldiers and surgeons of note since the time of Cromwell. The Sitwells, Foots and Huxleys haven't done so badly but the Graves must hold the record for the number of books written by one family. Charles Graves speaks of the hundreds of books three generations of his family produced, finishing with the casual line: 'If it comes to that, every one of my other six surviving brothers and sisters has written anything from one to five books; so had my Aunt Ida (Lady Poore), my Uncle Arnold and my Uncle Bob (Sir Robert Graves).' Add the Dr Graves of Graves' Disease, who also invented the mechanism for the second hand on watches, another Graves who was Queen Victoria's favourite preacher and an uncle who was asked to decide the US/Canadian boundary and you have some of the elements of one of the most gifted families in the country.

Perceval Graves is dead now, but when I met him in his middle nineties he still possessed the good looks for which the Graves are famous. Charles Graves wrote of him in 1951:

Perceval gay, goodlooking as his great-uncle the legendary Charles O'Malley, the playboy of the family, practised as a lawyer in places as far east as Rangoon and as far west as British Columbia, returned to England, married twice. His twin delights have always been Somerset cricket and English opera. Now he does gardening, writes occasional books and lives near St. Albans.

I first went to see Perceval Graves completely ignorant of the Ukridge attribution. I was certainly looking for Ukridge but my edition of *Goodbye to All That* was a late one and all I knew was that he had shared a flat with Wodehouse early in the century. In the course of our conversation he told me of the attribution by Robert and his annoyance at it. He had persuaded Robert to delete the passage in later editions but he gave me sufficient information to trace the rumour through various books of memoirs.

During a second visit, I mentioned that I was still having difficulty in my search for Ukridge. If Ukridge wasn't Townend or Perceval Graves, who was he? In their kindness Mr and Mrs Perceval Graves found the answer and gave me permission to use it.

Here is the letter to settle the question; from the creator of Ukridge to the putative Ukridge saying who the real Ukridge was:

Sept 26 1960

Dear Graves,

How nice hearing from you after all these years. I remember so well the time – gosh, it must be nearly fifty-five years! – when we shared rooms.

I can't imagine what Robert was thinking of when he said that I had drawn Ukridge from you! There couldn't be two more different people. Ukridge was drawn originally from what Townend told me about a man named Craxton, and shortly after that I met a man named Westbrook who was very much the same type of chap. Both now dead. Lots of people agree with you in not liking Ukridge. I suppose he is a bit too much of a crook.

Yes, I remember that stand in the Artists match. Great days!

I shall join you in being 79 next month.

Yours ever

P. G. Wodehouse

So we have two names and it was a straightforward matter of Somerset House, St Katherine's House and the reference libraries. I knew Westbrook's name already; he was the co-author with Wodehouse of *Not George Washington* (1907), a story written by the two of them about an author who sells his work by using the names of four strangers. Craxton I was unable to trace. It is an unusual name and there are few among the records of Somerset House between 1910 and 1970. Craxton was a friend of Townend's not of Wodehouse's, and since both were dead, it was impossible to say which Craxton I wanted. Townend says the chicken farm was in the West Country somewhere so our man might be the Walter Hugh Craxton who died in Blandford, Dorset, in 1949 at the age of 75. He might equally have been the Thomas William Henry Craxton of Surbiton, Surrey, who died in 1937 or Charles Sidney Craxton . . . The trail is too cold – but Westbrook is another matter.

In his *Portrait of a Master* Jasen relates how Westbrook came to see Wodehouse with a letter of introduction and also tells of certain incidents that confirm that Ukridge/Westbrook relationship.

Somerset House gave me the time and place of Westbrook's death and the people to whom he left bequests, and the British Museum holds copies of the books he wrote. Further, since he spent most of his time in London, Kelly's Directories have most of his addresses through the years. That is the detail; the fact/fiction relationship is that Ukridge is four men.

He is, first, the mysterious Craxton whom Townend described in the letter to Wodehouse. He is also and un-questionably Herbert Wotton Westbrook, both from the incidents Jasen describes and Wodehouse's letter to Perceval Graves. He is also William Townend himself. Townend's unusual methods of earning his living made a deep impression on Wodehouse and the most startling of these was Townend's habit of travelling the hard way – in the galley or stokehold of tramp steamers. Ukridge maintained his deus ex machina status by vanishing on such trips to reappear with Battling Billson or some new scheme for that elusive fortune. Because Townend told Wodehouse the original story, Wodehouse always associated him with Ukridge and used a facet of his life to develop Ukridge's character.

The fourth source is 'Shifter' Goldberg, 'Fatty' Coleman, 'Brer Rabbit' and those other impecunious eccentrics of the Pelican Club whose antics Wodehouse knew so well and whose ingenuity and unscrupulousness he followed to such effect when he wrote the Ukridge stories. But Westbrook is our main source.

Ukridge is an unusual name. There is not nor ever has been a

Ukridge in the London Telephone Directory nor could I find any trace of it in Somerset House. There were four brothers named Uridge at Dulwich with Wodehouse and perhaps they provide half the name with the second syllable of Westbrook's name providing the other half. There is certainly the same ring to Herbert Wotton Westbrook as there is to Stanley Featherstonhaugh Ukridge.

In *Love among the Chickens* Jeremy Garnet speaks of Ukridge's habit of addressing everybody as 'Old horse':

> . . . He had the painful habit of addressing all and sundry by that title. In his schoolmaster days – at one period of his vivid career he and I had been colleagues on the staff of a private school – he had made use of it while interviewing the parents of new boys and the latter had gone away, as a rule, with a feeling that this must be either the easy manner of Genius or due to alcohol, and hoping for the best.

When Westbrook first met Wodehouse, he was a schoolmaster at King-Hall's school at Emsworth in Hampshire and he invited Wodehouse down there. Wodehouse went, became friends with the headmaster, Baldwin King-Hall, and lived in a room over the stables for a couple of months. He lived in Emsworth for two years and although he never taught at the school, he certainly knew the routine there very well.

In 'First Aid for Dora', a story from *Ukridge*, young Corcoran returns to his digs in exalted mood to don his dress clothes before joining his friends at Mario's. He has drawn the third horse in the club sweep on the Derby and he is on top of the world. Wodehouse describes his euphoria as he greets his awe-inspiring ex-butler landlord Bowles:

> 'Mr Ukridge called earlier in the evening, sir,' said Bowles.
> 'Did he? Sorry I was out. I was trying to get hold of him. Did he want anything in particular?'
> 'Your dress-clothes, sir.'
> 'My dress-clothes, eh?' I laughed genially. 'Extraordinary fellow! You never know – '. A ghastly thought smote me like

a blow. A cold wind seemed to blow through the hall.

'He didn't get them, did he?' I quavered.

'Why, yes, sir.'

'Got my dress-clothes?' I muttered thickly, clutching for support at the hat-stand.

'He said it would be all right, sir,' said Bowles with that sickening tolerance which he always exhibited for all that Ukridge said or did. One of the leading mysteries of my life was my landlord's amazing attitude towards this hell-hound. He fawned on the man. A splendid fellow like myself had to go about in a state of hushed reverence towards Bowles, while a human blot like Ukridge could bellow at him over the banisters without the slightest rebuke. It was one of those things which make one laugh cynically when people talk about the equality of man.

The upshot is that Corcoran has to go off to Mario's in a suit lent to him by Bowles. Formerly the property of the late Earl of Oxted, it is far too small, smells strongly of mothballs and gives rise to uninhibited comment amongst his friends.

The real story is told three times by Wodehouse. It is his laughing butler story, which in the period it happened was something to tell your grandchildren.

In *Bring on the Girls* in 1954 Wodehouse tells Bolton how he had to attend a dinner-party in the evening dress belonging to his Uncle Hugh. Uncle Hugh (Captain Hugh Pollexfen Deane) was a very big man and his trousers were so large that they kept riding up over the embarrassed Wodehouse's shirtfront. Eventually they escaped altogether and shot right up over his tie. This was too much for the butler, who gasped like a paper bag exploding and dashed from the room. Bolton says: 'You should have had the things altered by a tailor.' 'Talk sense,' says Wodehouse. 'It would have cost about a quid.'

In 1957 in *Over Seventy*, we get a little more detail:

On a certain night in the year 1903 I had been invited to a rather more stately home than usual and, owing to the friend who has appeared in some of my stories under the name of

Ukridge having borrowed my dress clothes without telling me, I had to attend the function in a primitive suit of soup-and-fish bequeathed to me by my Uncle Hugh, a man who stood six feet four and weighed in the neighbourhood of fifteen stone.

In 1975 in Jasen's *Portrait of a Master*, we read the version:

On this occasion, Plum had been invited to a formal dinner party at a nearby stately home. Coincidentally, Westbrook, who was in residence, had been invited to a similar party elsewhere and had borrowed Plum's best formal clothes without bothering to tell him. Plum was therefore forced . . .

Borrowing a friend's clothes is common enough amongst young men. Do we have anything else?

In *Thank You, Jeeves*, we are introduced to Bertie Wooster's banjo:

I was still playing the banjolele when he arrived. Those who know Bertram Wooster best are aware that he is a man of sudden, strong enthusiasms and that, when in the grip of one of these, he becomes a remorseless machine – tense, absorbed, single-minded. It was so in the matter of this banjolele-playing of mine. Since the night at the Alhambra when the supreme virtuosity of Ben Bloom and his Sixteen Baltimore Buddies had fired me to take up the study of the instrument, not a day had passed without its couple of hours assiduous practice.

The banjo causes Bertie to be evicted from his flat, forces Jeeves to resign and eventually perishes in the flames of Bertie's cottage down at Chuffnell Regis.

The next banjo appears in 'Ukridge's Accident Syndicate', a story from *Ukridge*. In order to cash in on the insurance policies they have taken out with a dozen daily papers, Ukridge's syndicate have to persuade Teddy Weeks to have the accident on their behalf. He shows an understandable reluctance to do so and says he needs to be primed with champagne. Consternation strikes the syndicate of penurious young men, but Ukridge makes the big decision:

'Gentlemen,' said Ukridge, 'it would seem that the company requires more capital. How about it, old horses? Let's get together in a frank, business-like cards-on-the-table spirit and see what can be done. I can raise ten bob.'

'What!' cried the entire assembled company, amazed. 'How?'

'I'll pawn a banjo.'

'You haven't got a banjo.'

'No, but George Tupper has, and I know where he keeps it.'

Started in this spirited way, the subscriptions came pouring in.

Once again *Portrait of a Master* gives us the origins:

As if all this were not enough, he had a new endeavour in mind for 1905. One of his New Year's resolutions was to learn to play the banjo. This sudden thirst for musical accomplishment may have been the direct result of his still-recent introduction to the world of the theatre. . . . What heights he might have scaled as a banjoist will, alas, never be known. There was a fly, so to speak, in the ointment – namely Westbrook. That worthy was on one of his prolonged stays at Threepwood, which meant that almost anything could happen at any time. What actually did happen was that Westbrook – either because he had no ear for music or because he was temporarily out of ready cash – took advantage of one of Plum's absences from the house to rush the banjo off to an obliging pawnshop. This would not have irked Plum so much had the separation from his instrument been for a specified period. But Westbrook, whether by accident or design, lost the pawn ticket and thus put paid to a possible musical career . . .

Craxton, Townend's friend, provided the initial inspiration but thereafter Ukridge is firmly based on the eccentricities of Herbert Wotton Westbrook.

Wodehouse and Westbrook first met in 1903. Wodehouse moved down to Emsworth, where Westbrook was a teacher, and stayed there, either in the school or at a cottage called Threepwood. Westbrook was trying his hand at freelance writing and when Wodehouse was promoted to become chief writer of the 'By the Way' column of *The Globe*, he persuaded the editor to employ Westbrook as his assistant. They worked together for the next few years and, after Wodehouse returned from his second trip to New York, they continued in partnership till about 1913. That's about ten years collaboration, during which they produced that odd piece of autobiographical writing *Not George Washington*, collaborated in a play for Lawrence Grossmith, did a sketch for the theatre with music by Ella King-Hall and wrote articles under each other's name and split the proceeds. From 1913 their ways seem to have separated, although Ella King-Hall married Westbrook in 1911 and Wodehouse made her his agent in England.

The British Museum catalogue has six books under Westbrook's name:

The Cause of Catesby (1905) (a novel about the Gunpowder Plot)
Not George Washington (1907) (written jointly with Wodehouse)
The Globe By the Way Book (1908) (written jointly with Wodehouse)
The Purple Frogs (1914) (a musical written with Lawrence Grossmith)
Back Numbers (1918)
The Booby Prize (1924)

One of these, *Back Numbers*, is of interest and makes odd reading to a Wodehouse enthusiast. The stories owe something to Barry Pain and O. Henry and all reflect the short story style that started with the mass circulation magazines and newspapers of the 1890s. They concern a young man and the various jobs he tries – which leads to the question, were they autobiographical? Many of them do not have a happy ending and reveal a bitterness or cynicism that might be the trait we are looking for. If Westbrook was the origin of Ukridge he had to be egotistical to say the least.

In Westbrook's will in Somerset House there are various legacies mentioned, including one to his solicitor Mr Simons. Mr Simons of Simons and Vaizey is dead now but his son still practises and remembers Westbrook as an elderly man, sandy hair freckled with grey, very cheerful and with appalling writing. He says Westbrook wore thick spectacles with gold wire rims (no – not pince-nez), was not very tall and had left little in his will.

I still had little idea of what Westbrook was like and decided to try one of the relatives mentioned in the will. Mr Charles Westbrook is an optician in Lymington and kindly made time to tell me of his uncle.

In the 1870s two families living in North Kent intermarried and a Miss Wotton married Mr Westbrook. The families were successful small shipbuilders but were badly hit by the Baring's Bank crash of 1891. An aunt provided the money to send young Herbert Westbrook to school at Tonbridge and Ely and he went on to King's College, Cambridge (is this why so many early Wodehouse heroes went to King's?). He won a place in the Trial Eight but had an argument with his coach and did not get his Blue. He must have gone to King-Hall's school at Emsworth soon after getting his degree. He met Wodehouse, started working on *The Globe* with him and eloped in 1911 with Ella King-Hall, Baldwin King-Hall's sister.

He fought in the First World War, was commissioned, wounded and returned to writing articles for newspapers and magazines. *The Globe* was closed down during the war so he lost his income from that source although Ella King-Hall's literary agency kept them going. Charles Westbrook remembers his uncle's financial status as precarious but this did not seem to bother Westbrook, who enjoyed entertaining people to dinner and employing expensive caterers to do it. A series of family legacies helped him to maintain his standard of living. He died at 54 Flood Street, Chelsea, in 1959.

Two photographs show him to have been a goodlooking man. In the earlier photograph he is a young Edwardian with the fashionable high collar of the period. In the other, taken towards the end of his life, he is impressive in a double-breasted suit, with strong regular features. He had a patrician manner but remained fond of his wife to the end of her life and missed her sadly after her death in 1932. He could be inconsiderate or rude with little provocation, and was easily bored by men but was fascinating to, and was fascinated by, pretty women. He had no children.

In a note Charles Westbrook subsequently wrote to me, he sums up his uncle as having great natural charm and a delightful speaking voice. He had panache and never liked discussing such mundane things as cash problems or politics. He was a Greek and Latin scholar and retained an interest in algebra till the end of his life.

I have set out below a poem Westbrook wrote. It has the charm Wodehouse perceived in the writer which, when one thinks about it, is the secret of Ukridge's appeal. Nobody ever said no to Ukridge – they would do what he wanted against their better judgement. The clothes borrowing, the pawning of banjoes, the great schemes for the elusive fortune are the details that make us laugh. It is Ukridge's influence over all who meet him, his friends, his enemies, landlords and fierce dogs that is important – and charm and panache are the words Westbrook's nephew used of him.

'L'Hôtelier'
(Oscar Wilde died at the Hôtel d'Alsace, Paris, on 30 November 1900)

A little hotel is the Hôtel d'Alsace
Its rating is formally Fifth.

But le patron, Dupoirier, asks you to note
The electrical system of bells.
He works for his living, rises at dawn
And buys what he wants from Les Halles
Advised by Madame (yes, she sits at the caisse).
They're careful and, well, they contrive.

They contrive to be happy, these two, for it's fun
To master the tricks of the trade.
Here's an afternoon off. Shall we go to Chaville?
There's a fête in the forest today.
They contrive to see Coquelin (Cyrano's role),
Take a turn at the Bal Tabarin.
But these are rare outings. Thrift keeps them at home;
'We don't like to leave the hotel.'

The Rue des Beaux Arts is Dupoirier's world.
There he's known – and no further than that.
The sum of his life has created no stir
That captures the public and Press.
He dines with his neighbours without a display
Of brilliant and whimsical talk.
He is gentle and kind to his sick locataire,
His debtor, who dies in his arms.

H. W. Westbrook

Westbrook may have made a few more contributions to his friend's work, since three of Wodehouse's most disparate characters have something in common; the handsome Lionel Green of *Money in the Bank* and *Company for Henry*, the Rev. Harold Pinker and Lord Tilbury of The Mammoth Press. They are all known to their intimates as 'Stinker', which is the same soubriquet by which Westbrook always addressed his old friend Plum Wodehouse.

I don't know if Westbrook and Wodehouse met after the First War. I think they may have done. 'Ukridge's Dog College', a story from *Ukridge*, appeared in 1923. The action takes place at The White Cottage, Sheep's Cray, Kent.

Looking through Kelly's Directory for Kent for 1921, I note that the address for H. W. Westbrook is Barne's Cray, Crayford, Kent.

CHAPTER V

SNAKES, PEKES AND PARROTS

THE animal kingdom has a special place in Wodehouse's books. It is one of the most fruitful fields of investigation since we are on sure ground.

Animals appear in nearly every one of Wodehouse's ninety-seven books and are mentioned in every second letter in *Performing Flea*. A close comparison of the books and the letters to William Townend show that the fictional animals bear a remarkable resemblance to those Wodehouse owned at the time of writing.

For most people snakes are unpleasant animals, but not for Wodehouse. From about 1920, like all his animals, they are a force for good, and have a part to play in the stories in which they appear.

The first snake is Clarence, the property of Polly, Countess of Wetherby, in *Uneasy Money* in 1916. She is the pleasant chorus-girl who married England's poorest earl and she makes a fortune doing classical dancing in a New York nightclub. This isn't too Wodehousean – at least two English peeresses added considerably to their savings by doing just that before the First World War.

There is the friendly Peter in *Indiscretions of Archie* in 1921, Bobby Wickham's snake in *Mr Mulliner Speaking* in 1929, Joe Bishop's snakes in *Ice in the Bedroom* in 1961 and three or four others scattered through the novels, concluding with Legs Ponderby's attacker in *A Pelican at Blandings* in 1969.

I have no firm origin for this liking for snakes but perhaps childhood memories of Hong Kong or of grass snakes in

Shropshire may have something to do with it. There is an odd piece of information tucked away in Beverley Nichol's *Are They the Same at Home?* (1927). Describing a visit to the Zoo with Wodehouse he says of him:

> Apart from that he [Wodehouse] grew increasingly sombre and preoccupied. Perhaps that was because he could not find the snakes (for which he seemed to cherish an unnatural affection). Whenever there was a pause in the conversation he said, rather plaintively, 'I suppose there ARE snakes?' and the rest of us, who did not at all want to see the snakes, remarked quickly that of course there were snakes, lots of them, but that they were a long way off, and just *look* at that lovely antelope. He looked, sighed, and said, 'Yes, it is a beautiful antelope.' But one knew that in his heart of hearts he cherished a fierce resentment against that antelope, simply because it was not a snake.

Parrots are the next category and include Polly in *The Man Upstairs* in 1914, Bill in *Jill the Reckless* (1920) and the unfortunate Leonard in *Ukridge* (1924), who gives Wodehouse the chance to introduce one of his best tricks. Young Corcoran has returned to his flat and is met by his landlord Bowles carrying a bottle and a large cardboard hatbox. Bowles explains that Ukridge has left them.

> I had not seen Ukridge for more than two weeks, but at our last meeting, I remembered he had spoken of some foul patent medicine of which he had somehow procured the agency. This [the bottle], apparently, was it.
> 'But what's in the hat-box?' I asked.
> 'I could not say, sir,' replied Bowles.
> At this point the hat-box, which had not hitherto spoken, uttered a crisp, sailorly oath, and followed it up by singing the opening bars of 'Annie Laurie'. It then relapsed into its former moody silence.

There's another parrot in *The Small Bachelor*, Uncle Fred's famous patient in Mitching Hill from *Young Men in Spats* and the parrot that nearly frightened Lancelot Bingley to death in *Plum Pie*. The maltreated Leonard and Nelly Bryant's Bill in *Jill the Reckless* get star-billing and in Bill's case a section to itself and its adventures in the big, wide world – providing just the twist in the story that Wodehouse wanted.

A spread of parrots from 1914 to 1966, but the two best described occur in 1920 and 1924. Why at this period particularly? The first letter in *Performing Flea* is dated February 1920 and it concludes:

> We sail on the *Adriatic* on April 24, as follows: Ethel, carrying the black kitten, followed by myself with parrot in cage and Loretta, our maid, with any other animals we may acquire in the meantime.

The weird animals that Wodehouse's actresses kept for publicity were certainly not imaginary. Our pop stars nowadays maintain their publicity in different ways but Lottie Blossom's alligator, Lady Wetherby's snake and monkey and Madame Brodowska's snake Peter in *Indiscretions of Archie* were all reflections of the theatrical world Wodehouse knew and which his readers knew as well. In *Mrs A*, the biography of Gertrude Lawrence, her husband speaks of Tallulah Bankhead turning up for rehearsals in 1940 with her monkey and in 1941 with a lion cub. If a star like Miss Bankhead felt that animals could help her publicity, what lengths must lesser ladies have gone to?

Nor was it a modern phenomenon. Wodehouse was a lyric-writer in London in 1906 when one of the ladies of the Gaiety turned up with a young puma. Wodehouse's fictional actresses behaved as did the real ones he knew.

Cats crop up constantly in the novels, from the evil Captain Kettle in 1903 in *Tales of St Austin's* to the cat that is the cause of all the trouble in his last completed novel *Aunts Aren't Gentlemen*. He knews cats well, spoke often in his letters of his wife's collection of cats and wrote of them in his books. Some are heroic like the reprobate Webster, some merely light relief like the drowsy Augustus of Brinkley Court. All are important in the stories in which they appear – like every animal in the novels they have a part to play. Only in the case of one or two of the early stories can they be considered merely as background.

With dogs we come back to our main track – those small incidents in Wodehouse's life that appear in his novels. The characteristics he saw in his own animals are reflected in the animal scenes he wrote. This was not mawkish sentimentality. He simply took the behaviour of his animals in the same way that he took the surroundings in which he found himself – and used them. I think he would pause in his work, lean back, light his pipe, do whatever he did when stumped for a word, and idly watch the antics of his dogs and muse on their idiosyncrasies. Later that same idiosyncrasy would appear full-blown as though the whole plot had been built round it.

Pekinese were probably his favourites. He owned them for thirty years and they are mentioned constantly in *Performing Flea*, but they are only one breed among many.

The first dog in the novels was Bob, the stupid but amiable mongrel in *Love among the Chickens* (1906). It was with Bob that Jeremy Garnet went for his swim in the morning and with Bob that he mused on his love for Phyllis Derrick. I do not know whether any of the uncles or aunts with whom he spent his childhood had a dog. Perhaps they did, but when his parents came back to England in 1895 and bought the house in Shropshire he loved so much, they bought their first dog. It was a mongrel called Bob.

The next animal we know Wodehouse owned was a case of fiction-to-fact rather than fact-fiction. In *Mike*, written in 1909, one of the big incidents in the book is the painting of Sammy the bull-terrier. The next animal we read of Wodehouse owning, the first dog of his own that we know of, is the bulldog that he was 'given by one of the girls in the revue Guy and I wrote for the Century Theatre (Gosh, what a flop that one was!)'. The bulldog is mentioned in the first letter in *Performing Flea*, written in 1920. Wodehouse was given the animal in 1917, eight years after *Mike* was written, but he named the bulldog Sammy.

It is Sammy that we see reflected in all those bulldogs of frightening appearance but hearts of gold that occur throughout the novels. 'The Mixer' in *The Man with Two Left Feet* is a bulldog/terrier mixture; the animal Archie Moffam cures in 1921 in *Indiscretions of Archie* is Percy, a bulldog. In *The Girl on the Boat* in 1922 some of the best scenes are provided by Smith, another bulldog:

> Between Smith and the humans who provided him with dog-biscuits and occasionally with sweet cakes there had always existed a state of misunderstanding which no words could remove. The position of the humans was quite clear; they had elected Smith to his present position on a straight watchdog ticket. They expected him to be one of those dogs who rouse the house and save the spoons. They looked to him to pin burglars by the leg and hold on till the police arrived. Smith simply could not grasp such an attitude of mind. He regarded Windles not as a private house but as a social club, and was utterly unable to see any difference between the human beings he knew and the strangers who dropped in for a chat after the place was locked up. He had no intention of biting Sam. The idea never entered his head. At the present moment what he felt about Sam was that he was one of the best fellows he had ever met and that he loved him like a brother.

The line of bulldogs carries on with Amy in *Sam the Sudden*, William in *Meet Mr Mulliner* and Lysander in *Mr Mulliner Speaking*. There's a gap till the Second World War and we return again to the breed with George, the property of the sixth Viscount Uffenham, in *Something Fishy*. The last bulldog appears in *Bachelors Anonymous*; he is Percy, the only one of Wodehouse's bulldogs with blackness in his soul – 'the sort of dog that hangs about on street corners and barks out of the side of its mouth; a dog more than probably known to the police'. Even the evil Percy is a force for good, since he makes Ephraim Trout see the error of his misogynous ways. He ends the bulldog line in 1973, perhaps the most lasting result of that theatrical failure back in 1917.

Pekinese dogs appear in the novels from 1922 to 1954 and parallel exactly Wodehouse's ownership of them. He mentions them constantly in the letters in *Performing Flea*, and in *Portrait of a Master* Leonora Wodehouse is quoted:

> Susan is our Pekinese and Plum adores her. Just as we have planned some glorious voyage round the world, we remember that Susan would have to be left behind, so we stay in England to keep her amused, or see the world in relays. She is very pretty, small with a chestnut coat and that dancing way of walking that Pekinese have. Plum will leave anyone in the middle of a conversation to ingratiate himself with Susan if she gives him the slightest encouragement: and a man may be without morals, money or attractions, but if the word goes around that he's 'sound on Pekes' Plum will somehow find excuses for his lack of morals, lend him money, and invent attractions for him.

Despite his affection for Pekes, Wodehouse always kept his common sense when writing about them. Although he liked them so much, he realized that others did not always regard them in the same light.

> 'The one to which I allude is a small brown animal with a fluffy tail.'
> 'Yes, and a bark like a steam-siren, and in addition to that, about eighty-five teeth, all sharper than razors. I couldn't get within ten feet of that dog without its lifting the roof off, and if I did, it would chew me into small pieces.'
> *(The Girl on the Boat)*

More than any other animal, it is of Pekinese that strong men go in dread. It is Pekinese who go for your ankles and make you leap like lambs. It is Pekinese whose voices raised in emotion cause so many Wodehouse characters to shelve their immediate plans for a more propitious occasion:

At this moment just when their conversation promised to develop along interesting lines, it seemed to both men that the end of the world had suddenly come. It was, as a matter of fact, only Patricia barking, but that was the impression they got.

If there was one thing this Pekinese prided herself on, it was her voice. She might not be big, she might look like a section of hearthrug, but she could bark. She was a coloratura soprano, who thought nothing of starting in A in alt and going steadily higher, and when she went off unexpectedly under their feet like a bomb, strong men were apt to lose their poise and skip like the high hills.

Wodehouse owned at least six Pekes between 'the puppy' in 1922 and Squeaky in 1949. One of them, Susan, appeared under her own name in 'The Go Getter' in *Blandings Castle* and their fictional counterparts appeared in just about every novel Wodehouse wrote during that period. In *Ring for Jeeves* we meet Pomona:

Reference has been made earlier to the practice of the dog Pomona of shrieking loudly to express the ecstasy she always felt on beholding a friend or even what looked to her like a congenial stranger. It was ecstasy that was animating her now. . . . Meeting him now in this informal fashion, just at the moment when she had been trying to reconcile herself to the solitude which she so disliked, she made no attempt to place any bounds on her self-expression.

Screams sufficient in number and volume to have equipped a dozen Baronets stabbed in the back in libraries burst from her lips.

We will find Pomona's source in Wodehouse's letter to Townend of May 2nd 1949 in *Performing Flea* (p. 154).

Did I tell you that we were housing Guy Bolton's Peke, Squeaky, while Guy is in England? She is an angel and loves everybody. She is pure white, and her way of expressing affection and joy is to scream like a lost soul, or partly like a lost soul and partly like a scalded cat. When the Boltons were in Hollywood, the neighbours on each side reported them to the authorities, saying that they had a small dog which they were torturing. They said its cries were heartrending. So a policeman came round to investigate, and Squeaky fortunately took a fancy to him and started screaming at the top of her voice, so all was well.

Could there be a closer resemblance?

In 1960 in *Jeeves in the Offing* a new breed appears on the scene. Poppet is a dachshund belonging to Aubrey Upjohn's stepdaughter. He gives Bertie Wooster (and Wodehouse) the chance to air their views on dogs' names in general and dachshunds in particular.

'Talking of being eaten by dogs, there's a dachshund at Brinkley who when you first meet him will give you the impression that he plans to convert you into a light snack between his regular meals. Pay no attention. It's all eyewash. His belligerent attitude is simply – '

'Sound and fury signifying nothing, sir?'

'That's it. Pure swank. A few civil words, and he will be grappling you. . . . what's that expression I've heard you use?'

'Grappling me to his soul with hoops of steel, sir?'

'In the first two minutes. He wouldn't hurt a fly, but he has to put up a front because his name's Poppet. One can readily appreciate that when a dog hears himself addressed day in and day out as Poppet, he feels he must throw his weight about. His self-respect demands it.'

'Precisely, sir.'

'You'll like Poppet. Nice dog. Wears his ears inside out. Why do dachshunds wear their ears inside out?'

'I could not say, sir.'

'Nor me. I've often wondered. But this won't do, Jeeves. Here we are . . .'

65

The next year in *Service with a Smile* we meet Myra Schoonmaker walking sadly by Lord Emsworth's side:

> Her brow was furrowed, her lips drawn, and the large brown eyes that rested on George Cyril Wellbeloved had in them something of the sadness one sees in those of a dachshund which, coming to the dinner table to get its ten per cent, is refused a cut off the joint.

In 1964 in *Frozen Assets* Biff Christopher is described by his sister and the police as looking exactly like a dachshund, while another dachshund gives Joe Cardinal the chance to meet the girl he loves and to prove that, like Ginger Kemp and Beefy Bingham, he is one of the men who can jump into a dog-fight and stop it. In 1971 dachshunds join Wodehouse's animal metaphors:

> There was no doubt that I had impressed with the gravity of the situation. She gave a sharp cry like that of a stepped-on dachshund and her face took on the purple tinge it always assumes in moments of strong emotion.
>
> (Much Obliged, Jeeves)

The source of all these animals can be found on the dustcover of *Bachelors Anonymous*. The back cover shows Wodehouse looking out of a window with his pipe in his mouth. In the foreground of the picture is a dachshund, and from David Jasen we know its name is Jed.

One breed is missing. We know of the mongrel Bob, Sammy the bulldog, the Pekes, the cats and Jed the dachshund. They are all listed in *Performing Flea* or *Portrait of a Master*, but where did McIntosh and Bartholomew come from? These famous terriers belong to Aunt Agatha and Stiffy Byng. We first meet Bartholomew when he puts Constable Oates in the ditch:

> One moment he was with us, all merry and bright; the next he was in the ditch, a sort of macedoine of arms and legs and

wheels, with the terrier standing on the edge, looking down at him with that rather offensive expression of virtuous smugness which I have often noticed on the faces of Aberdeen terriers in their clashes with humanity.

Later in the same book Bartholomew forces Bertie to seek refuge on the chest of drawers while Jeeves flies to the top of the wardrobe.

A rather stiff silence ensued, during which the dog Bartholomew continued to gaze at me unwinkingly, and once more I found myself noticing – and resenting – the superior, sanctimonious expression on his face. Nothing can ever render the experience of being treed on top of a chest of drawers by an Aberdeen terrier pleasant, but it seemed to me that the least you can expect on such an occasion is that the animal will meet you half-way and not drop salt in the wound by looking at you as if he were asking if you were saved.

Wodehouse must have owned an Aberdeen terrier, but I could find no trace of one till in 1975 I was given a book of photographs taken by Elliot Erwin entitled *Son of Bitch*. The introduction of four pages was written by Wodehouse. He mentions some of the dogs he had owned, he tells of Sammy, as amiable and sweet-natured an animal as ever broke biscuit, and then he speaks of Angus. And Angus is the one we are looking for:

When Sammy succumbed to old age, I made what I think was a mistake by appointing as his successor an Aberdeen terrier who was supposed (though he seldom did) to answer to the name of Angus. Aberdeen terriers are intelligent and (if you don't mind those beetling eyebrows) handsome, but so austere and full of the Calvinistic spirit that it is impossible for an ordinary erring human being not to feel ill at ease in their presence. Angus had a way of standing in front of me and looking at me like a Scottish preacher about to rebuke the sins of his congregation. . . . It was a relief when I gave him to a better man than myself.

    After Angus my wife and I fell under the spell of Pekes . . .

The next time you read one of these Wodehouse books that are so difficult to date like *If I Were You* or *French Leave*, look at the animals. If there's a Pekinese in the book, it was written between 1922 and 1954. If there's a dachshund, it's 1956 or later.

What of his most famous animal creation, the Empress of Blandings? In 1981, a Wodehouse enthusiast discovered a book *The Pig – Breeding, Rearing and Marketing* by Sanders Spencer (1919), which contained a picture of a magnificent Berkshire sow with the ascription 'From a painting by Wippell'. Was this the source? If it was, when might Wodehouse have seen it? Was it sufficient on its own to change Lord Emsworth from a rose enthusiast to the pig fanatic he thereafter became?

The Empress first appeared in *Summer Lightning* (1929) but we know Wodehouse had been thinking about it for two years. In 1926, he spent the summer at Hunstanton Hall, the Norfolk estate of Charles LeStrange (see chapter VIII). His host was an enthusiastic and successful breeder of Jersey cows.

I think that at some time during that visit, with *Summer Lightning* slowly forming in his mind, Wodehouse escaped from his host and his hobbyhorse, picked up a book at random in the library and found himself looking at the picture by Wippell.

Charles LeStrange's special pride was a Jersey cow named Glenny 2nd. I find it no coincidence that we first read of the Empress' success at the Shropshire show the year after her original, Glenny 2nd, had become champion of Norfolk, Essex, Cambridge and Suffolk.

CHAPTER VI

MARY JANE PIGGOTT
AND BEALE

DO you remember Jeeves's aunts? Few are named, and then only by their Christian names, but one name at least has a factual origin. At some time in the long, hard process of writing, Wodehouse paused, searched for a name, bent forward to his typewriter again and inserted something he knew was appropriate. It might not be the best but it would fit exactly the impression he was trying to convey.

Aunts Aren't Gentlemen is Wodehouse's last complete novel; it was published in 1974 when he was ninety-three. Bertie and Jeeves are down in Somerset trying to extricate Bertie from the dreadful consequences of Aunt Dahlia's bright ideas for making some easy money. The story revolves around a cat which has become the stable companion to a race horse. The cat turns out to belong to Jeeves's aunt, who lives in the village. Jeeves asks Bertie for permission to spend the night at his aunt's house.

'. . . My aunt returned this morning and is at her home in the village.'

'Then go to her, Jeeves, and may heaven smile on your reunion.'

'Thank you very much, sir. Should you have any need of my services, the address is Balmoral, Mafeking Road, care of Mrs. P. B. Piggott.'

Having discovered where the real name came from, I assume Wodehouse's memory played him false. In *Ring for Jeeves*, published in 1953 when Wodehouse was a slip of a seventy-year-old, he got it right. *Ring for Jeeves* is the only book that features Jeeves without Bertie, as the manservant of Lord Rowcester. The final scene shows the cast listening to the commentary on the Derby on which the fortunes of Lord Rowcester depend. At the same time, the Chief Constable is carrying out his investigations into the theft of a necklace from the wealthy Mrs Spottsworth.

It is one of the grand finale scenes that Wodehouse did so well, which he realized every novel needed and which reflected so clearly his experience in the theatre. It is Bedlam, carefully written to arouse tension and excitement. The radio is blaring away as the commentator describes the race; seven people are listening to the commentary, arguing with each other and giving what little remains of their attention to the Chief Constable's questions about the necklace. Only Jeeves retains his self-possession as the Chief Constable asks for the names of the servants in the house.

One name is that of an old friend of Wodehouse enthusiasts:

> 'The gardener's name you said was what? Clarence Wilber-force was it?'
> 'Percy Wellbeloved, sir.'
> 'Odd name.'
> 'Shropshire, I believe, sir.'

The other servants are the housemaid and the cook – and the cook's name is Mary Jane Piggott.

The real Mary Jane Piggott was one of those servants or employees who, over the years, became part of the family. I found her in Somerset House, in the will of Wodehouse's favourite aunt, Miss Louisa Deane, who died in 1906. She was either cook/housekeeper or companion to Aunt Louisa and was left £50. Mrs Nella Wodehouse remembers the name and tells me that Mrs Piggott certainly attended the wedding of Wodehouse's younger brother in the 1920s.

I don't know what happened to her afterwards but she has gained an immortality denied to most of us.

✻   ✻   ✻

Beale is the ex-soldier who helps Ukridge and Jeremy Garnett run the chicken-farm in *Love among the Chickens* in 1906. He has red hair, an equable disposition and 'a passion for truth that had made him unpopular in three regiments'.

There are plenty of Army and Naval officers in Wodehouse, probably based on his own uncles, but very few rankers. I wondered idly where Beale came from but never thought about it too much till the real source fell into my lap.

When would Wodehouse have met a soldier? When might he have worn uniform himself? The book written immediately before *Love among the Chickens* was *The Head of Kay's* (1905). Some of the action takes place at the Schools' Cadet Camp at Aldershot. I don't know if Wodehouse was in the Dulwich OTC or not but, since all OTCs had a sergeant or sergeant-major to train them, the Dulwich NCO would proabably have been the first NCO Wodehouse would have known.

Browsing through a bookshop, I came across the *Dulwich Record* for 1901 (the year after Wodehouse left). It records a valediction to the NCO who had looked after the Dulwich Corps for ten years. His name was Sergeant-Major Beale.

71

CHAPTER VII

LONDON CLUBS –
WHICH WAS THE DRONES?

THERE are three categories of club in Wodehouse. There is the Drones, there are Wodehouse's other creations, the Junior Lipstick, the Junior Bloodstain and their fellows – and there is Wodehouse's own club, which he used often but which was well hidden.

The great London clubs, White's, Boodles, the Athenaeum and the Reform, still stand as proudly as ever they did, but we are looking at another type. The clubs Wodehouse drew were based on those that started in the 1880s and 1890s when better transport, more money and the new-found habit of eating out meant that more and more people wanted some facility in London for meeting their friends. The days of the Pickwick Club who met in the upstairs room of a public house have gone, although even today some pubs in the City still offer facilities to bodies with names like 'The City of London Clerks' Cycling Club'.

The new clubs were created when land and servants were still cheap. Their aim was that of clubs like Wodehouse's 'Junior Bloodstain', to meet the same sort of people as yourself, engaged in a common profession, with a standard of entry set by the members themselves. They served as a useful introduction to club life for those members who, as they grew older, would move on to more prestigious clubs but were not yet eligible to join the senior organizations.

Thus we have the creation of the 'Juniors'. Kelly's Directory for 1907 lists the Junior Army and Navy, the Junior Athenaeum, the Junior Carlton, the Junior Conservative, the

Junior Constitutional, the Junior Naval and Military and Junior United Service. The same volume lists the Aero Club (surely a select body in 1907), the Auto-Cycle, the Cobden and the Cromwell, the German Athenaeum, the New Era Ladies, the Quill and the Rehearsal. In the period between the death of Victoria and the Second World War, just about every one of Wodehouse's creations could be matched, covering every interest and every stratum of professional and middle-class life.

The 'Junior Lipstick' was no exception. It's surprising how many women's clubs existed and how early they came into existence. The first, the Alexandra, was founded with the support of Queen Victoria herself, who had noted the complaints from her ladies in waiting and the female members of the family that they found it undignified not to be allowed into their husbands' clubs. By forming their own club, they were able to turn the tables on the proud males who had themselves to wait while the hall-porter decided whether the lady was or was not in the club. In the 1907 Directory therefore the ladies had the Alexandra, the Alliance, the Calenda, the Empress, the Green Park, the Ladies' Automobile, the Ladies' Army and Navy, all flourishing and all with addresses that any club today would be happy to own.

For those people ignorant of its existence, the 'Junior Ganymede' is the club which has the honour to include Reginald Jeeves amongst its members. We hear of it early in the Bertie Wooster saga, and of the existence of the famous club book, but do we not enter its portals till *Much Obliged, Jeeves*, published on Wodehouse's ninetieth birthday. It is 'just off Curzon Street' but this is little help to us. Its membership is restricted to valets, butlers and gentlemen's personal gentlemen; it is cosy, select and well appointed.

Did any such club ever exist? I see no reason why not. Many people's ideas of servants' clubs are based on memories of Sam Weller's soirée with the footmen of Bath, but Dickens, like Wodehouse, described the truth so delightfully that people were reluctant to believe it was based on reality. In 1925 E. V. Lucas described a small public house in Mayfair. One bar was completely given over to the upper servants of the great houses nearby, and Lucas tells us of the way the senior gentlemen would refer to each other by the names of their employers:

'Another gin, two whiskies and a cigar for the Duke of Such-and-Such.'
'Threepenny or fourpenny cigar?'
'Fourpenny, of course! Did you ever know His Grace to smoke a *threepenny* cigar?'

The serious dignity of Hudson of the television series *Upstairs, Downstairs* is far nearer the truth than many realize, and circumspection and discretion were always the sign of good servants. Looking at the hundreds of clubs that flourished in London for their employers, I think it very likely that the servants who looked after them had at least one similar institution of their own. Unfortunately their discretion has proved an obstacle in my search for it. I believe Wodehouse certainly knew of such a club; as he says, he was always in the butler class and when he placed the Junior Ganymede 'off Curzon Street' he showed again his accuracy for description. 'Off Curzon Street' means Shepherd Market, which would be the perfect spot for a club like the 'Junior Ganymede', away from the great Mayfair houses but central enough to meet the needs of the men who served them.

The Drones is unquestionably Wodehouse's most famous club, and I never had any doubt that he had a real club in mind when he wrote it. The question is, which? Although the Pelican Club provided much of the background to his characters, it is not the Drones. We are looking for a young man's club and this is the first part of the problem. Looking at the list of clubs in the 1900 Kelly's Directory one name leaps off the page. Among the Athenaeum, Boodles, the Carlton and the rest is the Bachelors' Club at Hamilton Place, Piccadilly. It is certainly one of the places we are looking for. Only bachelors could become members; if they married they were fined £25 and had to re-submit their names for membership. The annual report for 1891 shows that twenty-eight members had been fined for the sin of matrimony and had submitted their names for re-election.

In 1891 Wodehouse was only ten years old, and it is possible that he never entered the Bachelors', whose members included some fifty peers of the realm, Whitbreads, Guinnesses and Count Metternich as well as young Colonel Kitchener. He certainly used it however in *The Swoop* in 1909 when he makes it the club Bertie Bertison belongs to. Jimmy Crocker of *Piccadilly Jim* is a member eight years later and in *My Man Jeeves* (1919) Reggie Pepper, who later became Bertie Wooster, watches his friend Bobbie Cardew: 'I stood at the window of our upper smoking-room, which looks out on to Piccadilly, and watched. He walked slowly along . . .' That is certainly the Bachelors' which stood on the corner of Piccadilly and Hamilton Place.

In *Jill the Reckless* (1921) we have the most interesting reference of all. Freddie Rooke is firmly established as a member of the Bachelors' but Chapter Eight finds him seated in the hall of the Drones Club waiting for Algy Martin to come and rescue him because 'the Drones was not one of Freddie's clubs.' So the Drones is not the Bachelors' – or is it? *Jill the Reckless* is the first time we see the Drones mentioned and it is introduced only to allow Wodehouse to describe Freddie's sombre thoughts as he awaits his host. The Drones was therefore brought in only to provide another club, similar in membership to the Bachelors' – so the implication is that the Bachelors' *was* a source.

If Wodehouse had the Bachelors' in mind, why is the Drones set so firmly in Dover Street? The Bachelors' stood down at the western end of Piccadilly but something caused Wodehouse to push it eastwards. Perhaps the reason was that when he realized that he could develop the Drones, the Bachelors' would be no longer suitable. Using a real club occasionally was one thing. To make it the mise-en-scène of a series was quite another. So in *Leave it to Psmith* the Drones is in Dover Street, and it stays there ever afterwards. The reason for its placing there is because Dover Street was the home of the second club that gave Wodehouse a background for the Drones.

Dover Street has been a 'club street' since the 1880s. In 1904, in its hundred yards length, it possessed the Atlantic, the Sesame, the Imperial Colonies, the Ladies' Field, the Bath Club, the Empress Club, the Arts, the London United and the Mayfair. Which of these was the Drones? Like everybody else I tried to work it out from *Uncle Fred in the Springtime*:

> The door of the Drones Club swung open, and a young man in form-fitting tweeds came down the steps and started to walk westwards. An observant passer-by, scanning his face, would have fancied that he discerned on it a tense, keen look, like that of an African hunter stalking a hippopotamus. And he would have been right. Pongo Twistleton – for it was he – was on his way to try and touch Horace Pendlebury-Davenport for two hundred pounds.
>
> To touch Horace Pendlebury-Davenport, if you are coming from the Drones, you go down Hay Hill, through Berkeley Square, along Mount Street and up Park Lane to the new block of luxury flats they have built where Bloxham House used to be . . .

Tantalizing, but insufficient to identify the building Pongo came out of. A better clue is the most famous incident in the Drones Club history as we know it – when Tuppy Glossop bet Bertie Wooster he could not swing himself across the swimming pool by the ropes and rings and then looped back the last rope so that Bertie had to drop into the pool in full evening dress. This can only be the Bath Club at 34 Dover Street. It was founded in 1864 by a group of gentlemen dissatisfied that there were so few places to swim, and a gymnasium was added later, thus providing both the elements in Wodehouse's story.

Wodehouse was not a member but at least two of his uncles were, as was his kinsman Lord Wodehouse, for whose son Wodehouse stood as godfather in 1924. Another member was Victor Cazalet MP, whom Wodehouse knew well and whose brother became Wodehouse's son-in-law. It is a fair assumption that Wodehouse visited the club and equally likely that at some time or another one member had played on another the dastardly trick Tuppy played on Bertie. Like so many other miscellaneous bits of information it must have been filed away in Wodehouse's extraordinary memory for future use. Further, by putting the Drones in Dover Street, Wodehouse took full advantage of its characteristic as a 'club street'. Pall Mall and St James's were and are far too well known to slip a fictitious club in amongst the venerable institutions that occupy them. Dover Street is a different matter; there were so many clubs in its short length, which changed their names often through the years, that it was easy for Wodehouse to slip another in. Dover Street it became and has remained.

The third source for the Drones is still going strong and the arguments here are even stronger. Wodehouse certainly used the Bachelors' up to the mid-1920s and the last mention of it is in *Leave it to Psmith*, which set the Drones firmly in Dover Street. Wodehouse made Freddie Threepwood a member of the Bachelors' to show that he and Psmith had not met before, since they were members of different clubs. After that book another real club takes over as the major source and was probably in Wodehouse's mind when he wrote *Young Men in Spats* and *Eggs, Beans and Crumpets*, the two books exclusively about the Drones and its members. They were published in 1936 and 1940, but Bertie Wooster has been speaking of the Drones since 1925; we are looking for a young man's club that flourished after the First War. How about Buck's?

During the First War a group of officers decided to form their own club after the war. Captain Buckmaster carried the project through and became the proprietor of Buck's Club, which still flourishes at 18 Clifford Street. In the 1920s and 30s it fitted exactly the pattern Wodehouse drew. Its members were young and wealthy and their golfing weekends at Le Touquet were famous. It was the Drones' weekend at Le Touquet that led to the trouble originally in *Uncle Fred in the Springtime* and the similarity is too close to be ignored.

Wodehouse's connection with Buck's stands close examination. A lot of people feel Buck's fits the bill more than any other. Not too much in that, but in his article on Wodehouse in 1961 in the *Sunday Times*, Evelyn Waugh said: 'He [Wodehouse] was an early member of Buck's Club.' Buck's Club disagree. By permission of the secretary I have looked through the members' lists from the foundation of the club and Wodehouse's name does not appear. So why did Waugh say it?

The answer lies in the excellent book on London clubs written by Charles Graves, *Leather Armchairs* (1963), which has a foreword written by Wodehouse. He speaks of his long acquaintance with the Graves family and goes on to describe his weakness for joining clubs which his friends felt he would enjoy. Unfortunately, he says, he finds that very soon he finds himself writing to the secretary resigning his membership because the club is not what he wanted. This may be the answer. The membership of Buck's in the 1920s was an impressive one; all the Royal princes were members, as were Winston Churchill and a couple of dozen peers. Wodehouse was a shy, even an unsociable man and Buck's does not sound the sort of club he would enjoy. If he joined then I think it highly probable that he resigned quickly, which would explain why his name didn't appear in the annual lists of members.

A second explanation which would fit Waugh's statement equally well was that Buck's developed the habit of electing one writer or actor each year. In 1921 Sir Charles Hawtrey was elected, in 1923 they voted in E. V. Lucas, in 1925 it was Hugh Walpole. In 1933 both Evelyn Waugh and Guy Bolton became members – and Bolton was Wodehouse's closest friend.

If Waugh, a member of Buck's himself, says that Wodehouse was a member, he must have had a reason. Either Wodehouse did join and resigned so quickly that his name never made the membership list or, as in the case of the Bachelors', he wasn't a member but his friends were. Both of these would fit Waugh's statement. As far as I know Waugh and Wodehouse did not meet before 1960; either from Wodehouse himself or from some common acquaintance Waugh may have been told: 'Oh, yes, Wodehouse (I) was in Buck's a lot in the early days.' This could easily be taken to mean that Wodehouse was a member but I don't think he was. There were enough of his friends amongst the membership to give him the background he needed or to have invited him to lunch there.

Although Buck's fits both in the age and type of membership and the famous weekends at Le Touquet, they are insufficient on their own. Luckily, Wodehouse gives us two more clues. In *If I Were You* (1931) Freddy Chalk-Marshall in the early chapters says that he is a member of Buck's. It is only mentioned once. Thereafter Freddy proclaims himself to be a member of the Drones, and does so three times to ensure there is no mistake. The other clue is even stronger and it comes from *The Inimitable Jeeves*, with ancillary information from *A Few Quick Ones* and *Plum Pie*.

In both the later collections of short stories there appears the same basic plot, which rests on the fact that McGarry, the barman of the Drones, is one of those gifted people who can tell the weight of anything by looking at it. Freddie Widgeon is the hero of one story, Bingo Little is the main character of the other, but McGarry is the man to concentrate on. In both stories of 1959 and 1966 he is firmly established at the Drones – but in *The Inimitable Jeeves* (1923), he is at Buck's! Bertie and Bingo are at the bar and Bertie is listening to Bingo declaim his love for Honoria Glossop:

> 'I worship her, Bertie! I worship the very ground she treads on!' continued the patient in a loud penetrating voice. Fred Thomson and one or two other fellows had come in, and McGarry, the chappie behind the bar, was listening with his ears flapping. But there's no reticence about Bingo. He always reminds me of the hero of a musical comedy who takes the centre of the stage, gathers the boys round him in a circle, and tells them all about his love at the top of his voice.

That must surely be the Drones, but on the previous page, Bertie says:

> I was still brooding when I dropped in at the oyster-bar at Buck's for a quick bracer . . .

I don't think it was deliberate; it was simply a Wodehouse slip. Buckmaster's autobiography reveals that his barman was indeed an ex-Irish Guardsman called McGarry, and a letter from Wodehouse, towards the end of his life, confirms that Buck's was the principal inspiration for the Drones, while the Bath Club was a secondary source. In the early books the club was a minor factor and he didn't have to hide it carefully since there was little to hide; only later as the Drones became famous in its own right did he have to take care over its disguise.

The Drones was born among the Bachelors' at the junction of Hamilton Place and Piccadilly sometime between 1900 and 1908. After the First War, probably during his visits to London of 1920 to 1922, Wodehouse shifted it to Buck's, the new young man's club, and perhaps because of the swimming-pool story or simply because he wanted a suitable 'club street', he set it firmly at the Bath Club at 34 Dover Street. The Bath Club has left Dover Street now and we shall never hear another Drones Club story, but Buck's is still there and long may it flourish.

Our last club is older than the Drones, and Wodehouse wrote of it from 1910 till the end of his life. Its name in the novels is the Senior Conservative and its members include Rupert Psmith, Lord Emsworth, Horace Wanklyn and J. B. Butterwick.

It is in the smoking-room and card-room of the Senior Conservative that Psmith wreaks his revenge on Mr Bickersdyke in *Psmith in the City*. It is in the dining-room of the Senior Conservative that Lord Emsworth dodders to and fro and meets Psmith for the first time. It is to the Senior Conservative that elderly gentlemen belong when Wodehouse wants to emphasize their respectability. In *Leave it to Psmith* Baxter's charges against Psmith are effectually countered by Psmith's membership of the club:

'Are you a member of the Senior Conservative Club?'
'Most certainly.'
'Why, then, dash it,' cried his lordship, paying to that august stronghold of respectability as striking a tribute as it had ever received, 'if you're a member of the Senior Conservative, you can't be a criminal. Baxter's an ass!'
'Exactly.'

In *Blandings Castle* in 1935 the dining-room of the club becomes the venue for a lesson in pig-calling:

> 'Pig-hoooo-o-o-o-ey!' yodelled Lord Emsworth, flinging his head back and giving tongue in a high, penetrating tenor which caused ninety-three Senior Conservatives, lunching in the vicinity, to congeal into living statues of alarm and disapproval.
>
> 'More body to the "hoo",' advised James Belford.
>
> The Senior Conservative Club is one of the few places in London where lunchers are not accustomed to getting music with their meals. White-whiskered financiers gazed bleakly at bald-headed politicians, as if asking silently what was to be done about this. Bald-headed politicians stared back at white-whiskered financiers, replying in the language of the eye that they did not know. The general sentiment prevailing was a vague determination to write to the Committee about it.

The Senior Conservatives never hit the headlines in the way the Drones did but it formed an invaluable mise-en-scène for Lord Emsworth and those like him. It may be this sense of respectability that kept its source a secret for so long and its address is not revealed till 1959 in *A Few Quick Ones*. It is in Northumberland Avenue and this can only mean one place – the Constitutional Club.

Wodehouse's first appearance in *Who's Who* was in 1908, and he is shown there as a member of the Constitutional Club. Later editions show that he joined the Garrick and the Beefsteak, where he came to know Kipling, but till 1939 the Constitutional is always the first listed. Till 1963 it stood halfway down the left side of Northumberland Avenue as you walk from Trafalgar Square. In *Psmith in the City* Wodehouse said:

> The club to which Psmith and Mr Bickerdyke belonged was celebrated for the steadfastness of its political views, the

excellence of its cuisine and the curiously Gorgonzolaesque marble of its main staircase.

That's exactly what it was and Wodehouse drew it accurately as a club of utmost probity for senior Conservatives with none of the slightly risqué connotations of Boodles or White's or the political significance of the Carlton.

In *Psmith in the City* we read that Psmith won his final victory in the Turkish Baths that were near the club:

> Thus, when approaching the Senior Conservative Club at five o'clock with the idea of finding Mr. Bickersdyke there, he observed his quarry entering the Turkish Baths which stand some twenty yards from the club's front door . . .

The Constitutional Club has left Northumberland Avenue now, but if you walk down there, past the large bank which occupies the site where the club stood, you will come to the Sherlock Holmes pub. Turn sharp left and walk up the little passage beside the Sherlock Holmes. About twenty feet along the passage, the smooth newness of the wall is broken by a tiled Moorish doorway. It is the last of the Turkish Baths that Wodehouse and Psmith used – as well as being the resort of Sherlock Holmes in at least two of Conan Doyle's stories.

I wondered why Wodehouse stayed a member of the Constitutional so long when his normal practice seems to have been to resign from his clubs early and often. Charles Graves suggests it was because the Savage, the Beefsteak and the rest were lively places with a high and constant level of conversation. The Constitutional was the other extreme. It was so large and impersonal that you could hide in a corner of the library or lunch alone in the dining-room. This, Graves reckons, was exactly what the quiet, shy Wodehouse wanted, peace and quiet, somewhere to eat and to work out his plots in peace.

Perhaps this is why the Constitutional appears only once under its real name in Wodehouse's ninety-seven books. In the preface to *The Girl on the Boat* Wodehouse apologizes for the fact that both in his story and one written by another author, the hero tries to get out of a tight corner by hiding in a suit of armour:

> Looks fishy, yes? And yet I call upon Heaven to witness that I am innocent, innocent. And, if the word of a Northumberland Avenue Wodehouse is not sufficient, let me point out that this story and Mr. Clouston's appeared simultaneously in serial form in their respective magazines . . .
>
> P. G. Wodehouse
Constitutional Club
Northumberland Avenue

In *Summer Lightning* the awful J. Frobisher Pilbeam has a club too. Wodehouse made him a member of 'the Junior Constitutional'.

CHAPTER VIII

※⁂※

NORFOLK

NORFOLK is not an obvious 'Wodehouse county' but it offers one of the few examples where we can say without any reservation that Wodehouse wrote *this* scene because of his knowledge of *this* place.

Money for Nothing (1928) is Wodehouse's fortieth book, and opens by describing the village where the action takes place:

> You will find Rudge-in-the-Vale, if you search carefully, in that pleasant section of rural England where the grey stone of Gloucestershire gives place to Worcestershire's old red brick. Quiet – in fact, almost unconscious, it nestles besides the tiny river Skirme and lets the world go by . . .

On page 22 we learn that the Skirme runs into the Severn, on page 47 the hero drives to London by way of Blenheim Park and Oxford. At page 90 we are told that Rudge is seven miles from Worcester and eighteen from Birmingham. The only good golf-course is at Stourbridge and it takes an hour to get to Wenlock Edge. The main line station is Shrub Hill at Worcester.

Despite all this, Wodehouse set *Money for Nothing* in just about the easternmost part of England one can find. In a letter of 1929 in *Performing Flea* he said:

> I think I like Hunstanton as well in the winter as in summer, though, of course, I don't get the moat in the winter months.

I laid the scene of *Money for Nothing* at Hunstanton Hall.

I don't know what influence, if any, it had on his allusions or references but Norfolk is the 'official' Wodehouse county. The head of the family is the Earl of Kimberley and the title comes from Kimberley in Norfolk. The Wodehouses have been there for hundreds of years and it was from Norfolk that Wodehouse's grandfather set out to fight in the Napoleonic wars. I have not been able to trace any visits by him to Norfolk before 1920, but with aunts as proud and as conscious of their family history as his were, he must have known of the connection.

In June 1926 Wodehouse dated his letter to Townend from Hunstanton Hall, Norfolk – 'The above address does not mean that I have bought a country estate. It is a joint belonging to a friend of mine, and I am putting in a week or two here.' From 1926 to 1933 he visited Hunstanton regularly and rented it himself on occasion. From his use of Norfolk place names in his early books (Lady Wroxham, Lady Waveney, the Duchess of Waveney and Lord Wisbech) he seems to have had some knowledge of it, but Hunstanton is the place to concentrate on.

Open a map of Norfolk and look at the area round Hunstanton. Hunstanton itself, which Wodehouse first visited in 1926, gave its name the following year to Lord Hunstanton, who sponged on Mrs Waddington in *The Small Bachelor*. Due south of Hunstanton is Heacham, which gave its name to Lord Heacham, Lord Emsworth's pompous young neighbour in *Blandings Castle*.

The next village is Snettisham; Jack Snettisham and his wife were the evil couple who tried to win Anatole away from Aunt Dahlia in *Very Good, Jeeves*. Go back to Hunstanton now and run your finger along the northern coast to Brancaster. It was Lord Brancaster whom Jeeves quoted as a precautionary tale to prevent Bertie rendering Gussie Fink-Nottle hors-de-combat before the famous prize-giving. And beyond Brancaster is Sheringham, which Wodehouse gave to our old friend Chimp Twist when he wanted to give his agency an air of respectability – J. Sheringham Adair. He only used the Wodehouse ancestral home, Wymondham, once for Algy Wymondham-

Wymondham in *Mr Mulliner Speaking* and I am surprised that Bertie Wooster's uncle Lord Yaxley is given a title from over the border in Suffolk.

Hunstanton itself is important since it reveals the train of thought by which to join factual background to fictional plot, and *Money for Nothing* shows how he did it. Despite all the references to the west of England, Wodehouse used a house from the other side of the country. He started the book in place A and continued it in place B, and in this instance both A and B are traceable.

Performing Flea and *Portrait of a Master* show that Wodehouse spent a great deal of time on his plots. He worked and reworked them very hard, and when he had them right he started on what he considered was the easy part, dialogue and background. It is the background we are looking at. Wodehouse was writing *Money for Nothing* when he wrote to Townend from Hunstanton:

> Anyway, bung-oh! I'm sweating blood over *Money for Nothing* and have just finished 53,000 words of it. Meanwhile I have to anglicize *Oh, Kay!* by 9 August, attend rehearsals, adapt a French play, write a new musical comedy and do the rest of *Money for Nothing*, as far as I can see, by about September 1st. It'll all help to pass the time.

Under pressure like that, can we be surprised that Wodehouse used the surroundings in which he found himself or that settings shift as their creator moved from one part of the country to another?

In *Money for Nothing* one of the characters states that Rudge Hall is seven miles from Worcester and eighteen from Birmingham. The gazetteer shows only one place that fits those limits – Droitwich – which is where Wodehouse was staying when he wrote the words. The timing looks like this:

June 1926	Hunstanton Hall
April 1927	Norfolk Street, London
May 1927	Impney Hotel, Droitwich
July 1927	Hunstanton

He started working out the plot (using Hunstanton) in 1926. The plot is firm in 1927 and he is working on it when he went to Droitwich, where he uses the local mileages. Then back to Hunstanton again to do the final draft. Norfolk was translated to Worcestershire and back again.

In *Portrait of a Master* Jasen describes Wodehouse's reaction to Hunstanton Hall:

> Everything about Hunstanton Hall appealed to him. It was a real-life Blandings Castle, the estate encompassing more than a thousand acres, which included a lake, a park, many gardens and a moat. Part of the original mansion, built in 1623, had been destroyed by fire in the early nineteenth century and rebuilt in Victorian style. The house was so large that at least two-thirds of it hadn't been lived in for almost a century.
>
> Plum spent much of his time on the moat, sitting in a punt with his typewriter on a small bedside table and wishing he could settle down permanently in a place like this – the Hall, of course, not the moat. And he watched in wonderment the way that life was lived there, regretting only that he couldn't use it in a story because no one would believe it. By this he meant such things as the late arrival of an unexpected guest because of car trouble – said guest arriving eventually at three o'clock in the morning to find that his host had roused the entire household and had a five-course dinner waiting for him.

Sadly, the owners of the Hall, the Le Stranges, have left it now, although they still live nearby. They are worth a mention in their own right. As their name implies they are an old Norman family and the head of the family has for centuries been hereditary Lord High Admiral of The Wash. It is one of the oldest offices in the country; the Romans appointed a Count of the Saxon Shore in this part of the coast and the Le Stranges' office is probably a continuation of it. The office must be retained by the holder riding a horse into the sea and flinging a spear. Where the spear lands is the limit of his jurisdiction, and if the practice is still carried out, then we are back to the Dark Ages when men prayed for delivery from the Norsemen.

Hunstanton Hall was originally built on its moated plateau by Sir Hamon Le Strange in 1309. The great gatehouse was added in 1490 and another Sir Hamon built wings in the reign of Elizabeth. Fire has destroyed some of the building and the Welfare State and income tax have wrought changes that hundreds of years failed to do. When the photograph at Plate 3 was taken, the moat had nearly vanished. The Hall is an old red-brick house with the Tudor gatehouse guarding the main entrance to the inner quadrangle. A small river was diverted to provide a moat around the house and was widened at one side to form a lake. A large estate surrounds the house with a church and smaller house lying to the northwest. If you read *Money for Nothing* with a large-scale map, you can trace every spot Wodehouse describes, including the moat, the small bridge across the head of the stream and the path across the fields to the village.

The moat was a favourite place of Wodehouse's and his letters to Townend refer to it often. He may have visited other houses with a moat but can have known none as well as he knew Hunstanton, and the first result was *Money for Nothing*. Two years later in *Very Good Jeeves*, the first story is 'Jeeves and the Impending Doom', which finishes with the rescue by Bertie and Jeeves of the Rt Hon. A. B. Fillmer, whom young Thomas has marooned.

Bertie describes Aunt Agatha's house at Woollam Chersey in Hertfordshire as impressive and surrounded by a splendid estate:

> But the feature of the place was the lake.
>
> It stood to the east of the house, beyond the rose garden, and covered several acres. In the middle of it was an island. In the middle of the island was a building known as the Octagon. And in the middle of the Octagon, seated on the roof and spouting water like a public fountain was the Right Hon. A. B. Fillmer.

Bertie describes the Octagon for us:

> This building was run up sometime in the last century, I have
> been told, to enable the grandfather of the late owner to have
> some quiet place out of earshot of the house where he could
> practise the fiddle. From what I know of fiddlers, I should
> imagine that he produced some pretty frightful sounds there
> in his time; but they can have been nothing to the ones that
> were coming from the roof of the place now.

Five hundred yards south of the Hall at Hunstanton, the
stream forms a lake and in the middle of the lake is a small
island. The Octagon, a small building, stands in the middle of
the island exactly as Wodehouse describes. Lady Townshend,
a neighbour of the Le Stranges, mentions the building in her
memoirs:

> The Stuart wings were built by Sir Hamon Le Strange, who
> carried the news of the death of Elizabeth to King James. Sir
> Hamon was a great music-lover and so fond of the violin that
> his wife, Dame Alice, insisted on him building a little house
> on an island called the Octagon where he could practise to his
> heart's content and not disturb those inside the hall.

So, Woollam Chersey, as well as Rudge Hall, is based on
Hunstanton. In the same book, *Very Good, Jeeves*, Bobby
Wickham's home Skeldings suddenly has a Moat Room and in
Blandings Castle the moat at Skeldings becomes the scene of
the rescue of Mr Potter by Clifford Gandle MP in 'Mr Potter
Takes a Rest Cure'.

It is tempting to attribute the origins of many houses in the
novels to Hunstanton. Certainly Aunt Agatha and Bobby
Wickham drew their homes from that source, and so did Bingo
Little in 'Jeeves and the Old School Chum'. How many others
are there? There is a simple test. What distinguishes Rudge
Hall from Blandings? Or Totleigh Towers from Bobby
Wickham's Skeldings? The moat is the thing to watch for; if
there's a moat mentioned anywhere then it's a fair bet that

we're back at Hunstanton again. It wasn't the only country house Wodehouse knew, but it was probably the one he knew best and it gives a pleasant postscript.

Jasen says Wodehouse found it a real-life Blandings, and the last Hunstanton reference appears in a Blandings story. In *A Pelican at Blandings* the heroine Vanessa Polk is not the daughter of the millionaire Lady Constance thinks she is, but the daughter of a Blandings parlour-maid who has heard so much about the old place that she encourages Lady Constance's error in order to be invited to stay. Who can blame her – but I thought this was a trifle unreal, even for Wodehouse. I was wrong. During my researches into Hunstanton, I received a letter from Mrs Meakin, a Le Strange by birth. She sent me a letter she received from Wodehouse talking of happy days at the Hall and ending:

> About a year ago I got a letter from a Mrs Hide, who used to kitchenmaid at Hunstanton and now we correspond regularly . . .

That's where he got the idea from, another of the small incidents in his life on which so much of his work was based.

CHAPTER IX

DULWICH OR 'VALLEY FIELDS'

DULWICH appears under three guises in Wodehouse's books. There is the school, the London suburb – and there is 'Valley Fields'.

Wodehouse's school stories – *The Pothunters, A Prefect's Uncle, Tales of St Austin's, The Gold Bat, The Head of Kay's, The White Feather* and *Mike* – are nearly all based on Dulwich. The exception is the Wrykyn cricket ground which comes from the Malvern playing fields where Wodehouse used to play during his holidays. They are good stories and were very popular. Most appeared in the old *Captain* magazine, and the appearance of Psmith led to a quiet revolution of speech amongst public schoolboys of the time. It is all long past but I have read many books of memoirs where the *Captain* and the early Wodehouse school stories were fondly remembered.

He used fictional locations for his schools. Beckford, Wrykyn and St Austin's are set in country districts – except once. In a perfect example of a 'Wodehouse slip' Babington of *Tales of St Austin's* decides to break bounds and accept an invitation from his brother to see a comedy in London. He catches the one-thirty train to Victoria and takes the Underground to Charing Cross. He is clearly coming from Dulwich rather than St Austin's, which is firmly set over a hundred miles from London.

Dulwich College is still what it was when Wodehouse knew it. Founded by the Elizabethan actor Edward Alleyn in 1619, its buildings date from the middle of the nineteenth century and are set amongst delightful grounds. It looks exactly how a school should look, and Wodehouse loved it from the moment he saw it.

He enjoyed his time at Dulwich. He played for both the First XI and XV, was editor of the School magazine and followed the fortunes of the Rugger team for the rest of his life. In *Performing Flea* (1953) he said:

> The impression these letters have left me with is the rather humbling one that I am a bad case of arrested mental development. Mentally, I seem not to have progressed a step since I was eighteen. With world convulsions happening every hour on the hour, I appear still to be the rather backward lad I was when we brewed our first cup of tea in our study together, my only concern the outcome of a Rugby football match.
>
> Though I believe there are quite a number of people like me in that respect. I remember lunching with Lord Birkenhead once, and my opening remark: 'Well, Birkenhead, and how are politics these days?' left him listless. He merely muttered something about politics being all right, and crumbled bread. But when I said 'Tell me, my dear fellow – I have often wanted to ask you – what came unstuck at Oxford in 1893, or whenever it was? Why was it that you didn't get your Rugger Blue?' – his eyes lit up and he talked for twenty minutes without stopping, giving me no chance to tell him what I did to Haileybury in 1899.

Dulwich has a memorial to him now – his desk, typewriter and books, bequeathed to the school he loved so much.

In the school stories Mike Jackson is what Wodehouse would like to have been and in *Psmith in the City* what Wodehouse assuredly was – an unhappy young man who loathed the job he was doing and was desperate for any means of escape from it. An alternative likeness is Charteris of *The Pothunters* and *Tales of St Austin's*. He is given a turn of speech extraordinarily close to Wodehouse's quotes of himself in *Performing Flea* and *Bring on the Girls* and is given the same position and status in the school that Wodehouse himself enjoyed.

When Beverley Nichols wrote his chapter on Wodehouse in *Are They the Same at Home?* he described him as having various secrets:

92

Every Saturday afternoon, Mr P. G. Wodehouse disappears. For many years the reasons why he went, and what he did when he got there, were insoluble problems to his family . . .

. . . I am able from a secret source to throw light upon the problem of Mr Wodehouse's Saturday afternoons . . . He goes to a football match. There! It is out . . .

It was not to Football League matches that Wodehouse used to go but back down to Dulwich to watch his beloved Rugger team doing its stuff; and if the match was a good one he would write to Townend telling him all about it. He had been brought up in the walking tradition of the Victorians and often travelled on foot the five or six miles between Dulwich and his West End house. He became famous in Hollywood later by adopting the same practice there and walking the five miles to the studio rather than travelling by car.

With his six years at school, including a short period in 1895 when his father took a house in Dulwich, and frequent visits thereafter Wodehouse knew the area well. So we read of 'Valley Fields' and of East Dulwich and the distinction between them. Have you noticed when you are walking through a town, how the whole atmosphere of a place can change in twenty yards? London is full of such instances; the most dramatic is probably the corner where the regal spendour of Kensington Palace Gardens meets Notting Hill. An extraordinary contrast in two or three yards.

The difference between East Dulwich and 'Valley Fields' is not so marked – but to a West Dulwich resident, East Dulwich is simply not Dulwich at all. One might as well speak of Streatham or Herne Hill, or even Tooting or Balham.

If you are of the proletariat like Miss Rhoda Platt, the waitress Bertie Wooster's Uncle George wanted to marry, you will live at Wisteria Lodge, Kitchener Road, East Dulwich. If you are a lady accompanied by Bertie Wooster to a nightclub and the place is raided, he will advise you in an urgent undertone to adopt the alias of Miss Matilda Bott of 365 Churchill Avenue, East Dulwich. If you are a retired ship's steward like Albert Pease-march, you will live at Chatsworth, Mafeking Road, East

Dulwich. Albert Peasemarch is based on a steward Wodehouse met during one of his innumerable Atlantic crossings, although the name itself belongs to the engineer of the *Dorinda* – the hell-ship belonging to Colonel Henry Savage, one of the American theatrical impresarios from whom one was lucky to escape alive. But if you are a Wodehouse hero or heroine then you are allowed to live in 'Valley Fields'.

At Plate 5 is a map of Dulwich. Croxted Road runs north–south to the left of the station and across Park Road. To the right Dulwich Common (Road) runs towards the College and is crossed by Alleyn Park Road and College Road. To the left is Rosendale Road and the small roads that run up the hill to West Norwood. Somewhere in the area has to be the fabled 'Burberry Road' and 'Mulberry Grove'.

In *Sam the Sudden* the heroine Kay Derrick catches a No. 3 bus from Piccadilly Circus:

> The omnibus stopped at the corner of Burberry Road, and Kay, alighting, walked towards San Rafael. Burberry Road is not one of the more fashionable and wealthy districts of Valley Fields, and most of the houses in it are semi-detached. San Rafael belonged to this class, being joined, like a stucco Siamese Twin, in indissoluble union to its next-door neighbour, Mon Repos. It had in front of it a strip of gravel, two apologetic flower beds with evergreens in them, a fence, and in the fence a gate, modelled on the five-barred gates of the country.

When Wodehouse made the bus stop 'at the corner of Burberry Road', he made things difficult. 'At the corner' can mean either that it ran along Burberry Road and stopped where it crossed another road or that Burberry Road is one of the smaller roads that comes up to meet the main route. The No. 3 bus still follows the same route and Burberry Road could be either Croxted Road itself or any of the roads off it.

A close comparison of the descriptions in the novels shows that the same house is meant each time, and a check of the addresses used gives us the answer:

Sam the Sudden (1925): San Rafael and Mon Repos in Burberry
Road
Company for Henry (1967): Mon Repos, Burberry Road
Do Butlers Burgle Banks? (1968): Restharrow, Croxley Road
Pearls, Girls and Monty Bodkin (1972): 11 Croxted Road (the real
name)
Bachelors Anonymous (1973): The Laurels, Burbage Road.

'Croxley Road' for Croxted Road is exactly the sort of disguise
to look for and the use of the correct name in *Pearls, Girls and
Monty Bodkin* confirms it. Burberry/Burbage/Croxley Road are
Croxted Road. All that is needed is the house.

It occurred to me that if Wodehouse could describe the interior
of the house so well, then it must have been the house his parents
took in Dulwich when they returned from Hong Kong. The
College houses he boarded in were all far too large. By no stretch
of the imagination can they be called semi-detached.

Wodehouse's father only took the Dulwich house for a few
months in 1895 and I had great difficulty in tracing it. I eventually
found it in the Kelly's Directory for Kent for 1899 as a belated
entry: 'H. E. Wodehouse CMG 62 Croxted Road, Dulwich'.
Number 62 Croxted Road is the first house on the left if you
come out of the station, turn left and then left again into Croxted
Road. It has gone now – a modern bungalow occupies the site –
but old maps show that the house was indeed the semi-detached
house Wodehouse described. On the off-chance I looked
through some even older maps and they show that some fifteen
years before the Wodehouses stayed there, the two houses had
been one. This is the factor that produces the happy ending of
Sam the Sudden.

62 Croxted Road fits exactly with the directions given in the
novels. Kay Derrick's journey on the bus will take you to it and in
Company for Henry forty years later, Jane Martyn is described as
reaching her destination:

> . . . .the morning was still reasonably young when she alighted
> from the train at Valley Fields and emerged into the sunlit street.
> And she was looking about her for someone who would direct

her to Burberry Road, when she became aware that a few yards from where she stood a certain liveliness was in progress.

(A cat is up a tree, the hero comes along, gets it down at Jane's request and then dashes for his train.)

But he has gone . . . she addressed the gentleman of leisure, who had begun to speak of the possible necessity of amputation.

'I wonder if you can direct me to Burberry Road?'
He seemed to ponder deeply.
'Burberry Road?'
'Yes.'
'Burberry Road?'
'Yes.'
'Burberry Road, eh? Lady, you're in it.'
'In it?'
'You couldn't be more in it if you tried for a month of Sundays,' said the gentleman of leisure, elaborating his point. 'If Burberry Road's what you want, you've got it.'

That's Croxted Road again, and Jane Martyn's tree stood in what had been the Wodehouses' garden.

In the early 1970s Wodehouse's English publishers brought out new editions of many of his books and Wodehouse wrote new introductions to some of them. The preface to the 1972 edition of *Sam the Sudden* reads:

I hope that in the thirty years since I have seen it Valley Fields has not ceased to be a fragrant backwater. Though I did read somewhere about a firm of builders wanting to put up a block of flats in Croxted Road where I once lived in the first house on the left as you come up from the station. Gad, Sir, if anyone had tried to do that in my time, I'd have horsewhipped them on the steps of their club, if they had a club.

So – San Rafael, the home of Kay Derrick, is No. 62 Croxted Road and Mon Repos, the home of Sam Shotter and of Bill Hardy forty years later, is No. 64. We also now know where

Wodehouse got that sub-plot in *Company for Henry* about Algy Martin's method of making money.

Here is Algy explaining things to Bill Hardy:

> 'Are you by any chance acquainted with a wayside inn called the Green Man in Rosendale Road, Valley Fields?'
>
> 'No.'
>
> 'Nice little pub,' said Algy approvingly. 'Good beer and they give you credit which is the vital thing. I was in there yesterday, and I met a man who has a house in Croxley Road. . . . I got into conversation with this bloke, as I say, and I found him in a peevish mood. It seemed that he was an old inhabitant and it was his opinion that all these building operations that were going on in its midst were turning Valley Fields from a peaceful rural retreat into a sort of suburban Manchester. He said he was thankful he was clearing out . . . Fortunately he said he would be able to sell his house, because some syndicate or association or whatever you call these concerns wanted to build a block of flats in Croxley Road and his residence came right into the middle of the chunk of land they were planning to do it on.'

Algy immediately put in a higher bid knowing that he could hang on for a higher price than the owner who had to go abroad. It's a perfect Wodehouse allusion – a minor piece of news in his life, the long process of building up a good plot, the need for a sub-plot for Algy Martin and, from the back of Wodehouse's mind, the recollection of the flat-building. Croxley/Croxted Road plays its part again thirty years after Wodehouse had last seen it.

If Burberry/Burbage/Croxley Road is Croxted Road, where is Mulberry Grove? We must know its three houses, The Nook, Peacehaven and Castlewood, nearly as well as Blandings, but there is no 'Mulberry Grove' in Dulwich. It is a small cul-de-sac and is the centre of activity for Dolly and Soapy Molloy, Freddie Widgeon, Lord Uffenham, Keggs the butler and other old friends.

Of all the delectable spots in Valley Fields (too numerous to mention) it is probable that the connoisseur would point with greatest pride at Mulberry Grove, the little cul-de-sac bright with lilac, almond, thorn, rowan and laburnum trees which lies off Rosendale Road, and it was here that the sun was putting in its adroitest work. At the house which a builder with romance in his soul had named Castlewood its rays made their way across the neat garden . . .

(Something Fishy, 1957)

The only small cul-de-sac off Rosendale Road is Elmworth Grove, but Kelly's Directories show that from 1870 to 1910 there was never anything there other than Joseph King's Laundry and Akerman's Cottages. In any event *Big Money* and *Ice in the Bedroom* put Mulberry Grove firmly in Croxley Road and near the station. *Big Money* further aggravates the problem by giving Mulberry Grove a small stretch of ornamental water on which two swans, Egbert and Percy, have their being:

. . . and both birds then sneered audibly. Swans, like sub-editors, are temperamentally incapable of understanding love's young dream.

I spent a long time looking for Mulberry Grove. Pond Cottages over to the right just beyond the College had the ornamental water and the swans but nothing else, and these on their own were insufficient. I found it at last by doing what Wodehouse must have done often but described only once in his books.

I parked my car by West Dulwich Station (the station where Wodehouse waited as a schoolboy for the next edition of *The Strand* to come in) and walked down Croxted Road to Acacia Grove. It was to Acacia Grove that Mike Jackson came to look for lodgings in *Psmith in the City*. In one of the few sad passages in his novels Wodehouse described what he felt himself when he left the school he loved for the bleak loneliness of London. He felt it so deeply that he described things Mike saw that only a Dulwich boy would recognize, and Mike is meant to be a complete stranger to the area.

Mike wandered out of the house [in Acacia Grove]. A few steps took him to the railings that bounded the College grounds. It was late August and the evenings had begun to close in. The cricket-field looked very cool and spacious in the dim light, the school buildings looming vague and shadowy through the light mist. The little gate by the railway bridge was not locked. He went in and walked slowly across the turf towards the big clump of trees which marked the division between the cricket and football fields. It was all very pleasant and soothing after the pantomime dame and her stuffy bed-sitting room. He sat down on a bench beside the second eleven telegraph board and looked across the ground at the pavilion. For the first time that day he began to feel really home-sick . . .

. . . The clock on the tower over the senior block chimed quarter after quarter but Mike sat on, thinking. It was quite late when he got up, and began to walk back to Acacia Grove. He felt cold and stiff and very miserable.

I did what Mike Jackson and Wodehouse did. I walked down Acacia Grove, turned to the right as it does and, after a few yards, found myself under the railway bridge. Across the road, through the little gate and across the turf towards the big trees that still stand there. The College buildings loomed through the gathering dusk exactly as Wodehouse described them. I walked back to Acacia Grove and as I passed the last house, I saw it.

'It' was the doorway of the last house but one as you come out of Acacia Grove into Croxted Road. On either side of the door crouched two sphinxes – and sphinxes were one of the landmarks I was looking for. I collected my car, drove back to Acacia Grove and flipped through the pages of *Big Money*. I had found Mulberry Grove at last.

Try it yourself one day, using *Big Money* as your guide. Walk out from West Dulwich station, turn left, then left again down Croxted Road. There are some new roads on your left – ignore them. The first road on the left in Wodehouse's day was Acacia Grove; ignore that as well for the moment and continue for fifty yards past Ildersley Grove till you come to the crossroads where Croxted Road meets Park Hall Road.

The crossroads is the shopping centre for this section of Dulwich. It is a trifle scruffy now but just to your right is the estate agents (Messrs Matters & Cornelius perhaps?) and to your left is the Alleyn Arms. Turn to Chapter Five of *Big Money*, where the Biscuit concludes his conversation with Mr Cornelius. The Biscuit leaves Cornelius and espying a pub 'just around the corner', goes in to test the beer. That's the Alleyn Arms. He 'came out of the hostelry with a buoyant step, and a moment later the full beauties of Mulberry Grove were displayed before him.' Do as he did, out of the Alleyn Arms, across the road and walk up Acacia Grove with the railway embankment on your right hand. Follow the bend of Acacia Grove round to the left and walk along the left-hand side towards Croxted Road.

> . . . he passed on and came to a gate on which was painted in faded letters the word
>
> *Peacehaven*
>
> Peacehaven was a two-storey edifice in the Neo-Suburban-Gothic style of architecture, constructed of bricks which appeared to be making a slow recovery from a recent attack of jaundice. Like so many of the houses in Valley Fields, it showed what Montgomery Perkins, the local architect, could do when he put his mind to it. It was he, undoubtedly, who was responsible for the two stucco sphinxes on either side of the steps leading to the front door.

The houses on your left are exactly the colour and material that Wodehouse described. Some have greyhounds in front of them, some have lions and a couple have a simple ball and pillar. Just before you come to Croxted Road, you will find the sphinxes (Plate 6). You are at Peacehaven.

Test the theory by turning to Chapter Six of *Big Money*, where Lord Hoddesdon starts his ill-advised sortie into Valley Fields. He also walks past Acacia Grove and finds himself at the pub on the 'corner of Benjafield Road'. He is completely lost and inquires of a little boy directions to Acacia Grove. The rest of the chapter purges the emotions with pity and terror and takes us down Acacia Grove and around the corner to Peacehaven again and its neighbour, Castlewood, the residence of Major Flood-Smith, late of the Loyal Royal Worcestershires. (Wodehouse had an uncle in the Worcesters.)

In Chapter Nine of *Big Money* Lady Vera Mace sets out on the same task as her brother. She, of course, finds Peacehaven with no difficulty at all and causes her nephew some disquiet by her unexpected arrival.

> His emotion was understandable. He was just on his way to Castlewood to collect Miss Valentine and take her to the Bijou Palace (One Hundred Per Cent Talking) at the corner of Roxborough Road and Myrtle Avenue, the meeting place of all that is best and fairest in Valley Fields. And, while he knew that he was doing this merely because he was sorry for a lonely little girl, a stranger in a strange land, who had few pleasures, the last thing he wanted was a prominent member of the family dodging about the place, taking notes of his movements with bulging eyes.

The Biscuit discovers his aunt has only a few minutes to spare.

> 'Ah!' said the Biscuit, relieved. 'That puts a different complexion on the matter. Well, I'll walk to the station with you.'
>
> He hurried her round the corner and into the asphalt-lined passage that led thither. Only when they were out of sight of Mulberry Grove did the composure return.

At the railway end of Acacia Grove, you will still find that path to the station. It is the final proof that we are in Mulberry Grove. There was once some ornamental water on the other side of Croxted Road but this has gone and council flats occupy the site.

It's not important. You can still wander down Croxted Road and turn into Acacia Grove and admire the sphinxes. Dulwich is still a pleasant spot on a summer evening and Wodehouse would still recognize it as the setting of the school he loved and the background for some of his best stories.

CHAPTER X

THE REVEREND AUBREY UPJOHN
AND HIS FELLOWS

THERE are three categories of headmaster in Wodehouse's
books. The fatherly, remote figures of the early school
stories are followed by the high-farce headmasters of the
Mulliner stories – and there is the Rev. Aubrey Upjohn.

The headmasters and schoolmasters of the early books have
little for us. They are drawn as human beings, although more
respect is given to those who have a good Blue as well as a good
degree. The headmasters of St Austin's, Wrykyn, Beckford
and Sedleigh are drawn as they appear to a boy. They are
elderly and dignified, they are remote, they are the fount of
justice. They are descendants of the headmaster of Westminster who kept his hat on while showing Charles II round
the school. When charged with discourtesy, his simple reply
was: 'The boys must not see that there is one greater than I.'

They reflect the respect and awe that Wodehouse felt for his
own headmaster at Dulwich, the great A. H. Gilkes. Although
Wodehouse's affection for his school and respect for Gilkes
stopped him using Dulwich by name, it played an important
part in his success as a writer.

He used to grumble to Townend about those books written
by people saying how unhappy and misunderstood they had
been at their schools. He followed Dulwich football and
cricket matches all his life and some people thought him rather
a bore on the subject. Frederick Lonsdale expressed his
disappointment with his conversation at the Savage Club and
said that Wodehouse only appeared to be interested in plots,
Pekes and Dulwich Rugby football.

He was conscious that his interests were limited and admitted it to Townend. Or, he asked, was it just that Dulwich was a particularly good school in their day? It was, and Wodehouse's success owed more to Dulwich than perhaps he realized. The Dulwich record in the Nineties was extraordinarily good. It was one of those periods of excellence which happen to schools and much of the success came from Gilkes. Wodehouse did Classics, and in those days that meant constant Greek and Latin, prose and verse, into both languages and out of them. By the time he was sixteen he was writing Greek and Latin verse with ease. It is unlikely that any other subjects occupied more than a quarter of his time – and it is the significance of this that has often been overlooked.

I discussed the matter once with a famous headmaster. His view was unequivocal – that Wodehouse was the end of a line. Never again would any writer have the solid grounding in the Classics that Wodehouse had, unmarred by radio and television. He felt that the combination of the Classics background, the printed word as the only medium of communication and Wodehouse's own temperament and omnivorous reading produced an almost Shakespearean range of language that we shall never see again.

Like so many of us, Wodehouse didn't appreciate what his schooldays had given him. He said once that all he could remember from them was an odd little limerick; but there was an influence that stayed with him all his life even though perhaps he didn't realize it.

In *Bachelors Anonymous* Ivor Llewellyn says that his knowledge of literature started with his love for his English schoolmistress. Bill Shannon, the 'Old Reliable', tells Phipps that she quotes Shakespeare so much because that was all there was to read on the boat on which she was a stewardess. (The job as a stewardess is an echo of Bill Townend but the volume of Shakespeare was more than an echo. When Wodehouse was bundled into internment by the Germans, the Complete Works was what he took with him – he foresaw that internment would at least afford him the opportunity to read them.) In his autobiography Raymond Chandler, who was also at Dulwich during Gilkes's régime, speaks of his days there with a strong recognition of the advantages it gave him.

Chandler lists Caesar, Livy, Ovid and Virgil as the Latin authors he read and Thucydides, Plato and Aristophanes amongst the Greeks. He describes Gilkes as being unusual among headmasters in being a published novelist and having a passion for English literature. He would read a favourite passage to the class and ask them to say why it was good English. He was a stickler for clear prose and when he set a translation, he would make the class revise and revise their work till in his opinion the translation reflected the virtues of the original. The following week he would make them translate their final version back again! Could there be a better education for a writer?

Chandler makes an important point:

A classical education saves you from being fooled by pretentiousness, which is what most current fiction is too full of. Having read dead languages wholly lacking in immediate practicality, one is able to look at later literary fads with some scepticism.

In this country [USA] the mystery writer is looked down upon as a sub-literary being merely because he is a mystery writer rather than a writer of social significance twaddle. To a classicist, even a very rusty one, such an attitude is merely a parvenu insecurity.

. . . if I hadn't grown up on Latin and Greek, I doubt if I would know so well how to draw the line between vernacular or what I should call illiterate or faux naif. There's a hell of a lot of difference.

Isn't that exactly why Wodehouse stands out from his contemporaries? He created a new mythology consistent through fifty years and enriched by language that makes full use of precise adjectives and unrivalled metaphors. I think Dulwich and Gilkes had a lot more to do with Wodehouse's success than he ever realized. He had a high regard for Gilkes,

although he says he was terrified of him; from all accounts
Gilkes, six foot four with a beard, deep-blue eyes and a
resonant voice, was certainly a man to be held in awe. In
Performing Flea Wodehouse tells Townend that the book
recently (1938) published about Dulwich and Gilkes gives a
wrong impression:

> I liked the Gilkes book. I thought Leake had made a good job
> of it. Though you rather get the impression of Gilkes as a man
> who was always trying to damp people, to keep them from
> getting above themselves. ('So you made a century against
> Tonbridge, did you, my boy? Well, always remember you
> will soon be dead, and in any case, the bowling was probably
> rotten!')

From Gilkes and the awe in which Wodehouse held him,
echoed in the respect given to the headmasters in the school
stories, we move to Mr Arnold Abney.

Arnold Abney is the headmaster of Sanstead House School,
the setting for *The Little Nugget*. He is the first headmaster we
see through adult eyes. Peter Burns, the narrator, describes his
own (and Wodehouse's) feelings as an adult going back to
school:

> My view, till then, had been that the assistant-master had an
> easy time. I had only studied him from the outside. My
> opinion was based on observations made as a boy at my own
> private school, when masters were an enviable race who went
> to bed when they liked, had no preparation to do and
> couldn't be caned. It seemed to me that those three facts,
> especially the last, formed a pretty good basis on which to
> build up the Perfect Life . . .
> 'Taking duty' makes certain definite calls upon a man. He
> has to answer questions; break up fights; stop big boys
> bullying small boys; prevent small boys bullying smaller
> boys; check stone-throwing, going-on-the-wet-grass,
> worrying-the-cook, teasing-the-dog, making-too-much-
> noise, and, in particular, discourage all forms of hara-kiri

such as tree-climbing, waterspout-scaling, leaning-too-far-out-of-the-window, sliding-down-the-banisters, pencil-swallowing, and ink-drinking-because-somebody-dared-me-to.

Wodehouse no longer wrote of schoolmasters as a school-boy sees them but as a schoolmaster sees a colleague. The reason for the change was that between 1903 and 1909 he had been in constant contact with a small school exactly as he described – Emsworth House, in Hampshire. It was here that Westbrook taught when Wodehouse met him and it was here that Wodehouse lived for a couple of years.

The year after *The Little Nugget* we meet Mr Blatherwick, the headmaster of Harrow House in *The Man Upstairs* (1914). He is drawn like Mr Abney and they set the pattern for the high-farce headmasters that join the Wodehouse Valhalla.

We meet the Rev. Trevor Entwhistle, known to his contemporaries as 'Catsmeat', the Rev. Mr Waterbury, who bedevils young Sipperley with his little articles on old Etruria, and the Rev. J. G. Smethurst, now disguising himself as the Bishop of Bognor. They are superb creations, although none of them faces the tribulations of 'the bearded bloke' who holds the fortunes of the Market Snodsbury Grammar School in his hands. (Gussie Fink-Nottle's presentation of the prizes in *Right Ho, Jeeves* must be the chapter that lives in the memory of Wodehouse readers more than any other.) And there is the Rev. Aubrey Upjohn.

Despite the Rev. Aubrey's portrayal as a force of repression, one has a certain sympathy for him. To be responsible for the young Bertie Wooster, Gussie Fink-Nottle, the infant Bingo Little and Freddie Widgeon is enough to turn any man into a bad-tempered Old Testament prophet.

The Rev. Aubrey has been with us a long time, but his eventual appearance in a full-length novel (*Jeeves in the Offing*) causes no shift of emphasis either in Wodehouse's writing or our view of Upjohn himself. It's a tribute to Wodehouse's consistency that he could introduce a character after thirty years of allusion and only have to add a moustache.

If, as Usborne says, the relationship of Bertie Wooster's thoughts to those of his creator are very close, and if any of Wodehouse's creations had a factual origin, then there had to be a real Aubrey Upjohn somewhere. In common with other faithful readers I blinked when Aubrey Upjohn was replaced by Arnold Abney in *Much Obliged, Jeeves* in 1971. It is of Arnold Abney that Bertie has memories in that book and he specifically refers to his old master six times in fifty pages.

Perhaps the reason is that *Much Obliged, Jeeves* was written for publication on Wodehouse's ninetieth birthday. At that age one is entitled to make the odd slip, and a very useful slip it was. *Much Obliged, Jeeves* was written to order if ever a book was. The world knew Wodehouse would be ninety, suddenly realized how long he had been writing and wanted another book on his birthday. He wasn't hounded but there was certainly pressure on him, and I think this is reflected in the book.

It is the book which tells us Jeeves's Christian name and takes us inside the Junior Ganymede Club for the first time. These are great events in the Wodehouse world and more than offset the two Wodehouse 'slips'. The first is the mix-up over Brinkley's name. Brinkley was Bertie's temporary valet years before and burnt down Bertie's cottage at Chufnell Regis. Bertie reminds Jeeves that Brinkley is a member of the Junior Ganymede and therefore Jeeves is wrong to state there are no men of ill will amongst the members. Jeeves says the name is Bingley, not Brinkley, and in any event he, Bingley/Brinkley, is only a country member.

This is very strange. The name was Brinkley and Wodehouse must have known it – so why did he say the name was Bingley? One explanation is that when Wodehouse drafted the plot he must have realized that if he was going to set the book chez Aunt Dahlia and use Bertie's old valet as a character, then he had a problem. Every Wodehouse reader knows Aunt Dahlia's address is Brinkley Court, Market Snodsbury, commonly referred to as Brinkley. Something had to go and Brinkley lost his patronym. Oddly enough, the precaution proved unnecessary. Although almost the entire book takes place at Aunt

Dahlia's country house, it is not actually named once – presumably so that Wodehouse need not explain any further Brinkley/Bingley problems.

The second slip is the Arnold Abney/Aubrey Upjohn changeover. If Wodehouse could make a mistake like that, there must be a reason for it. Remembering his age and the pressure he was under to complete it on time, it is a fair assumption that the slip came about because Arnold Abney of *The Little Nugget* of 1913 and Aubrey Upjohn of the later novels *were based on the same person*.

In *Portrait of a Master* Jasen says:

After two years at Elizabeth College, where 'life was very pleasant', Plum was designated by his father for a career in the Navy. He was to continue his education at Malvern House, a Navy preparatory school in Kearnsey, Kent, near Dover.

This is an astonishing piece of information. Was it possible that all Wodehouse/Bertie's comments on membership of the Malvern House chain-gang were deliberate? Malvern House was well known to thousands of Wodehouse enthusiasts, and the nub of *Jeeves in the Offing* revolves exactly round this point. Kipper Herring hears that Bertie is going to stay at Brinkley with the Rev. Aubrey.

'I envy you, Bertie,' he went on, continuing to chuckle. 'You have a wonderful treat in store. You are going to be present at the breakfast table when Upjohn opens his copy of this week's *Thursday Review* and starts to skim through the pages devoted to comments on current literature. I should explain that among the books that recently arrived at the office was a slim volume from his pen dealing with the Preparatory School and giving it an enthusiastic build-up. The formative years which we spent there, he said, were the happiest years of our life.'

'Gadzooks!'

'He little knew that his brainchild would be given to one of the old lags of Malvern House to review. I'll tell you

108

something, Bertie, that every young man ought to know. Never be a stinker, because if you are, though you may flourish for a time like a green bay tree, sooner or later retribution will overtake you. I need scarcely tell you that I ripped the stuffing out of the beastly little brochure. The thought of those sausages on Sunday filled me with the righteous fury of a Juvenal.'

'Of a who?'

'Nobody you know. Before your time. I seemed inspired.'

And Wodehouse himself attended Malvern House! I set off on the comparatively easy task of finding out who had been the headmaster down there at Kearnsey in the 1890s. There were various sources I could try, and I had a fair idea of the name I was looking for – Arnold Abney in 1913, Aubrey Upjohn thereafter – I was prepared to bet the name would be two words each of two syllables and the same initial letter to each.

Arthur Aarvold? Alfred Ampersand? Osbert Oswalds? It was none of these, but I was near the mark. The fat volume of Kelly's Directory for Kent for 1895 shows that the headmaster of Malvern House was Mr *Harvey Hammond*. He retired in 1909 and died in 1911, well before his alter ego appeared. I acquired one bit of information that I'm sure Wodehouse didn't know. Three years after Wodehouse left Malvern House, Hammond became a JP. Just think what Wodehouse could have done with that – Bingo and Bertie in the dock at Bramley-on-Sea and finding that the beak was their old mentor and that the six of the best of former years had been replaced by seven days without the option! What a pity he didn't pick up that snippet.

CHAPTER XI

◄§ ►

HOLLYWOOD

WODEHOUSE only spent a short time in Hollywood but it gives us some of the best examples of factual background to his work.

After a good deal of persuasion from Sam Goldwyn in 1929, Wodehouse went out there in 1930, rented a house from Norma Shearer and awaited the call from the MGM studio to write for them. Odd jobs came his way but little of any significance, and he continued writing such dialogue as he was asked for till the day he shook the movie industry to its foundations by telling a newspaper reporter that he regretted the little work he had done for the large amount of money he was being paid. The interview caused uproar across America and the bankers of the East Coast started their investigations into the extravagance which they had suspected but for which they had hitherto obtained no proof.

Wodehouse left Hollywood in November 1931 but was invited back by MGM in October 1936 on a year's contract. His thirty months in Hollywood gave us *Laughing Gas* and *The Old Reliable*, half a dozen short stories and the emergence of Ivor Llewellyn and his colleagues. His first Hollywood stories appeared in *Blandings Castle* and introduced us to Jacob Z. Schnellenhamer, Isidore Fishbein, Ben Zizzbaum and other moguls. These characters and the other Hollywood stories rest on certain factors which Wodehouse used constantly.

In his stories heads of studios are first-generation Americans, mostly Jewish, dictators of all they survey and

110

with poor command of English and less of its literature. They employ numbers of their own relatives and an even larger number of their wife's. They run organizations which have their own laws and where 'a contract' means what they want it to mean.

Here is Ivor Llewellyn reacting to his sister-in-law's suggestion that he hire Reggie Tennyson as adviser on his English sequences:

> 'And you,' boomed Mr Llewellyn, turning his batteries on his sister-in-law, 'you stop saying "Ikey!" So you want that I should hire more loafers to pick my pockets, do you? It's not enough, your brother George, and your Uncle Wilmot and your cousin Egbert and your cousin Genevieve?'
>
> Here Mr Llewellyn had to pause for an instant in order to grasp at the receding skirts of his self-control. He was greatly affected by those concluding words. There had always been something about that weekly three hundred and fifty dollars paid out to his wife's cousin Egbert's sister Genevieve which for some odd reason afflicted him more than all his other grievances put together. A spectacled child with a mouth that hung open like a letter-box, Genevieve was so manifestly worth a maximum of thirty cents per annum to any employer.
>
> *(The Luck of the Bodkins)*

When Wilmot Mulliner discovers that Little Johnny Bingley, the child movie-star, is a middle-aged midget, Mr Schnellenhamer does not hesitate;

> 'You would not reveal the Corporation's little secrets, thereby causing it alarm and despondency, would you, Mulliner?'
>
> 'Certainly he wouldn't,' said Mr Levitsky. 'Especially now that we're going to make him an executive.'
>
> 'An executive?' said Mr Schnellenhamer, starting.
>
> 'An executive,' repeated Mr Levitsky firmly. 'With brevet rank as a brother-in-law.'

Mr Schnellenhamer was silent for a moment. He seemed to be having a little trouble in adjusting his mind to this extremely drastic step. But he was a man of sterling sense, who realized that there were times when only the big gesture will suffice.

'That's right,' he said. 'I'll notify the legal department and have the contract drawn up right away.'

Wodehouse could have exaggerated the point far more and still been able to prove his case. In the heyday of Hollywood, from 1925 to 1935, the seven big studios were headed by men who kept their places by bullying, chicanery and forceful personality. All except one were Jewish – Darryl Zanuck was renowned as the only Gentile and the only studio head who was happy to speak and write English.

Carl Laemmle of Universal left it in 1935. The accountants brought in by the new owners discovered seventy of his relatives and friends on the payroll, including two who had died years before but to whose widows the pay-packet still went. Nick Cohn had twenty-nine members of his family on the Columbia payroll; there were a dozen relatives of Nick Schenk at Loewe studios and L. B. Mayer had six of his at MGM. Paramount had enough members of two families to have fielded a football team from either.

Those studio heads were incredible people. I read only four books of Hollywood memoirs but it is clear that Wodehouse didn't have to exaggerate anything. Sam Goldwyn's 'Goldwynisms' were famous and were undoubtedly the source of the pseudo-English spoken by Wodehouse's Mr Schnellenhamer and his friends. He is credited with remarks like:

'Include me out.'
'For this part, I want a lady. Someone that's couth.'

When listening to the advertising campaign for a new film which concluded with the words '... and the genius of Goldwyn have united to make the world's greatest entertainment', Goldwyn's comment was:

'That's the kind of advertising I like. Facts, no exaggeration.'

One of the factors of *The Luck of the Bodkins* was that Ivor Llewellyn thought Ambrose Tennyson the writer was *the* Tennyson, the poet. This is based on the occasion when Goldwyn solemnly issued orders for Shakespeare to be brought to Hollywood to tidy up *Othello*. Ludicrous, but even David Selznick felt he could offer Czar Nicholas of Russia a job by a telegram which concluded: 'Hear you are now out of work. Regards to you and the family.'

Conrad Nagle's autobiography describes the confusion and chicanery that went on and includes an anecdote of the time his studio wanted some English dialogue written:

'Nobody can write this except P. G. Wodehouse or a man of his calibre.'
'That's it. Get P. G. Wodehouse.'
They started calling, looking all over for him. They couldn't find him anywhere. It turned out he was right there in the studio. He had had an office there for six months and had been drawing a salary right along.

Probably the single factor that infuriated Wodehouse and his colleagues more than any other was the lack of decision. The story here is 'The Castaways' from *Blandings Castle* and deals with Bulstrode Mulliner, his fiancée and their colleagues. They travel to Hollywood and find themselves trapped for ever in the studios of the Perfecto-Zizzbaum Motion Picture Corporation.

'My nephew' Mr Mulliner hastened to explain, 'was not an author. Nor was Miss Bootle. Very few of those employed in writing motion-picture dialogue are. The executives of the studios just haul in anyone they meet and make them sign contracts. Most of the mysterious disappearances you read about are due to this cause. Only the other day they found a plumber who had been missing for years. All the time he had been writing dialogue for the Mishkin Brothers. Once having reached Los Angeles, nobody is safe.'

'Rather like the old Press Gang,' said the Sherry and Bitters.

'Exactly like the old Press Gang,' said Mr Mulliner.

It transpires that there are dozens of poor wretches engaged in writing the script for *Scented Sinners*, a film described by Mr Schnellenhamer as a 'powerful drama of life as it is lived by the jazz-crazed, gin-crazed Younger Generation whose hollow laughter is but the mask for an aching heart.' They have all been forced to sign contracts which commit them to write until the film is complete – which will never happen. Eventually Mr Schnellenhamer discovers that the rights of the film belong to another studio, and all is well.

There's a nice twist here. Wodehouse was undoubtedly thinking of his own experience with *Rosalie*, a musical that opened on the New York stage in 1928. Wodehouse and Bolton had been involved in it and it had then been passed to other authors and composers to complete. It did very well and reflected credit on its team of creators; MGM bought the movie rights and when Wodehouse went to Hollywood, there it was again waiting for him. In October 1930 he wrote to Townend (see *Performing Flea*):

MGM bought that musical comedy *Rosalie* – the thing Guy Bolton, Bill McGuire, George Gershwin, Sigmund Romberg, Ira Gershwin and I did for Siegfield for Marilyn Miller – for Marion Davies. Everyone in the studio had a go at it, and then they told me to try. After I had messed about with it with no success, Irving Thalberg, the big boss . . . worked out a story on his own and summoned me to Santa Barbara . . . to hear it. . . . Unfortunately, for some inscrutable reason Thalberg wants me to write it not in picture form but as a novelette, after which I suppose it will be turned into a picture. The prospect of this appals me, and I am hoping that the whole thing will blow over, as things do out here.

In the famous interview he gave that caused so much trouble, he said:

> 'Then they set me to work on a story called *Rosalie* which was to have some musical numbers. It was a pleasant little thing, and I put in three months on it. When it was finished, they thanked me politely and remarked that as musicals didn't seem to be going too well they guessed they would not use it.'

Wodehouse left Hollywood and came back to live in France and wrote short stories for *The Strand*. Some of them were about Hollywood, including 'The Castaways'. He didn't write them with any malice; they were funny and they made people laugh. In 1936 MGM decided they wanted him again and back he went to Hollywood. The first job they gave him was *Rosalie* again!

Like those of the Pelican Club, his Hollywood stories were based on fact. He took what he saw, rewrote it and made us laugh. He didn't have to invent too much; the crazy world of Hollywood did that for him.

‏‏‎ ‎

CHAPTER XII

KENT AND MILORD UFFENHAM

K ENT does not play a major part in the novels, but, like Norfolk, the background it does give is firm and undeniable. There are various references to it, and Beevor Castle of *Spring Fever* bears a very close resemblance to Hever Castle, then the Kent home of the Astors. Wodehouse went to school at Malvern House near Dover, later to become the nursery of the Drones Club, and he paid occasional visits to his brother at Birchington and to his old friend Bill Townend at Folkestone. These are minor references, and this chapter concentrates on one man and his house.

We meet George, sixth Viscount Uffenham, in *Money in the Bank* and *Something Fishy*. They both deal with his attempts to ensure that his two nieces marry the right young men and not the Gawd-help-us characters they have chosen for themselves. Lord Uffenham's ancestral home is Shipley Hall in Kent. It is gracious and pleasant and it is unfortunate that he has lost his memory and is therefore unable to remember where he hid the diamonds which represent the family fortune. The difficulty is that he has enjoyed finding new and more ingenious hiding places and is forced to remain as butler to Mrs Adela Cork, to whom he has let his house, so that he can follow up any clues his errant memory might bring to the surface.

Money in the Bank is one of the books Wodehouse wrote during his internment, and the language reflects it; it is full of beautifully turned phrases and metaphors. For us, its interest is the firm identification of Lord Uffenham and his house.

Shipley Hall, the ancestral seat of George, sixth Viscount Uffenham, and rented furnished from him by Mrs Cork, stood on a wide plateau backed by rolling woodlands, a white Georgian house set about with gay flower-beds and spreading lawns, commanding a comprehensive view of the surrounding countryside.

At page 29 of *Money in the Bank* (1946) we learn that Shipley is seventy minutes drive from London; at page 48 we read it is thirty miles from London and at page 69 we are told the drive is two hundred yards long. There is a small pond in the grounds and a sunken garden with a wall from the top of which our old friend Dolly Molloy can precipitate stone vases on to the heads of those who have incurred her displeasure. The nearest town is Tunbridge Wells; there is a rhododendron walk in which young lovers can be discovered in an embrace.

In *Something Fishy*, written eleven years later, it is described in similar terms:

Shipley Hall stood on a wide plateau, backed by rolling woodland, a massive white house set about with gay flower beds and spreading lawns. The sight of it, as the car turned in at the iron gates and rolled up the drive, drew from Lord Uffenham a low gurgle such as might have proceeded from the lips of his bull-dog George on beholding a T-bone steak, and Bill, always sympathetic, knew how he was feeling. Some poignant stuff was written by the poet Thomas Moore in the nineteenth century descriptive of the emotions of the Peri who was excluded from Paradise, and those of the British landowner who is revisiting the old home which poverty has compelled him to let unfurnished to a rich American are virtually identical.

As if to underline and emphasise his state of exile, the Jaguar of the new owner was standing at the front door, and Lord Uffenham eyed it askance. He had overcome his momentary weakness, and his long upper lip was stiff once more.

'That feller Bunyan's here,' he said.

117

Here the house is an hour and a quarter's drive from London and it is still near Tonbridge.

I started my search by drawing a line through Kent describing a thirty-mile radius from London. Somewhere on the line of the quadrant I drew was Shipley. Unfortunately so were Knole, Penshurst, Chiddingstone and Hever, and I found Shipley only by chance when following a completely separate line of investigation. In my work on Wodehouse's family I had traced aunts up and down the country and had completed my chapter on them when I realized that I had ignored the younger generation.

If you are in a prison camp, what do you miss most? Dozens of answers but one of the first must be one's family. Mrs Wodehouse was at least on the Continent and Wodehouse knew he would rejoin her eventually, but separated from him by the English Channel, and therefore in wartime a million miles away, was the second woman in his life, his stepdaughter Leonora. And she lived, not at 'Shipley, Kent' but Shipbourne, Kent!

When Leonora Wodehouse married Peter Cazalet in 1932, they went to live at Fairlawn, the Cazalet estate at Shipbourne in Kent. It is as Wodehouse described it, thirty miles from London, seventy minutes drive (faster nowadays if you use the motorway), and it is indeed a massive white early Georgian house set on a plateau looking out over Kent. The sunken garden is still there with urns on the wall, ideal for Dolly Molloy's fell purposes. It is smack on the line of the quadrant I drew. It is without doubt Lord Uffenham's ancestral home.

Lord Uffenham himself is one of the few characters who I knew was based on fact; Wodehouse said so without any equivocation in his letter to Townend of 24 February 1945 (*Performing Flea*):

In camp you don't see much of people who aren't in your dormitory. Did I tell you that Lord Uffenham in *Money in the Bank* was drawn from a man in my dormitory? It isn't often that one has the luck to be in daily contact with the model for one's principal character.

The problem was that there were dozens of names mentioned in Wodehouse's journal of his captivity and unless I had an unusual stroke of luck, it seemed as if Lord Uffenham's source would remain unknown. Guy Bolton, when I met him, did not know the name, there was no reason why he should, and the trail went cold for several months till I read a newspaper article by Anthony Lejeune, who mentioned that his uncle had been the original of Lord Uffenham. My stroke of luck had turned up.

Anthony Lejeune made time to see me, gave me some excellent suggestions on the Drones Club and told me of his uncle. The characteristics Wodehouse emphasized were Lord Uffenham's size and his habit of going into trances on thoughts that seemed important to him and irrelevant to everybody else. A typical passage from *Money in the Bank* reads:

> Lord Uffenham came suddenly out of his coma, and at once gave evidence that, though the body had been inert, the brain had not been idle.
>
> 'Hey,' he said, once more subjecting Jeff to that piercing stare.
>
> 'Yes?'
>
> 'Do you know how you can tell the temperature?'
>
> 'Look at a thermometer?'
>
> 'Simpler than that. Count the number of chirps a grass-hopper makes in fourteen seconds, and add forty.'
>
> 'Oh yes?' said Jeff, and awaited further observations. But the other had had his say. With the air of a man shutting up a public building, he closed his mouth and sat staring before him, and Jeff returned to Anne.

Wodehouse based Lord Uffenham on the man who acted as interpreter for their group in camp – Max Enke. He is mentioned often in Wodehouse's account of his internment and his daughter, Mrs Ruth Chambers, has provided the following information, including an answer to my specific question: did Max Enke know that Wodehouse had used him to create Lord Uffenham?

> You ask about my father, Max Enke. He was born March 12, 1884 in Manchester England and died January 29, 1971 in Victoria (B. C.). His parents were born in Germany, moved to England and became naturalized citizens. They moved to Belgium in the 1890s and had a factory there, buying rabbit skins and treating them, selling to the felt hat trade. After my grandfather died and my father's elder brother retired, my father managed the factory and was in charge of it in 1940 when Hitler broke through the Netherlands and Belgium. My father tried to escape through the south of France but left it too late and failed to get through. . . . He turned himself in in July 1940 as the Nazis were rounding up all British citizens. And that was it till 1945.
>
> Yes, I read *Money in the Bank*. Lord Uffenham was a cruel caricature of my father, who read the book, chuckled ruefully that Wodehouse had caught some of his peculiar ways.
>
> Max was very large, over six feet, 270 lbs when first interned but lost 70 lbs in the first two months. He was also very deaf, very bald, had a beautiful brain, very interested in chess, mathematics and scientific matters. He was never bored as he could always amuse himself working out maths or chess problems.
>
> He emigrated to Canada in 1907, bought a farm on Galiano Island and eventually gave a tract of land to the people of the island to be held in trust and perpetuity as a park . . .
>
> He was an eccentric but true, honest and utterly dependable.

To make a man funny is not necessarily to make fun of him, and a moment's reflection on *Money in the Bank* or *Something Fishy* shows that Lord Uffenham is the hero. There is a young man who wins the heroine but he is not the hero. In Lord Uffenham we see another of the elderly gentlemen, led by Gally Threepwood and Uncle Fred, who from about 1933 are the centre of the novels. It is Gally, Uncle Fred and Lord Uffenham who find answers and thwart villains, not the young men. It is Lord Uffenham who finds the diamonds in *Money in the Bank*, Lord Uffenham who makes his nieces see where their true love lies. It is Lord Uffenham we remember as the genius who solves everyone's problems in *Something Fishy* by his inspiration of facing Roscoe Bunyan with our old friend Battling Billson.

Lord Uffenham has gone and the Cazalets have left Fairlawn but it is still the beautiful house Wodehouse described, a fit setting for a beloved daughter where Wodehouse must have been happy to think of her as he sat in the crowded room in Tost Prison tapping out his chapters of *Money in the Bank*.

❧

CHAPTER XIII

'BILL'

NO, not the famous song that Wodehouse wrote for *Showboat* but the other 'Bill' – Bill Townend, the co-editor of *Performing Flea*, the series of letters written by Wodehouse to Townend from 1920 to 1950 which proved invaluable for the information it gave on the journeys, houses and friends on which this book is based.

It was only after I had dredged every reference I could from the letters that it struck me that perhaps I should be looking at their recipient as well. If my theory about Wodehouse drawing his characters from real people was correct, then some of Townend's personality or characteristics should appear in the novels somewhere.

This chapter looks at William Townend, traveller, adventurer, artist and author, and his place in the Wodehouse stories.

William Townend was born in 1881, the son of the Reverend A. J. Townend, a Service chaplain. His friendship with Wodehouse started when they were boys together at Dulwich. They kept in contact in London when Wodehouse started to write and Townend, a struggling artist, illustrated one of Wodehouse's books (*The White Feather*) and appeared under his own name in a Wodehouse story in the *Windsor Magazine* in 1908. Townend eventually became a writer helped, encouraged and often subsidized by Wodehouse. He wrote forty-one books, most of them about the sea. From 1920 to 1952 the friends corresponded regularly, and we can assume that they continued to do so till Townend's death near Folkstone in 1962.

Wodehouse was the most innocent and unworldly of men, yet his attitude towards Townend was that of an elder brother, giving firm, sound advice on agents, publishers, style and plots. They met comparatively rarely after the early days. Townend married in 1919 but had no children. He and Wodehouse lived near each other for a couple of years in the 1920s and again in the 1930s, but, apart from these two short periods, they seem to have maintained their friendship through the letters that make up *Performing Flea*. The two of them swapped plots and stories; Wodehouse envied Townend his eye for material and relied on him for anything to do with the sea and ships. In turn Townend sought Wodehouse's advice on style and layout and Wodehouse canvassed publishers on his behalf.

It is the detail of Townend's life that concerns us. Although Wodehouse may have been the adviser, the elder brother, there was one aspect in which he looked up to Townend, and it is this that comes through in the novels. While Wodehouse was working in the bank, starting his newspaper work on *The Globe* and making his way as a writer, Townend was out in the world, in Europe and America, keeping himself alive in outlandish places in a way that Wodehouse never forgot. There was no envy in this – Wodehouse knew from the start he wanted to be a writer. Townend, like so many of us, didn't know what he wanted to do.

We know that early in the century, probably in 1904, Townend sent Wodehouse a long letter describing the adventures of a friend of his on a chicken farm. Wodehouse used the idea to write *Love among the Chickens* (1906), his first adult novel and the first appearance of Ukridge. He shared the profits with Townend, who appears in the book as 'Lickford'. In the autumn of 1906 someone suggested to Townend that he should go for a voyage in a tramp-steamer to get material for his pictures. He says in *Performing Flea*:

> Plum said that if I really wanted to go – and 'rather you than me' – he would pay my expenses. I went for my voyage, to Sulina in Roumania, and returned after three months with a

broken nose, no hat, with no pictures, but with notebooks
filled with stories I had heard on board . . .

In 1986 that may not sound too exciting but we are talking of
the turn of the century. There are thousands of young people
hiking across Africa, and the streets of Khatmandu may be
thronged with Californian students, but seventy years ago
things were very different.

Reader's *Victorian England* puts it succinctly:

> . . . politics, the Church and the Services were the natural
> career for the young men of upper and middle-class back-
> grounds or the maintenance of the Empire that was at its
> zenith. Medicine and the law were acceptable alternatives
> while certain bold spirits turned to journalism or the stage,
> which were both regarded as déclassé except by those who
> were engaged in them.

How much more exotic was the public school man who
travelled the world by tramp-steamer. Between 1911 and 1915
Townend was on the Pacific Coast. He worked on a ranch up
near the Canadian border and picked lemons down at Chula
Vista near Hollywood. In 1923 he was in Switzerland and in
1937 he was in Brazil, and Wodehouse used to complain that
his address took longer and longer to write. Townend's
journeys and adventures made an impression on his friend that
stayed with him all his life. When Wodehouse wanted to
describe a certain sort of person or give him a certain attribute,
he remembered Townend and used something of his career.

As Usborne points out, Wodehouse heroes fall into two
categories, the Reggies, Freddies, Berties, Gussies and Montys
of the farces and a second group of straightforward young men
with names like Nick, Jeff, Mike or John. The most straightforward name of all in Wodehouse's books is Bill. William
Bates the solid golfer, Bill Dawlish the honourable, straight-
as-a-die peer, Bill Brewster who becomes Archie Moffam's
brother-in-law, Bill West, Bill Hollister, Bill Lister, Bill
Oakshott, Bill Bailey the honest curate, Bill Hardy and Bill

Rowcester are all in the same pattern. If we switch the sexes we have Bill Shannon the 'Old Reliable' herself, Billie Bennett and Billie Dore, although these ladies form a slightly livelier group.

The Reggies, Pongoes and Freddies are immediately classifiable as the Drones who need twenty quid to pay their bookmaker, or who are putting the bite on their guardian for the money to start a nightclub. The Bills, Jeffs and Nicks are different; they may have been to school with Bertie Wooster or Freddie Widgeon but they are poor men who have to work for their living. They have no valets and augment their income from their dull office job by writing detective stories or painting.

They are often given some physical attribute to impress the reader as well as the heroine; they either play Rugger for England or have represented their University in the boxing ring. Hugo Carmody, Ronnie Fish, even Bertie Wooster himself achieved a surprisingly high standard on the squash court, but for the straight heroes, the tougher sports of Rugger and boxing are more appropriate.

Ginger Kemp in *The Adventures of Sally* uses his skills as a scrum-half to hurl Sally on the train and Stinker Pinker gets his vicarage because of his Rugger skill. Ricky Gilpin met Polly Pott by sailing into a gang who were trying to beat up her father, probably with some justification, and the Reverend Bill Bailey met Myra Schoonmaker in similar fashion . . .

> '. . . and I came along just as someone was snatching her bag. So, of course, I biffed the blighter.'
>
> 'Where did they bury the unfortunate man?'
>
> 'Oh, I didn't biff him much, just enough to make him see how wrong it was to snatch bags.'

As early as 1909 another category of hero appears, the adventurers. They are the men who go off into the wilds, doing extraordinary things (in the eyes of their friends), living from hand to mouth and thoroughly enjoying themselves. Ukridge is the most obvious example but the first was Wyatt, who was expelled from Wrykyn and went out to South America to engage in gun-fights to defend his employer's sheep. In 1919 we have the prospector Hank Jardine, companion to the hero Kirk Winfield in *The Coming of Bill* (another 'Bill'), and in 1925 we meet Sam Shotter, the old Wrykynian, who goes on hunting trips in the depths of Canada and comes to England to win his bride in the Wodehouse tradition:

'When does Mr Shotter arrive?'
'I don't know. He says it's uncertain. You see, he's coming over on a tramp steamer.'
'A tramp steamer? Why?'
'Well, it's the sort of thing he does. Sort of thing I'd like to do too.'

In 1931 we meet Berry Conway in *Big Money*. He wants to get away to the wide open spaces but his sense of honour forces him to wait till he can repay a loan to his crusty-but-heart-of-gold solicitor and pension off his old nurse. He describes his dream to his old friend Lord Biskerton (archetypal second hero, a Drone and man-about-Town):

'And the really damnable part of it is that at the time when the crash came I was just going to buzz off around the world on a tramp steamer. I had to give that up, of course.'

Over the page he says:

'If I could find anybody who would give me enough to pay back old Attwater's loan I wouldn't stay here a day. I'd get on the first boat to America and push West. I can just picture it, Biscuit. Miles of desert, with mountain ranges that seems to change their shape as you look at them. Wagon trucks. Red porphyry cliffs. People going about in sombreros and blue overalls.'
'Probably fearful bounders, all of them' said the Biscuit. 'Keep well away is my advice.'

In 1935, in 'Pig-Hoo-o-o-ey', a story from *Blandings Castle*,

James Belford wins his bride by teaching Lord Emsworth the hog-call he learnt on a farm in Nebraska. In 1957 in *Summer Moonshine* Joe Vanringham has an equally colourful career:

'The last I heard of you, you were a sailor on a tramp steamer.'

'And after that a waiter. And after that a movie extra and a rather indifferent pugilist. I was also, for a time, a bouncer in a New York saloon. That was one of my failures. I started gaily one night to bounce an obstreperous client and unfortunately he bounced me. This seemed to cause the boss to lose confidence in my technique, and shortly afterwards I sailed to England to carve out a new career.'

Joss Weatherby (*Quick Service*) was holding an executive position at the local soda-fountain when he saved James Buchanan from drowning, and even the shy Bill Oakshott of *Uncle Dynamite* breaks away from the confines of Ashenden Oakshott to go exploring. Uncle Fred is curious:

'. . . And why did you commit this rash act? Wanted to get some girl out of your system, I suppose . . . In my day we used to go to the Rocky Mountains and shoot grizzlies. What made you choose Brazil?'

'I happened to see an advertisement in *The Times* about an expedition that was starting off for the Lower Amazon run by a chap called Major Plank, and I thought it might be a good idea to sign on.'

Another Bill, Bill Shannon the 'Old Reliable', has similar habits:

'Is that a favourite bedside book of yours?'

'I glanced through it, madam, when I was in the service of the Earl of Powick in Worcestershire. There was very little else to read in his lordship's library and it rained a great deal.'

'I've come across that sort of thing myself. I once went to Valparaiso as a stewardess on a fruit boat, and the only book on board was The Plays of William Shakespeare, belonging to the chief engineer. By the time the voyage was over, I knew them by heart.'

In *Weekend Wodehouse* (1939) are four extremely funny pages from an introduction Wodehouse wrote to one of Townend's books. He speaks of his own sybaritic existence, describes how he and Townend were at school together and worked as fellow authors on 'The Luck Stone' for *Chums*, and talks of Townend's journeys:

> . . . but this time he went in a tramp steamer, was nearly wrecked off the coast of Wales, messed about in the engine-room, and came back, looking perfectly foul in a stained tweed suit and a celluloid collar, resolved to write stories about men of the deep waters.
>   . . . Some years ago, after a long separation, I met him in The Strand and immediately noticed something peculiar in his appearance and bearing. 'That man,' I said to myself, 'has been sorting lemons.' And so it proved. He had just returned from a long stay on a ranch in Chula Vista, California, and the only thing you can do on a California ranch is sort lemons. You get up about five, breakfast, and go out and sort lemons. Lunch at twelve-thirty, followed by a long after-noon of lemon-sorting. Then dinner, and perhaps sort a few small ones before bed-time and the restful sleep. Next morning you get up at five, breakfast, and go out and sort lemons. Lunch at . . . But you have gathered the idea . . .

The hero of *Company for Henry* (1967) is Thomas Hardy, known as 'Bill'. He lives in Dulwich, is a writer who wants to break into the American market (with an agent whose name sounds suspiciously like that of Wodehouse's own agent), and like Bill Townend he has a broken nose. The heroine asks him about his life:

> 'And you ran away to sea?'
> 'It sounds pretty conventional, but that is what I did.'

'Sailor before the mast?'

'I didn't quite rise as high as that in the social scale. I worked in the galley, assisting the cook.'

'And after that?'

'I had various jobs.'

'Such as?'

'Well, there were quite a number of them. Picking lemons for one.'

'I knew it. The moment I saw you, I said to myself "That man has been picking lemons." Where was this?'

'Chula Vista, California.'

'Are there lemons out there?'

'Several.'

'And you climbed trees and picked them? That's where you got your cat technique, I suppose. Did you enjoy it?'

'Not much.'

'Still, better than exporting and importing, I should imagine.'

'Oh yes. Very healthy life. But I wasn't sorry to give it up.'

'For what?'

'Oh, a series of jobs.'

A thought struck Jane. 'Have you ever told this saga of yours to Algy?'

'I did once.'

'Did your example shame him?'

'Not in the least. He said the mere idea of working like that made him sick, and my story confirmed the view he had always had that I ought not to be allowed at large.'

All of us have a favourite name and Wodehouse's was 'Bill'. The song he wrote for *Showboat*, all those likeable and adventurous young men – all came from the same source, Bill Townend. And when Wodehouse described the career of Bill Hardy in *Company for Henry* in 1967, he was writing his epitaph for an old friend.

CHAPTER XIV

※

THREE LITTLE GIRLS OR WHERE DID MIKE JACKSON GET HIS SISTERS FROM?

WHEN Wodehouse wrote *Mike*, the book that introduced Psmith to the world, where did the Jackson girls come from? Mike Jackson, the schoolboy hero, is the youngest of the Jackson brothers, who are all good cricketers and are clearly based on the Foster brothers who played cricket for Worcestershire between 1895 and 1910. In *Mike*, published in 1909, Wodehouse writes of three younger sisters, Marjorie, Phyllis and Ella. Only one plays a part in the plot – but why bring them in at all?

Six years earlier, in 1903, in *Tales of St Austin's*, one of the stories revolves around the headmaster's daughter, aged about six or seven, who saves Charteris when he is up for judgement.

'Do you mean to tell me, Dorothy, that it was Charteris who came to your assistance yesterday?'

Dorothy nodded energetically. 'He gave the men beans,' she said. 'He did, really,' she went on, regardless of the Head's look of horror. 'He used right and left, with considerable effect.'

Dorothy's brother, a keen follower of the Ring, had been good enough some days before to read her out an extract from an account in *The Sportsman* of a match at the National Sporting Club, and the account had been much to her liking. She regarded it as a masterpiece of English composition.

'Dorothy,' said the Headmaster, 'run away to bed.' A suggestion which she treated with scorn, it wanting a clear two hours to her legal bedtime. 'I must speak to your mother

130

about your deplorable habit of using slang. Dear me, I must certainly speak to her.'

And, shamefully unabashed, Dorothy retired.

Nothing much to stir the blood – but that touch about bedtime, a child does indeed treat such a suggestion with scorn when it wants two clear hours to her 'legal bedtime' – but how did Wodehouse know? He was twenty-two years old, he was not married, he had no sisters of his own. Where did Dorothy and the Jackson sisters come from?

Not many of Wodehouse's books have a dedication. A few are dedicated to friends or men he admired and the early books are inscribed to his father, mother or brothers, but, surprisingly, the first book of all, *The Pothunters*, is dedicated to three girls – Joan, Effie and Ernestine Bowes-Lyon. Who were they? The name is well known enough to send me to *Burke's Peerage* and this revealed that the three girls were grand-daughters of the thirteenth Earl of Strathmore. I was still puzzled by the dedication since it seemed so at odds with Wodehouse's reputation as a shy man. When he wrote *The Pothunters* he was only twenty and a dedication to three girls seemed completely out of character.

The Pothunters was written over eighty years ago but, out of idle curiosity, I went back to *Burke's Peerage* to find out what happened to the three young ladies. Effie, Lady Winter as she became, died in 1982 but two letters from her take us back to the 1890s, and must surely be the last first-hand account of Wodehouse as a schoolboy:

I first met PG Wodehouse when I was staying with my cousins, the Corbetts in what used to be Shropshire. PG was then still at school but I forget where. His family lived near to Stableford and PG used to come out whenever my sister Joan or myself used to go out riding on the pony – of course on a leading rein accompanied by a groom (such was life in those days).

. . . but soon after that he came to live in London which is where we lived in those faraway times. PG had started to write but he was still working for some firm or another and he used to come around to tea with us three sisters. Joan, my elder sister and Teenie (Ernestine) my younger. He had already had some stories published in 'The Captain' (a boy's magazine) and he asked our advice as to whether he should give up his job and take up writing as a full-time career and of course we said 'yes'. So he did and with what astonishing results . . .

When we were all young, he used to propose to us in turn and we always made him go down on his knees and propose in proper fashion . . . PG never came to Scotland when we used to go there though I do remember he used to send us copies of 'The Captain'. My Aunt Maud was very surprised to find a copy of a boy's magazine on her table with on the cover 'With my blessing'. The fact was that Collingwood the butler used to unpack all the newspapers and put them on the table in Aunt Maud's room and this was from PG to us three.

. . . he used to come to tea with us in London and we used usually to play card games or writing games. PG did once come down to stay with us at Lyme Regis. That was after my Grandfather Glamis was dead and consequently we did not go to Glamis as we used to when he was alive.

I think it was important to remember that we three were all little girls when he used to visit us in Ovington Square . . . I think he could be friends with us because we were little girls.

I found Mike Jackson's three sisters and reached back to a world that vanished for ever in the holocaust of 1916. Little girls on ponies in country lanes with a groom solemnly holding the lead rein; the splendidly named Collingwood gravely submitting *The Captain* with its warm greeting to the chatelaine at Glamis Castle, and the twenty-year-old Wodehouse taking nursery tea and musing aloud whether he should go against his father's wishes and leave the security of the Bank he loathed. One sentence had me turning the pages of *Love among the Chickens*. The book is set at Lyme Regis and was published in 1906. That means that since the thirteenth Earl died early in 1904, Wodehouse could have visited Lyme Regis in 1904 or 1905 to get his setting for Ukridge's chicken farm.

In *Love among the Chickens* Ukridge's house is on a hill above Lyme Regis with a paddock between it and the edge of the hill. You can see the waves between the trees and it is five minutes walk to the famous Cob. It was indeed the house Wodehouse knew from his stay with the Bowes-Lyon girls. Lady Winter's second letter recalled that: 'The house at Lyme Regis was up a hill above the town and from its garden one overlooked the sea from under the trees . . .' So, when Bill Townend sent the famous letter that Wodehouse used for his first adult novel, Wodehouse was able to use a house and a place he knew. And, thanks to Lady Winter, we know where it was and how he knew it.

Perhaps that's not the only thing we should thank her for. Wodehouse's first book, dedicated to the three girls, came out two months after he left the Bank. Perhaps the encouragement he received round the fire at those tea-times at Ovington Square was important. Perhaps those three little girls did just tip the scale as to whether he should go against his father's wishes – if so then the world owes Lady Winter and her sisters a great deal.

CHAPTER XV

WRITING AND WRITERS

WODEHOUSE made his reputation writing of the moneyless/moneyed upper classes but he was equally funny about his fellow writers and their problems. Till the end of his long life he never forgot how a young writer felt about his work, but was able to step aside from his profession and see it as others did.

He was editor of the Dulwich school magazine *The Alleynian*, went on to write pieces for newspapers and magazines, celebrated his release from the Hong Kong and Shanghai Bank by seeing his first book published, and spent the next twenty years writing a daily column for *The Globe*, lyrics for musical comedies and earning his reputation through the novels he wrote at annual intervals. The result is that there are far more writers in his novels than there are Drones, clergymen or earls. We may think of Bertie Wooster, Jeeves, Lord Emsworth and Bingo Little as the main characters but it is a rare book where one of the characters isn't writing away at something. Like so much of the background he put in, it is so credibly described that it slips in almost unnoticed.

Writers appear in eighty-two of the ninety-seven books he wrote, and for a long time they are a direct reflection of their creator. He was editor of his school magazine – so, in the first two books, Charteris of St Austin's edits the official *Austinian* as well as the unofficial *Glow Worm*. I have heard mention of Wodehouse writing a similar unofficial publication when he was at Dulwich. In December 1904 the Pelican, Owen Hall, asked him to write a lyric for a musical comedy and the next year – in *The Head of Kay's* – we get our first glimpse of the theatre behind the scenes.

In 1906 we meet Ukridge for the first time and the narrator, the young author Jeremy Garnet, introduces himself with an entry in *Who's Who* which is extraordinarily like Wodehouse's own that appeared in the real *Who's Who* two years later. In *Not George Washington*, written jointly with Herbert Westbrook in 1907, the coincidences are so many that it is easier to set them out in a table. James Cloyster is drawn on Wodehouse, while the other main character, Julian Eversleigh, is written around Westbrook.

Cloyster	*Wodehouse*
Newspaper for which Cloyster works is *The Orb*.	Paper for which Wodehouse works is *The Globe*.
First humorous article published: 'Men Who Missed Their Own Weddings'.	First humorous article by Wodehouse in *Tit-Bits* Nov. 1900: 'Men Who Missed Their Own Weddings'.
Cloyster's second London address 23 Walpole Street, Chelsea.	Wodehouse's second London address 23 Walpole Street, Chelsea.
Column written by Cloyster is 'On Your Way'.	Wodehouse's column 'By the Way'.
Actor-manager who employs Cloyster is Stanley Briggs.	Actor-manager who employs Wodehouse is Seymour Hicks.
Theatre is the Briggs Theatre.	Theatre is the Hicks Theatre.
Show for which Cloyster writes lyrics, *The Belle of Wells*.	Show for which Wodehouse wrote lyrics, *The Beauty of Bath*.

In 1910 Wodehouse paid his second visit to America and *A Gentleman of Leisure* introduces a hero who is, like Wodehouse, an ex-newspaperman. *Psmith, Journalist* takes Wodehouse's best-known character and involves him with a New York newspaper as his creator was, while *The Man Upstairs* of 1914 has a plethora of similarities. We read of George Callender, a hopeful playwright (Wodehouse by then had written lyrics for seven shows), of James Datchett, a schoolmaster at a school very like Emsworth House who wants to become a journalist, and of Rutherford Maxwell.

Rutherford Maxwell is the hero of that strange story 'In Alcala' from *The Man Upstairs*, and the description of him is as near Wodehouse's own career as we will get: Wodehouse was a third son, his parents could not afford to send him to Oxford, and they put him in the Hong Kong and Shanghai Bank, which he loathed.

> Rutherford Maxwell was an Englishman, and the younger son of an Englishman; and his lot was the lot of younger sons all the world over. He was by profession one of the numerous employees of the New Asiatic Bank, which has its branches all over the world. It is a sound, trustworthy institution and steady-going relatives would assure Rutherford that he was lucky to have got a berth in it. Rutherford did not agree with them. However sound and trustworthy, it was not exactly romantic. Nor did it err on the side of lavishness to those who served it. Rutherford's salary was small. So were his prospects – if he remained in the bank. At a very early date he had registered a vow that he would not. And the road that led out of it was the uphill road of literature.

'In Alcala' is as near a tragedy as Wodehouse wrote, and its description of the humid discomfort of working in a small bedsitter in the heat of a New York summer has the ring of veracity that only personal experience can give.

When Wodehouse turned to the Drones for his heroes he involved them with people like Bruce Corcoran, a writer, Rocky Todd the poet, Rosie M. Banks, George Caffyn the playwright and Boko Fittleworth. And who can forget Bertie Wooster's pride in his article 'What the Well Dressed Man Is Wearing'? Wodehouse used Bertie to describe his fellow authors as others saw them so in *Joy in the Morning* we read Bertie's opinion of his friend Boko Fittleworth:

> The first sight of Boko reveals to the beholder an object with a face like an intellectual parrot. Furthermore, as is the case

with so many of the younger literati, he dresses like a tramp cyclist, affecting turtleneck sweaters and grey flannel bags with a patch on the knee and conveying a sort of general impression of having been left out in the rain overnight in an ash-can. The only occasion on which I have ever seen Jeeves really rattled was when he met Boko for the first time. He winced visibly and tottered off to the kitchen, no doubt to pull himself together with cooking sherry.

Later, he says of Boko:

His hair was disordered and his face flushed, presumably with literary composition. In appearance, as I have indicated, this man of letters is a cross between a comedy juggler and a parrot that has been dragged through a hedge backwards, and you never catch him at his nattiest in the workshop.

Wodehouse liked comfortable clothes himself, the older the better, and Mrs Nella Wodehouse tells me that he used to protest vigorously when forced by his family to smarten himself for interviews. In *Performing Flea* he said in a letter of January 1930:

I'm glad Christmas is over. I came in for the New Year festivities at Hunstanton and had to wear a white waistcoat every night.

He was quite happy to use 'fringe writers'. Pretentious young poets are satirized for fifty years unless, like Rocky Todd, they realize how pretentious their poetry is and are happy to continue writing it so long as the customer is mug enough to pay for it. However, poets become worthier citizens if, like Rodney Spelvin and Percy Gorringe, they take to writing detective stories instead:

'But Percy, darling, you surely can't make much out of your poetry?'
He twiddled his fingers for a moment. You could see he

was trying to nerve himself to reveal something he would much have preferred to keep under his hat. I have had the same experience when had up on the carpet by my Aunt Agatha.

'I don't,' he said. 'I only got fifteen shillings for that 'Caliban at Sunset' thing of mine in *Parnassus* and I had to fight like a tiger to get that. The editress wanted to beat me down to twelve-and-six.

'But I have a . . . an alternative source of revenue.'

'I don't understand.'

He bowed his head. 'You will. My receipts from this – er – alternative source of revenue amounted last year to nearly eight hundred pounds, and this year it should be double that, for my agent has succeeded in establishing me in the American market.

'Florence, you will shrink from me, but I have to tell you. I write detective stories under the pseudonym of Rex West.'

(*Jeeves and the Feudal Spirit*)

Bertie and Florence express admiration and respect at this revelation. As a poet, Percy Gorringe is a butterfly. As a writer of detective stories he joins that band whom Wodehouse admires – the professional writers. He says in one of his essays that anyone who doesn't get what he can for his writing is an ass, and that Dickens and Lord Tennyson insisted on their half-guinea and to hell with allowing the world to enjoy their genius without some monetary consideration.

When Wodehouse wanted Ashe Marson to meet Joan Valentine in *Something Fresh*, he made them both writers for the Mammoth Publishing Company. When he wanted to give Bingo Little an occupation, he made him editor of *Wee Tots*. He introduced us to Monty Bodkin in the splendid scene where Lord Tilbury sacks him from his job as acting editor of *Tiny Tots*. When we see what the four-year-olds of England were given that week, we can appreciate Lord Tilbury's point of view:

'Uncle Woggly To His Chicks'
'Well, chickabiddies, how are you all? Minding what Nannie
says and eating your spinach like good little men? That's
right. I know the stuff tastes like a motorman's glove, but
they say there's iron in it, and that's what puts hair on the
chest.'

Lord Tilbury, having taken time out to make a noise like a
leaking siphon, resumed his reading.
'Well now, let's get down to it. This week, my dear little
souls, Uncle Woggly is going to put you on to a good thing.
We all want to make a spot of easy money in these hard times,
don't we? Well, here's the lowdown straight from the horse's
mouth. All you have to do is to get hold of some mug and lure
him into betting that a quart whisky bottle holds more than a
quart of whisky . . .'

The emotions of a young writer struggling hard, looking for
the break, last right through Wodehouse's books for seventy
years. As late as 1973 Joe Pickering, the young playwright, is
consoled in his distress by the heroine Sally Fitch, also a writer,
and their happy ending is the acceptance of Joe's play by
Hollywood. Wodehouse seems to have known that anxiety all
his life – that this time, as he put it, he had picked a lemon in the
garden of literature.

Up to 1924 or so, the young man/author/playwright/
journalist/hero is Wodehouse himself. After that it is his vivid
memory of the young writer he had been. Two at least of the
other littérateurs he drew are traceable. The first is Lord
Tilbury, the dynamic founder of the Mammoth Publishing
Company. He first appears as the small, Napoleonic, Sir
George Pyke in 1924 in *Bill the Conqueror* and pops up at
intervals thereafter. A mellower version finds true love forty
years later in *Frozen Assets*, and the shift in emphasis reflects
the ninety-year-old Wodehouse's way of showing he had
reached the age of confidence when there were no figures of
authority left to frighten him.

I had a candidate in my mind as the original of Lord Tilbury
for years, but I had to read many books on Fleet Street to
confirm the theory. It wasn't Lord Astor of *The Times* nor

Lord Burnham and the Berry brothers of the *Telegraph*. It wasn't Lord Glenesk of the *Morning Post* or Lord Beaverbrook. I hadn't realized how many Press barons there were until I started my research but one name remains the most likely – Alfred Harmsworth, Lord Northcliffe.

Wodehouse probably chose him because he was 'good copy'. He was well-known, famous or notorious as the most autocratic of publishers. He started at the bottom and made himself head of the largest newspaper organization the world had seen. When Wodehouse joined the *Globe* in 1902, it was run by Sir George Armstrong. In 1907 it became part of the Harmsworth empire and was edited by Hildebrand Harmsworth, who insisted on exercising far tighter control over Wodehouse's column. It is unlikely that this was enough in itself to make Wodehouse satirize Northcliffe; it is more likely that Northcliffe's personality and career simply fitted better with the character Wodehouse wanted to draw.

Both Northcliffe and Tilbury (as drawn by Wodehouse) were renowned for their determination. Both are Napoleonic in manner, fully aware of it and use it to their advantage. Both are described as building up the largest publishing concern in the country and keeping a close personal eye on their publications. *Bill the Conqueror* and *Heavy Weather* both give directions to find Lord Tilbury's office. If you take them, you will find yourself at Northcliffe House off Fleet Street.

In *Bill the Conqueror* we are told that *Pyke's Weekly* never looked back from the moment it ran the competition 'How Many Pins Does the Prime Minister's Hat Hold?' Alfred Harmsworth's breakthrough came when his paper *Answers* ran a competition promising £1 a week for life to the person who guessed 'How Much Gold Is There in the Bank of England?' Although Newnes had achieved some success with *Tit-Bits*, Harmsworth grasped the idea of advertising through competitions before his rivals, and when Wodehouse wrote of the Prime Minister's Hat competition, Harmsworth was the only man he could have had in mind.

Women novelists are a special case in Wodehouse. If young they can be heroines, but if elderly, they are forces of authority and repression. Mrs Hignett, Lady Wickham and Mrs Delane Porter are all against true love and have to be defied or defeated before happy endings can be achieved. They and their colleagues are led by Miss Julia Ukridge, an elderly female writer and an aunt – the worst combination in the Wodehouse world. If she had a source, then undoubtedly the best candidate was Wodehouse's Aunt Mary (Miss Mary Deane, 1845–1940). Mrs Nella Wodehouse remembers her well as an autocratic lady, proud of her family and of her writing. In *Portrait of a Master* Jasen describes her:

> A professional writer, Mary was something of a tyrant; and her demeanour made an indelible impression on her young nephew that was to manifest itself in Bertie Wooster's unsympathetic Aunt Agatha.

Aunt Mary certainly provided the foundation for aunts and their evils but she is equally important as the prototype elderly female writer with a high idea of her own importance and a low opinion of everybody else's. She wrote half a dozen novels, some poetry and a history of the family. Her will in Somerset House mentions some family portraits that were obviously the cause of a long-standing family dispute. She seems to have combined exactly the qualities of pride of family, literary background and forcefulness of character that we see in Miss Julia Ukridge and the other elderly female writers.

Then something odd happened. Suddenly they become admirable in their own right and a force for good. Miss Ukridge is still a representative of authority, but how do we explain those pleasant ladies Bill Shannon, Barbara Crowe and Leila Yorke? They appear in the later books, they are writers and middle-aged, yet they are heroines in their own right.

Was this because, like Gally Threepwood and Uncle Fred who were the elderly heroes of the books in which they appear, they were of Wodehouse's own age and he had come to accept that middle-aged women could love as well? Or was it perhaps that Aunt Mary retained her influence over her nephew during the whole of her long life? Was it that, so long as she remained alive, Wodehouse felt in – well, *in statu nepotis* perhaps? I find it not surprising that Bill Shannon, the first literary, middle-aged heroine, appeared seven years after Wodehouse would have learnt of Miss Deane's death.

The year later would be too soon, but allow a few more years for drafting and writing and a couple more for the realization that never again would he have to worry about that fierce old lady who made him feel so foolish, and Bill Shannon, 'The Old Reliable', might be the first sign that he was free of 'the aunts' at last.

CHAPTER XVI

WIMBLEDON COMMON
AND THE LAW

WIMBLEDON Common is where Ukridge's Aunt Julia lives; it is where Mr and Mrs Bingo Little have their ménage so that Bingo can meet his bookie on the Common and lose money betting that his baby is uglier than the bookmaker's. It is the home of Flick Sheridan, who runs away in *Bill the Conqueror*. It is at The Larches, Wimbledon Common, that Bertie Wooster spends that hour of horror purloining the letter that Gussie Fink-Nottle has written breaking off his engagement to Madeline Bassett. It is at The Oaks, Wimbledon Common, that Lord Tilbury lives in *Frozen Assets*.

This favoured spot lies eight miles southwest of Hyde Park Corner. The approach from London is by the Portsmouth Road out of London, over Putney Bridge, up Putney Hill and the Common is on your left.

The Common is triangular; the vertical right-hand side runs due north–south from Putney to Wimbledon and the left-hand side runs down the Portsmouth Road to Kingston Vale, whence the bottom of our triangle runs east back to Wimbledon. We are looking at the right-hand side, the road that runs from Wimbledon to Putney. It is called Parkside, and somewhere along it was the house that Wodehouse described so often.

When Ukridge forces young Corcoran to go to Wimbledon to plead with Aunt Julia . . .

Four o'clock on the following afternoon found me entering a cab and giving the driver the address of Heath House,

Wimbledon Common.

My emotions on entering Heath House were such as I would have felt had I been keeping a tryst with a dentist who by some strange freak happened also to be a duke. From the moment when a butler of super-Bowles dignity opened the door and, after regarding me with ill-concealed dislike, started to conduct me down a long hall, I was in the grip of both fear and humility. Heath House is one of the stately homes of Wimbledon; how beautiful they stand as the poet says; and after the humble drabness of Ebury Street it frankly over-awed me. It keynote was an extreme neatness which seemed to sneer at my squashy collar and reproach my baggy trouserleg.

In *Bill the Conqueror* the same year (1924) we read:

Mr Sinclair Hammond . . . basked in the sunshine in the garden of Holly House, his residence on Wimbledon Common. There was a notebook on his knee and he was scribbling industriously with a stubby pencil.

Mr Hammond was fond of his garden. It was – for a suburb – quite an Eden. Several acres in dimension and shut off from the outside world by high brick walls, it contained almost more than its fair share of trees: and later on, when summer came, it would, he knew, blaze very nobly with many-coloured flowers. There were smooth lawns, hedges of lavender, and a decent-sized stone pool with goldfish.

In *The Mating Season* of 1949, Wodehouse is in full cry:

The Larches, Wimbledon Common, was one of those eligible residences standing in commodious grounds with Company's own water both h. and c. and the usual domestic offices and all that sort of thing, which you pass on the left as you drive out of London by way of Putney Hill. I don't know who own these joints, though obviously citizens who have got the stuff in sackfuls, and I didn't know who owned The Larches. . . . That was why on the following morning the commodious grounds of The Larches, in addition to a lawn, a summerhouse, a pond, flower beds, bushes and an assortment of trees, contained also one Wooster, noticeably cold about the feet and inclined to rise from twelve to eighteen inches skywards every time an early bird gave a sudden cheep over its worm. This Wooster to whom I allude was crouching in the interior of a bush not far from the french windows of what, unless the architect had got the place all cock-eyed, was the dining-room.

In *Frozen Assets* (1964):

Standing in the hall of The Oaks, Wimbledon Common, and taking in his surroundings with an appraising eye, Biff had become conscious of a cloud darkening his normally cheerful outlook on life. All the houses on Wimbledon Common are large, having been built in the days when householders did not consider home was home unless they had families of ten and domestic staffs of fourteen, and Lord Tilbury's little nest was in keeping with those of his neighbours.

Wodehouse clearly knew a house on The Common very well – but which? Time has caught up with Wimbledon. Parkside is still the epitome of moneyed respectability and still the place where wealthy aunts and newspaper proprietors would live, but many of the original mansions have gone.

Parkside is a mile and a quarter long; most of the houses Wodehouse knew were built in the 1860s and 1870s, all with eight or ten bedrooms, staff quarters for half a dozen and at least one coach house, set in grounds of an acre or more. Today only a few of the original monsters remain; the others have been replaced by their modern equivalent – 'architect-designed houses in Queen Anne style' each with its double or triple garage – and ten or fifteen nestling in the space occupied by one of their forebears. But enough of the originals remain to give a clear idea of their vanished fellows.

I started my search with the assumption that:
a)   Wodehouse knew the house well.

b) He hadn't lived there but had certainly visited it.
c) Apart from the account in *Frozen Assets* (1964), the best description is in *Bill the Conqueror* of forty years earlier. The house must therefore be one Wodehouse knew before that date.

The first thing I did was to walk the length of Parkside to see if Heath House, The Hollies or The Larches appeared either by name or by physical resemblance. They didn't; too many of the houses have gone. The next step was to see what the local library had to offer and, fortunately, they had an excellent local history section. The original houses of Parkside were all listed and marked:

Wimbledon House	Heathlands	Westcombe Lodge
Elmhurst	Castle Tower	Chivelston
Parkside	The Chestnuts	Spencer House
Oxford Lodge	The Oaks	Elmley House
Westfield	Belmont	Broadheath
Windfield Lodge	Heathside	Tyndale House
Wressil Lodge	Brant House	Richmond House
Heathfield House	Feldheim	Fairlawns
Manor Cottage	Albemarle	Tudor Lodge
Mill House	Gayton Lodge	Beech Lodge

No Larches, no Heath House, no Holly Lodge but names very like them, and one had to be the house I was looking for. The Wimbledon library also possessed lists of residents from the 1880s onwards, but there were no Wodehouses, Deanes, Matthews or any family names I recognized. There were plenty of medical knights, a sprinkling of peers and a French duke but nobody I knew.

It was possible that Wodehouse had no particular house in mind at all. He was an enthusiastic pedestrian all his life and would certainly have walked from Chelsea when he visited the Graves family at Wimbledon. The Red House, Lauriston Road, where they lived is on the southern edge of the Common and Wodehouse had to walk along Parkside to reach it. Perhaps he simply absorbed the atmosphere the Parkside houses represented. It certainly wasn't the Graves's house he described. It is still standing in Lauriston Road and bears no

1   London in the 1890s. As Wodehouse knew it as a young man

2   Wodehouse's Mayfair

1. The Bachelor's Club
2. The Bath Club in Dover Street
3. Buck's Club
4. Hay's Mews – 'Halsey Court'

5. Dunraven St – once Norfolk Street
    The home of PGW and Lord Emsworth
6. Gilbert Street – PGW's home before
    Norfolk Street
7. Claridge's Hotel – 'Barribault's'

3 The Octagon,
Hunstanton Hall

4 Hunstanton Hall (See chapter VIII)

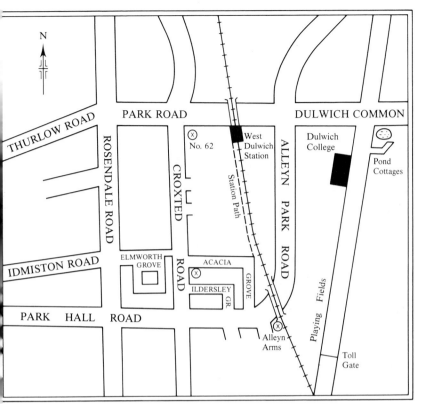

5 'Valley Fields' – Dulwich as Wodehouse knew it (See chapter IX)

6 'Peacehaven of Mulberry Grove'
The sphinxes of Acacia Grove, Dulwich (See chapter IX)

7 Threepwood in Emsworth, Hampshire, Wodehouse's cottage in the first years of the century; it gave its name to a dynasty (See chapter XX)

8 The Old House at Stableford, Wodehouse's boyhood home in Shropshire (See chapter XXIII)

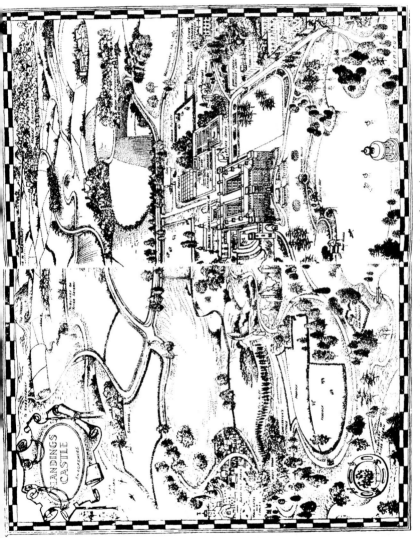

9 Blandings as Ionicus drew it

10　George Grossmith –
the man who brought the
'dude' to the London
stage, and who put
substance into Bertie
Wooster (see chapter
XIX)

11　Château Impney Hotel at Droitwich: Wodehouse stayed
here often and described it in his novels (See chapter XXIII)

12   Corsham Court, Wiltshire

13   Weston Park, Shropshire

14 Sudeley Castle, Gloucestershire

15 Sudeley Castle from ground level as Wodehouse would have seen it

resemblance to the enormous mansions he described.

Somewhere amongst the houses of Parkside there was a house he knew, but there seemed no way of finding it – till I had a stroke of luck, and that came from the second part of this chapter – Wodehouse and the law.

There are lots of solicitors in Wodehouse's novels. They are a natural part of the plots he wrote. But would everyday, normal knowledge have given him the following?

> 'What's the book today?'
>
> 'Widgery on Nisi Prius Evidence,' said Sam, without looking up.
>
> 'Capital!' said Sir Mallaby. 'Highly improving and as interesting as a novel – some novels. There's a splendid bit on, I think, page two hundred and fifty-four where the hero finds out all about Copyhold and Customary Estates. It's a wonderfully powerful situation. It appears – but I won't spoil it for you. Mind you don't skip to see how it all comes out in the end!'

And further down the page:

> 'All right,' said Sam absently. He was finding Widgery stiff reading. He had just got to the bit about Raptu Hàeredis, which as of course you know, is a writ for taking away an heir holding in socage.
>
> (*The Girl on the Boat*, 1929)

He had been summoned for jury duty, a thing that might happen to the best of us, and was about to sit on a hard bench and diligently enquire and true presentment make, as the legal slang has it . . . it was just his luck, he had felt, that he was not a borough treasurer, a registered dentist, a gaoler's sub-officer or one of the Brethren of Trinity House, for these pampered pets of the System are for some reason exempted from jury duty.

(*The Girl in Blue*, 1970)

The case in *The Girl in Blue* is Onapoulos and Onapoulos

versus The Lincolnshire and Eastern Counties Glass Bottling Company. It was:

> one of those dull disputes between business firms where counsel keep handing books to the judge and asking His Lordship with the greatest respect to cast an eye on the passage marked in pencil on the right-hand page, upon which he immediately looks at the left-hand page. ('Who is this Mr Jones? I have nothing about him in my notes.' 'Your Lordship is looking at the wrong page. If Your Lordship would kindly look at the right-hand page instead of the left-hand page.' 'But why should I *not* look at the left-hand page?' 'Because, my lord, with great deference there is nothing there concerning this particular case.')

In *Barmy in Wonderland* (1952) we have in five pages mention of feoffees of any fee, fiduciary or in fee simple, replevin, double burgage and heirs taken in socage. And how many people can cite a legal reference properly? In *Frozen Assets* there is a series of incidents where character A is shut in a flat with no trousers and secures them from B, and B in due course secures them from C and so on. Lord Tilbury is one of the protagonists and goes off to ask his lawyer Mr Bunting if he can arrest the man who took his trousers. Mr Bunting's reply gives Wodehouse the chance to slip in another 'allusion' – another private joke that only a dozen people would pick up:

> 'I was asking you if depriving a man of his trousers is a felony for which an arrest can be made?'
>
> Mr Bunting shook his head. 'It would be a matter for civil action.'
>
> 'You're sure of that?'
>
> 'Quite sure. The case would be on all fours with that of Schwed versus Meredith, L.R. 3. H.L. 330, though there the casus belli was an overcoat. Schwed sued before the magistrates of South Hammersmith sitting in petty court and was awarded damages.'
>
> Lord Tilbury choked on his steak. The disappointment

had been severe . . .

That's all it is, but when Wodehouse wrote it he must have checked the style of a citation and then smiled to himself and put in the names of the two people in his life most likely to go to law with each other – his agent and his publisher. When he wrote those names, his agent was Scott Meredith and his American publisher's representative with whom Meredith dealt was Peter Schwed!

A nice touch – but where did all those lawyers come from? Some of the later ones, I suggest, came from Wodehouse's own family. Johnny Halliday, Sam Bagshott and Joe Pickering are heroes of the later books and are all barristers or want to be. Their arrival on the Wodehouse scene, a change from the curates, Drones and young playwrights of earlier years, dates from the year his own grandson, Edward Cazalet, became a barrister. Perhaps some of his legal knowledge came from that source. Certainly the legal phrases of *Frozen Assets* and *The Girl in Blue* reflect what I call 'new knowledge'. But he was writing of solicitors and the law long before that; he got it from somewhere and the likeliest source takes us back to the Graves family again.

When Perceval Graves (see chapter IV) started his career, he joined the same solicitor's office as a young man called Edward Swinton Wodehouse Isaac. Isaac was Wodehouse's cousin, and it was he who introduced Graves to Wodehouse as a flat-mate.

Kelly's Directory, Somerset House and the Law Society gave me information on Isaac. One of Wodehouse's aunts, Miss Lucy Apollonia Wodehouse, married the Reverend Edward Whitmore Isaac in 1867. Edward was their son, brought up at Hanley Castle in Worcestershire. He went to Oriel College, Oxford, and came to London to serve his articles as a solicitor. Someone told Wodehouse enough about solicitors and their ways for him to write of one in *Something Fresh* back in 1915 and in *Uneasy Money* the following year. Was it Edward Isaac?

From the Law Society I found Isaac's address when he died.

It was in Wimbledon, where his widow still lives. She and her son gave me their time and information. Edward Isaac and Wodehouse did know each other well and Isaac's mother was one of the aunts with whom Wodehouse stayed while his parents were in Hong Kong. As far as Mrs Isaac remembers, they didn't meet after the First War but were quite close before then. Certainly they were close enough to share digs or recommend friends to each other.

I think Isaac is the best source of Wodehouse's legal knowledge; they certainly knew each other well and the surest way to pick up the jargon of any profession is to be friendly with someone who is taking or has just taken his final exams in the discipline. In his middle period Wodehouse may have learned legal terms from his own solicitors and picked up more from his grandson in the 1960s, but for the first accounts of Mainprice, Mainprice and Boole and the cheerful Gerry Nichols of *Uneasy Money*, then Edward Isaac is the man.

Mrs Isaac lives in that corner of Wimbledon touching Raynes Park and Morden. As I thanked them for their help and prepared to take my leave, I mentioned to Mrs Isaac and her son the difficulty I was having with the house on Wimbledon Common. I explained my theory and how, by every analogy I had discovered, there ought to be an aunt involved – but I had been unable to find her. Mrs Isaac and her son promptly told me there had been an aunt, but an Isaac aunt, not a Wodehouse one!

They couldn't remember the name offhand, but the name of the family was the same as the name of the small park around the corner from the Isaac house – and that was easy. The following day I made two telephone calls, one to the local library to find the name of the park and the other to Mrs Isaac to confirm it was correct, and from the lists of names I had for the residents of those splendid Parkside houses, I was at last able to identify Gayton Lodge, the home of the Hon. Mrs Holland.

Gayton Lodge has gone now and has been replaced by a GLC estate of high-rise flats, but it is easy to imagine it since its neighbours are still there. Walk along Parkside from the

Putney end and you will pass Tudor Lodge, Broadheath, Spencer House, Chivelston and Westcombe Lodge as large and impressive as when they were built a hundred years ago. Immediately beyond Westcombe Lodge you will come to where Gayton Lodge used to be. It was from here that Wodehouse drew his Wimbledon houses, it was here that so many of his characters from Ukridge's Aunt Julia onwards had their being.

Mrs Holland herself was no Isaac at all but the daughter of no less a person than Lord Chief Justice Gifford. She married Mr Holland of Worcestershire in the middle of the nineteenth century and they lived at Gayton Lodge for most of their married life. It took me some time to find her connection with the Isaacs but, through Somerset House, I discovered that Mr Holland was a partner of John Swinton Isaac of Boughton Park, Worcester. This John Isaac was brother to the Rev. Edward, vicar of Hanley Castle and therefore uncle to Edward Isaac. Since the Hanley Castle Isaacs lived only eight miles or so from their relatives (and the Hollands), it seems likely that Edward Isaac would have come to know the Hollands well and grown up to regard them as 'honorary' uncles and aunts, as so many of us do our parents' friends.

Wimbledon and the law run together in Wodehouse's life and in his novels. There was a house on Wimbledon Common – I never had any doubt of that – but to find which one it was and why Wodehouse knew it, took a long time. Perceval Graves, whom Wodehouse used to visit at Wimbledon, gave the first clue about Edward Isaac. Isaac in his turn led me through his own career and friendship with Wodehouse back to his widow, still living in Wimbledon. How fortunate that of all the people to whom I mentioned the house on Parkside, I should have chosen the widow and son of the one man in the world who could turn to young Pelham Wodehouse eighty years ago, and invite him to come along and take tea with Aunt Cynthia Holland of Gayton Lodge, Wimbledon Common.

※ ❧

CHAPTER XVII

THE LADIES OF GIRTON

THIS famous Cambridge college gave its name to a certain type of woman for fifty years. The world has moved on, and university education for women is no longer the cause of humorous newspaper articles as it once was, but Girton has always had a significance as one of the first women's colleges.

Girton was the result of years of work by Sarah Emily Davies, a pioneer suffragette who organized the foundation of the College at Hitchin in 1869 and moved it to Cambridge in 1873. She started a tradition of hard work and scholarship but, like many pioneers, her single-minded enthusiasm made her and the college easy targets for satire. For forty or fifty years a 'Girton woman' was a synonym for a lady of strong principles and high mental and moral endeavour.

Let us look at four of Wodehouse's ladies. The first appears in *Tales of St Austin's* back in 1903. She is Miss Florence Beezley and she is the Dragon of the short story 'The Babe and the Dragon'. The Babe is the schoolboy MacArthur, whose sister is at Girton. The sister brings home Miss Beezley for a stay and thereby ruins MacArthur's home life for that period:

Breakfast was a nightmare, lunch was rather worse, and as for dinner, it was quite unspeakable. Miss Beezley seemed to gather force during the day. It was not the actual presence of the lady that revolted the Babe, for that was passable enough. It was her conversation that killed. She refused to let the Babe alone. She was intensely learned herself, and seemed to take a morbid delight in dissecting his ignorance, and showing everybody the pieces. Also, she persisted in calling him Mr MacArthur in a way that seemed somehow to point out and emphasise his youthfulness. She added it to her remarks as a sort of after-thought or echo.

'Do you read Browning, Mr MacArthur?' she would say suddenly, having apparently waited carefully till she saw his mouth was full.

The Babe would swallow convulsively, choke, blush and finally say –

'No, not much.'

'Ah!' This in a tone of pity not untinged with scorn. 'When you say "not much", Mr MacArthur, what exactly do you mean?'

. . . 'Ah!' said Miss Beezley. She made frequent use of that monosyllable. It generally gave the Babe the same sort of feeling as he had been accustomed to experience in the happy days of his childhood when he had been caught stealing jam.

The next lady is Miss Heloise Pringle. She appears in 1925 in *Carry On, Jeeves*, the second collection of Bertie and Jeeves stories. Bertie finds himself forced to stay with the Pringles at Cambridge. His fortitude is severely dented by the Pringle family who 'gazed at me like a family group out of one of Edgar Allan Poe's less cheery yarns', and is further battered by his introduction to Miss Heloise Pringle:

I suppose everybody has had the experience of suddenly meeting someone who reminded them frightfully of some fearful person . . .

Well, Heloise Pringle, in the most ghastly way, resembled Honoria Glossop . . . Her voice put the lid on it. It might have been Honoria herself talking. Honoria Glossop has a voice like a lion tamer making some authoritative announcement to one of the troupe, and so had this girl.

Bertie finds his fears well-founded; Heloise is Honoria's first cousin. But worse is to come.

She was one of those girls you're always meeting on the stairs and in passages. I couldn't go into a room without seeing her drift in a moment later. And if I walked in the garden she was sure to leap out at me from a laurel bush or the onion bed or something.

Eventually, Bertie realizes to his horror that the look he has noticed in Heloise's eyes is familiar:

It had been the identical look which I had observed in the eye of Honoria Glossop in the days immediately preceding our engagement – the look of a tigress that has marked down its prey.

He consults Jeeves:

'I mean to say, I know perfectly well that I've got, roughly speaking, half the amount of brain a normal bloke ought to possess. And when a girl comes along who has about twice the regular allowance, she too often makes a bee line for me with the love light in her eyes. I don't know how to account for it, but it is so.'

'It may be Nature's provision for maintaining the balance of the species, sir.'

'Very possibly. Anyway, it has happened to me over and over again. It was what happened in the case of Honoria Glossop. She was notoriously one of the brainiest women of her year at Girton, and she just gathered me in like a bull pup swallowing a piece of steak.'

'Miss Pringle, I am informed, sir, was an even more brilliant scholar than Miss Glossop.'

Jeeves manages to rescue Bertie once again but it is a close-run thing.

Our third Girton lady is Honoria Glossop herself. She is the daughter of the loony-specialist Sir Roderick Glossop and ranks high in Bertie's calendar of ghastly females to whom he has become engaged. Incredibly, she only appears in two stories; the reputation she possesses is based on Bertie's frequent mentions of her. She is spoken of, referred to in action off-stage and is constantly on Bertie's lips as an example of how a guardian angel can act in an emergency, viz. by saving him from the fate worse than death.

> I looked at the poor fish anxiously. I knew that he was always falling in love with someone, but it didn't seem possible that even he could have fallen in love with Honoria Glossop.
>
> To me the girl was simply nothing more than a pot of poison. One of those dashed large, brainy, strenuous, dynamic girls you see so many of nowadays. She had been at Girton, where, in addition to enlarging her brain to the most frightful extent, she had gone in for every kind of sport and developed the physique of a middle-weight catch-as-catch-can wrestler. I'm not sure she didn't box for the 'Varsity while she was up.
>
> The effect she had on me whenever she appeared was to make me want to slide into a cellar and lie low till they blew the All-Clear.
>
> I was interrupted in my meditations by a noise like the Scotch express going under a bridge. It was Honoria Glossop laughing.
>
> *(The Inimitable Jeeves, 1923)*

> Honoria, you see, is one of those robust, dynamic girls with the muscles of a welter-weight and a laugh like a squadron of cavalry charging over a tin bridge. A beastly thing to face over the breakfast table. Brainy, moreover. The sort of girl who reduces you to pulp with sixteen sets of tennis and a few rounds of golf and then comes down to dinner as fresh as a daisy, expecting you to take an intelligent interest in Freud.
>
> *(Carry On, Jeeves, 1925)*

The last member of our quartet is Lady Florence Craye:

> She was a girl with a wonderful profile, but steeped to the gills in serious purpose. I can't give you a better idea of the way

things stood than by telling you that the book she'd given me to read was called *Types of Ethical Theory*, and that when I had opened it at random I struck a page beginning:

'The postulate or common understanding involved in speech is certainly co-extensive, in the obligations it carries, with the social organism of which language is the instrument and the ends of which it is an effort to subserve.'

(Carry On, Jeeves, 1925)

In *Joy in the Morning* in 1947, Bertie has time to consider and evaluate:

Scanning the roster of the females I've nearly got married to in my time, we find the names of some tough babies. The eye rests on that of Honoria Glossop, and a shudder passes through the frame. So it does when we turn to the B's and come upon Madeline Bassett. But taking everything into consideration and weighing this and that, I have always been inclined to consider Florence Craye the top. In the face of admittedly stiff competition, it is to her that I award the biscuit.

In 1954 in *Jeeves and the Feudal Spirit* we read that:

This Florence Craye is . . . well, I suppose you would call her a sort of step-cousin of mine or cousin once removed or something of that nature. She is Lord Worplesdon's daughter, and old W. in a moment of temporary insanity recently married my Aunt Agatha *en secondes noces*, as I believe the expression is. She is one of those intellectual girls, her bean crammed to bursting point with little grey cells, and about a year ago, possibly because she was full of the divine fire but more probably because she wanted something to take her mind off Aunt Agatha, she wrote this novel and it was well received by the intelligentsia who notoriously enjoy the most frightful bilge.

In *Much Obliged, Jeeves*, published on Wodehouse's ninetieth birthday, she is back again, engaged to Ginger Winship, and still the same overbearing female who has been putting the wind up Bertie for forty-six years.

If there were to be a factual origin for these ladies, how would we recognize her? Florence Beezley appears very early in 1903, and we are back to Wodehouse's youth again. Was there somebody, related like Florence Craye, who attended Girton, who was interested in philosophy and who wrote books?

It may be pure coincidence, but turn your mind back to Uncle Philip. The Reverend Philip John Wodehouse was Rector of Bratton Fleming in Devonshire from 1875 to 1913. He was one of the many uncles we looked at in chapter III and we know from *Portrait of a Master* that Wodehouse spent summer holidays with him, as a schoolboy. If you stay with an uncle you meet his children, and Uncle Philip had four. Helen Marion, Christine Lucy, Philip George and Charles Gilbert. To a shy third son like Wodehouse, a girl a year older than you are, and used to dominating her own brothers and sisters, can make a deep impression. Helen Marion was a year older than Wodehouse, the eldest of the family, and her career is of interest.

1898–1902	Girton College (exact contemporary of Florence Beezley)
1903–11	Lecturer in Philosophy, Birmingham University
1907	Doctorate in Philosophy
1911–19	Principal, Bingley Teachers Training College
1919–31	Professor of Education, Bristol University
1931–42	Mistress of Girton
1942–44	Director of Crosby Hall
1942–43	President of the Federation of University Women

A distinguished career. She wrote books on religion, education and philosophy and, speaking of books on philosophy, here are two extracts. The first is from *Carry On, Jeeves* in 1925 and is what Bertie reads to us from *Types of Ethical Theory*, forced

on him by Florence. The second is from *The Logic of Will* by
Dr Helen Marion Wodehouse, published in 1908.

In ordinary action the conative side is the more prominent
but even here a cognitive presentation is being developed. In
ordinary observation the cognitive side is the more prominent but even here there is activity in perception. I begin on
the cognitive side, not with a heap of sensations, preceptions
and ideas but with a single presentation-continuum.

Of the two antithetic terms in the Greek philosophy one only
was real and self-subsisting; and that one was Ideal Thought
as opposed to that which it has to penetrate and mould. The
other corresponding to our Nature was in itself phenomenal,
unreal without any permanent footing, having no predicates
that held true for two moments together; in short redeemed
from negation only by including indwelling realities appearing through.

It could just be complete coincidence . . .

CHAPTER XVIII

WODEHOUSE AND THE THEATRE

To talk of Wodehouse without mentioning the theatre is like discussing Shakespeare without referring to the sonnets. The second part is so essential that it must be considered as an integral part of the whole. He said often what an important part the theatre played in his writing, but because he said it in such simple language, it didn't seem to make much impact. We have become so used to writers who speak of trends, of influences, of streams of consciousness that when a straightforward man like Wodehouse said that he considered his novels as musical comedies without music, we don't listen.

If Wodehouse had been a pretentious writer, he might have received more acclaim from the literary world. He certainly knew how pompous his fellow writers could be. In the introduction he wrote in the 1930s to Hutchinson's *A Century of Humour*, he said:

It is a bare thirty-four years since I started earning my living as a writer, yet already I am the author of an Omnibus Book, and now the world is ringing with the news that Messrs Hutchinson have asked me to edit their *Century of Humour* – a job which entitles me to wear pince-nez and talk about Trends and Cycles and the Spirit of Comedy and What is The Difference Between Humour and Wit.

My only trouble is that I have so little to say on these matters. Trends, now. Well, I suppose trends are all right, if you are able to take them or leave them alone. It is more a question of will-power than anything. And very much the same thing applies to Cycles. (Remind me to tell you some time how I once cycled from Portsmouth to London.)

When he said to Townend in *Performing Flea*: 'The principle I always go on in writing a long story is to think of the characters in terms of actors in a play . . .' he meant exactly what he said. In another letter of 1924, two years later, he said:

I believe I told you once before that I classed all my characters as if they were living salaried actors, and I'm convinced that this is a rough but very good way of looking at them.

The one thing actors – important actors, I mean – won't stand is being brought on to play a scene which is of no value to them in order that they may feed some less important character, and I believe this isn't vanity but is based on an instinctive knowledge of stagecraft. They kick because they know the balance isn't right.

In 1936, he said it again: 'Some actors are natural minor actors, some are natural major ones. It's a matter of personality. Same in a book. Psmith, for instance is a major character. If I am going to have Psmith in a story, he must be in the big situation.' If you take out Wodehouse's superb language and the intricacy of his plots – far more intricate than they seem – you are left with a stage play. He liked working this way and it is an easy task to trace the improvement in his writing from his early novels, written with no stage experience, to his final perfected style which he reached in about 1930.

We have to go a long way back to Wodehouse's first theatre work, to the Pelican, Owen Hall (real name James Davis). This remarkable gentleman was an entrepreneur who was equally ready to stage shows, run newspapers or write for them and to get himself into debt. For a short period he even ran his newspaper from a prison cell and was universally known to his colleagues and stage audiences as 'Owing All'. In 1904 he used Wodehouse's lyrics for one of the songs in his show *Sergeant Brue*.

Two years later Wodehouse was engaged by Seymour Hicks

to write songs for *The Beauty of Bath* and the following year he was engaged for another show *The Gay Gordons*. Between then and 1916 he wrote lyrics or plots for half a dozen other plays and in 1916 *Miss Springtime* came out, the first of a long and successful series of musicals written with Guy Bolton.

It is strange that Wodehouse's skill as a lyric writer has been forgotten. Perhaps this is because the written word outlasts the spoken, but there must be some reason, since even the most ardent theatrical historian has difficulty in answering the question: Which lyric writer has the record for the greatest number of shows on Broadway at one time? The answer is, of course, P. G. Wodehouse.

Portrait of a Master and *Bring on the Girls* record all the facts we want. Wodehouse and Guy Bolton achieved the position of the leading book and lyric writing team in the American theatre. With Jerome Kern, they were the first to make a successful break from the Viennese operetta tradition of musical interludes interspersed with minimal plot or action. Richard Rodgers said in his book that, until Hart started writing 'only P. G. Wodehouse had made any real assault on the intelligence of the song-listening public.'

Between September 1916 and November 1918, Bolton and Wodehouse clocked up no less than twelve New York openings, and Wodehouse's record as a lyric writer with five shows on Broadway at the same time and Bolton's six as author will never be equalled. In the ten years up to 1927, Wodehouse wrote three plays and lyrics for twenty-three musicals, as well as publishing twenty-one books. Is it any wonder that, from about 1918, the theatre and its personnel began to play a part in his novels?

Wodehouse didn't write his lyrics in isolation. He and Bolton worked together, sweated out plots and lyrics together and went through all the agonies of rehearsals and pre-New York tours. They saw all the strain, effort and frenetic activity that makes a successful musical and they remembered it in that most amusing of theatrical memoirs *Bring on the Girls*. Guy Bolton is dead now but I met him on his last visit to London to see the revival of his show *Very Good, Eddie*. It was still a good show sixty years after its first opening night, which was the occasion when Jerome Kern introduced Mr Guy Bolton to Mr Plum Wodehouse and started a collaboration that lasted for over fifty years.

Between 1904 and 1954 Wodehouse wrote lyrics or the book for fifty-one shows, and this is reflected in eighty theatrical characters who appear in his novels. The eighty are split equally between those who appear in novels about the theatre, and theatrical characters with whom the other personae of the novels become involved. Wodehouse didn't work with Seymour Hicks till 1906 but met him first in 1904 – and a year later in *The Head of Kay's* we meet the actor-manager 'Higgs' while in 1907 in *Not George Washington* we meet him again under the name of 'Stanley Briggs' of the 'Briggs Theatre'. Seymour Hicks had opened the Hicks Theatre the year before; it is now the Aldwych.

Wodehouse's first lyrics for Hicks were for *The Beauty of Bath*. That name may strike a chord in your memory, since he used remarkably similar titles for his fictional shows. *The Belle of Wells*, *The Belle of Boulogne* and *The Beauty of Brighton* are a few of the echoes Wodehouse used in the novels, and variations on the title of a song he wrote, 'Ask Dad', occur frequently for thirty years. The original was one he wrote in 1918 for the show *Oh My Dear* – and that phrase suddenly reappeared in the novels of the 1960s.

If you want to find the famous Regal Theatre in London, base of George Bevan of *A Damsel in Distress* (1919), of Sue Brown and Mortimer Mason in *Summer Lightning* (1929) and of Joe Pickering of *Bachelors Anonymous* (1973), walk along to the Shaftesbury Theatre at the top of Shaftesbury Avenue. It was originally the Prince's Theatre (hence 'Regal' connotations). It is brought into the novels as somewhere he knew and could describe in the same way as his old friend Guy Bolton appears, in name at least, as 'George Bevan', 'George Benham' or 'George Caffyn'. All of them are drawn as hardworking, pleasant young men of the theatre and a compliment to their original.

I wondered whether the close similarity of these names,

these Wodehouse allusions, was deliberate or whether they simply arose from his stated desire to write his characters as if they were living actors. When he was actually writing of the theatre and of actors he knew, was the similarity so strong that he couldn't stop the resemblances coming through? Actors appear in the novels within a year of his own first experience of the theatre, mainly as supporting characters, till *A Damsel in Distress* (1919). This started the Wodehouse formula of Anglo-American, theatre/stately home plots with an American hero who writes songs, the English girl he falls in love with and the earl who marries an American chorus girl. With the stage as the background, it was written to appeal to both his English and American readers and came out when Wodehouse had just seen his fifth Broadway opening.

The next novel, *Jill the Reckless*, used the same formula. American playwright, described as a friend of George Bevan (Guy Bolton) of the previous book, loves nice English girl who has become a chorus-girl in America. To balance this, second English hero loves nice American chorus-girl. This time the stage is the predominant feature. We meet the deaf choreographer 'Johnson Millar' who bears a close resemblance to Julian Mitchell, the famous deaf choreographer with whom Wodehouse and Bolton had worked. The novel covers the vicissitudes of the show *The Rose of America*, named after the real *The Rose of China* on which Wodehouse was working when he wrote the book.

The manager of the show described in *Jill the Reckless* is the unpleasant Isaac Goble of Goble and Cohn – who bears a similarity to the famous dictatorial producer A. L. Erlanger. Erlanger is also the original of the theatrical producer Blumenfeld, who scares the pants off Bertie Wooster and who is always accompanied by his son, whom he uses to assess all theatrical ventures. If his son likes it, so will the public. In real life Erlanger used a nephew in the same role.

Jill the Reckless was the book that Lord Asquith said cheered him so much after his defeat at the Paisley election. (This led Wodehouse to dedicate *Meet Mr Mulliner* to him and *that* snippet of information is going to excite some historian in a hundred years' time.) Jill's unpleasant American uncle is given the same address in Long Island that Wodehouse happened to be living at at the time and in chapter ten we meet Mr Otis Pilkington and Mr Roland Trevis. They are given a passage which seems to be a straight echo – a recollection by Wodehouse of what he and Bolton had said to each other.

Look through *Bring on the Girls* and see how Wodehouse narrates his exchanges with his old friend, then read the conversation in *Jill the Reckless* when Jill Mariner leaves the office:

> The silence which had fallen upon the room as she left it was broken by Mr Trevis.
>
> 'Some pip!' observed Mr Trevis.
>
> Otis Pilkington awoke from day-dreams with a start.
>
> 'What did you say?'
>
> 'That girl . . . I said she was some pippin!'
>
> 'Miss Mariner,' said Mr Pilkington icily, 'is a most charming, refined, cultured and vivacious girl, if you mean that.'
>
> 'Yes,' said Mr Trevis. 'That was what I meant!'

It is very slight, just a turn of phrase more relaxed than in the rest of the book, somehow nearer fact and more realistic in tone. As with the conversations between Trevor and Clowes or Charteris and Welch of the early school stories, the conversation is not essential to the plot. Wodehouse uses these minor exchanges to show an outsider's view of the hero or heroine; he seems for a moment to relax his concentration and we get this odd shift from imagination to memory.

Jill the Reckless is his best theatrical novel, and its successor of 1924 *The Adventures of Sally* moves away from the stage the same way Wodehouse himself seems to have done. He was still busy writing lyrics, but it came out the same year as the last of the Wodehouse/Bolton/Kern shows that had been so successful, and it ends not with the successful first night but with the hero and heroine happily running a kennels on the southern shores of Long Island. Incidentally, their address is again the same as the Wodehouses' at the time of writing, but the stage has lost its glamour for them as it was beginning to do for their creator.

The next book, *The Inimitable Jeeves*, brings in the cameo parts that characterize his use of the theatre for the next twenty years. We meet Mr Blumenfeld, based on the dreaded Erlanger, George Caffyn (Guy Bolton) and Marion Wardour, who sounds very like Marion Davis, the actress with whom the Wodehouses were friendly. In *Bill the Conqueror* we meet Prudence Stryker, the aggressive chorus-girl, and in *Sam the Sudden* the hero takes the heroine to a show at the Winter Garden. (At the time he wrote the passage the Winter Garden in Drury Lane just happened to be the theatre where Wodehouse's current show was running.) In 1929 in *Summer Lightning* we meet the delightful Sue Brown, the chorus-girl engaged to Ronnie Fish; she and others like her, making single, minor appearances in the short stories, are all we see of the theatre till Wodehouse's last theatrical novel, *Barmy in Wonderland*.

Barmy in Wonderland (1952), in racing jargon, is out of *Eggs, Beans and Crumpets* by *Jill the Reckless*. Barmy Fotheringay-Phipps, Dinty Moore and Mervyn Potter are amongst his best combinations of characters and Wodehouse wrote one of his funniest books around them. The reason why he suddenly returned to the stage for a plot after so many years is the obvious one, that he wrote it after he had spent some weeks touring with a company trying out a play of his. At the age of seventy, however, even Wodehouse had to admit that five hundred or a thousand miles' journey each weekend was too much, and he left the company rather than continue with such a punishing routine.

One of the sub-plots of *Barmy in Wonderland* is that Mervyn Potter, an actor, is not only America's leading leading man but also America's leading drunk, and the ups and downs of the show in the novel depend on his sobriety or otherwise. In *Performing Flea* Wodehouse told Townend of his efforts to catch the company as they whizzed to and fro across America until he eventually decided not to bother:

I was told later I hadn't missed much. Our star had laryngitis and was inaudible, and the principal comic character started drinking, became violent, wrecked the house where he was staying, and was taken to prison. The police let him out each night to play his part and on Saturday for the matinee and then took him back to the jug again . . .

With a few later mentions of such people as Joe Pickering of *Bachelors Anonymous*, who is a typical Wodehouse hero (boxing champion, public school, destined for the Bar but family funds no longer permit so grinds away in office and writes plays by night) and whose theatre is still the Regal at the top of Shaftesbury Avenue with old Mac, the doorkeeper, still firmly in charge, Wodehouse's theatrical coincidences come to an end.

He found the stage more exciting than his short stories or his movies and his early years on *The Globe* trained him in writing humorous verse to order. With the pressing timings the theatre forced on him, it was a useful skill to have acquired. Remember that extract from *Performing Flea* written in July 1927:

> I'm sweating blood over *Money for Nothing*, and have just finished 53,000 words of it. Meanwhile, I have to anglicize *Oh, Kay!* by August 9, attend rehearsals, adapt a French play, write a new musical comedy and do the rest of *Money for Nothing*, as far as I can see, by about September 1st. It'll all help to pass the time.

The effect of the theatre on Wodehouse's novels cannot be overestimated. As he learnt to appreciate the importance of dialogue and pace, it gave his writing a polish, a balance and rhythm that he acknowledged time and time again. It also gave him, in part, his most famous character of all – Bertram Wilberforce Wooster.

CHAPTER XIX

⋘§⋙

BERTIE WOOSTER AND JEEVES

WE first meet Bertie Wooster in 1917 in *The Man with Two Left Feet*. We bid him farewell in *Aunts Aren't Gentlemen*, Wodehouse's last complete novel, in 1974. Every critic of Wodehouse's work has stressed Bertie's universality. He is the hero who succeeds by his own innocence, who comes to his reward by the Providence that looks after the pure in heart. He occurs throughout English literature, he is ageless – but Wodehouse gave him a new lease of life.

There is no single source for Bertie; he is too well drawn, too complex to be anything other than a slow development over the years. He is like Ukridge, who originated in the mysterious Craxton, travelled in tramp-steamers like Townend, and was rounded out by the idiosyncrasies of Herbert Westbrook.

There are various clues to his origins and we start with the most surprising. It is what Wodehouse said in 1963 when he was being interviewed by Alistair Cooke. Cooke asked:

'Was there a particular man – a living human being that gave you the idea of Bertie Wooster?'
'I wouldn't say any definite individual but that type was very prevalent in the days when I was in and about London – 1911, 12 and 13.'
'Before the War?'
'Yes. The late Anthony Mildmay – Lord Mildmay the steeplechaser, he was very much the type of Bertie Wooster.'

A name from Wodehouse's own lips but one that raises

167

many questions. Lord Mildmay was born in 1909 and died in 1950. He was eight years old when Wodehouse wrote his first Bertie Wooster story, so he can't have been the original source. *Ergo*, if he was 'very much the type' then there were others – the others that Wodehouse mentioned he knew before the First War. But there were a lot of Bertie Wooster stories between 1918 and 1930. Was there a 'link-figure' in those middle years? And what was the connection between Wodehouse and Lord Mildmay anyway?

When we first meet Bertie in 1917, he is a shadowy figure with Aunt Agatha looming over him. He has an aunt who used to be a Principal Boy and a friend who married a Gaiety Girl. He has little personality. Two years later in *My Man Jeeves* we find a change. Bertie and Jeeves are settling into the relationship of the next fifty years; we meet Bingo Little and, somehow, in the agonies he goes through on Bingo's behalf, Bertie is no longer a cardboard figure. He has developed into a man we can believe in. He is a member of Buck's Club (soon to become the Drones); he can remember brave nights at Covent Garden Balls.

In 1925 in *Carry On, Jeeves* the pattern is set. Florence Craye and Sir Roderick Glossop appear, as do Aunt Dahlia and Uncle Tom. In *Very Good, Jeeves* we discover that Bertie is a horseman, and in *The Mating Season* we find that he played rackets well enough to get his Blue.

In *Performing Flea* in November 1938, Wodehouse says:

A real character in one of my books sticks out like a sore thumb. You're absolutely right about Freddie Rooke [*Jill the Reckless*]. Just a stage dude – as Bertie Wooster was when I started writing him. If you look at the early Jeeves stories, you'll find Bertie quite a different character now.

There can be no doubt that much of Bertie Wooster is Wodehouse himself. Usborne's *Wodehouse at Work* makes the point decisively. The trains of thought that wander irrelevantly around the topic of the moment, the misplaced half-forgotten – or, more cleverly, the half-remembered – quotation, the guileless approach to the world: Bertie's thoughts are his creator's thoughts. But who did Wodehouse think of when he wrote of Bertie?

The first clue we have is Wodehouse's reference to Lord Mildmay. What was his connection with Wodehouse? Anthony Bingham Mildmay was the son of the first Baron Mildmay of Flete, who received his peerage for political services. Our Lord Mildmay was born in 1909, educated at Eton and Trinity and joined Baring Brothers for a short time. Thereafter he devoted himself to becoming a successful steeplechase jockey. He rode twenty-one winners in 1937–38 and thirty-two winners in 1946–47. In the words of the *Concise Dictionary of National Biography*, he was 'beloved by racecourse crowds for his courage and skill'. He was drowned while bathing in 1950.

Lord Mildmay worked closely with a trainer with whom he had been at school. The trainer was Peter Cazalet, Wodehouse's son-in-law! He had also been an amateur rider from 1930–38 and became a trainer in 1939. We know that Bertie once said he liked visiting places 'where there was something in the stables worth riding' and we know that towards the end of the saga he discusses with Ginger Winship the dangers of being engaged to Florence Craye. Ginger has joined that cohort of the damned and is explaining to Bertie (who already knows Florence far better than Ginger does) why it is essential that he win the Market Snodsbury by-election.

'Gorringe,' said Ginger, continuing, 'was a loser and it dished him. And long ago, someone told me, she was engaged to a gentleman jockey and she chucked him because he took a spill at the canal turn in the Grand National. She's a perfectionist. I admire her for it, of course.'

'Of course.'

'A girl like her is entitled to have high standards.'

'Quite.'

I don't know if Lord Mildmay ever came off at the canal turn. He may well have done, since he rode in many Grand

Nationals and was placed twice.

MPs appear early in the Wodehouse list of characters. The villain in *Jill the Reckless* was an MP who put his political career before true love, and the unhappy Mr Gandle, enamoured of Bobby Wickham, was another. The best description of MPs and their habits comes from the famous prize-giving at Market Snodsbury Grammar School. Bertie, describing Gussie Fink-Nottle's performance on the platform, says:

> It went well, and I wasn't surprised. I couldn't quite follow some of it, but anybody could see that it was real ripe stuff, and I was amazed that even the course of treatment he has been taking could have rendered so normally tongue-tied a dumb brick as Gussie capable of it.
>
> It just shows, what any Member of Parliament will tell you, that if you want real oratory, the preliminary noggin is essential. Unless pie-eyed, you cannot hope to grip.

In Beverley Nichols's *Are They the Same at Home?* published in 1927 we read:

> When I first met him [Wodehouse], we were both lunching at the House of Commons, and I noticed that whenever he opened his mouth the faces of the politicians seated around him prepared to twitch up into set smiles.

In 1929 Wodehouse paid a short visit to Hollywood to have a look at the place. Marion Davies invited him to the lunch being given by MGM for Winston Churchill, and in *Performing Flea* Wodehouse says:

> I have reluctantly come to the conclusion that I must have one of those meaningless faces which makes no impression whatever on the beholder. This was – I think – the seventh time I had been introduced to Churchill, and I could see that I came upon him as a complete surprise once more.

I don't know when MPs or the Cazalet family first entered

Wodehouse's life but it must have been well before 1928. In *Portrait of a Master* Peter Cazalet is described as 'the son of one of Plum's friends'. Peter Cazalet married Leonora, Wodehouse's stepdaughter, in December 1932 so presumably the Wodehouses knew the Cazalets before then – and Peter Cazalet's brother Victor was MP for Chippenham from 1924 till his death in 1943.

The Cazalets probably provide another clue to Bertie Wooster's origins in *The Mating Season* (1949). In that book Bertie suddenly turns out to be a rackets Blue, and Wodehouse's son-in-law represented Oxford at rackets, cricket and tennis, while Victor Cazalet not only got his Blue in rackets but was Amateur Squash Champion in 1925, 1927, 1929 and 1930!

Bertie Wooster was a Magdalen man. We are told so specifically. But this does not square with Bertie's avowed penchant (well, he did it once and his friends seem never to forget it) for either singing in, or riding bicycles around, the College fountain. Every right-minded person knows that can only mean Christ Church, not Magdalen. I would like to think that the reason was that both Peter and Victor Cazalet went to Christ Church. Unfortunately the first mention of the College fountain incident comes in 'Extricating Young Gussie', the first Bertie Wooster story back in 1917 – a pity. But the rackets Blue, the riding and the Lord Mildmay connection fit exactly in time with the Cazalet brothers, and I add them to the list of people whose attributes helped to make Bertie.

Although the Cazalets and Lord Mildmay may have helped to round out Bertie, they are too late to have been more than ancillary sources. They probably entered Wodehouse's life in what one might call his 'London social period' – roughly 1926 to 1933. They do not explain the important difference between the stage dude of the early Bertie of 1917 and 1919 and the much firmer character of *The Inimitable Jeeves* of 1923 and *Carry On, Jeeves* of 1925. Something happened in the intervening four years.

It is tempting to say simply that Wodehouse matured or that he started to draw his characters better. I think there is a better answer. If a straightforward man like Wodehouse says that he now imagines his personnel as if they were actors on a stage and if he has just spent six years in intensive theatrical work, isn't it a sensible idea to look at some of the theatrical people he was working with?

Most of Wodehouse's stage work was done in New York, but in England he worked closely with the man who, for my money, is as close to Bertie Wooster as we will get – George Grossmith Junior.

Some years ago we enjoyed watching Ian Carmichael playing Bertie Wooster on television. If Wodehouse had been commissioned to write stories specifically for the series, isn't it fairly certain, with his theatrical experience, that he would have put some of Ian Carmichael into them? I find it no coincidence that Bertie 'grew' during and immediately after the period when Wodehouse worked closely with George Grossmith.

In one of the interviews with Wodehouse in the 1920s he said that G. P. Huntley and George Grossmith were perfect likenesses of the sort of person he visualized Bertie to be. Many autobiographies of the 1920s make the same remark about these two actors as being examples of the young men of the Drones Club. The point is that when Wodehouse first wrote of Bertie in 1917, Grossmith and Huntley had created the part already. Wodehouse didn't invent Bertie. He took him off the stage and put him in print.

George Grossmith was born into the theatre although, like his father and uncle, he was trained for something else. His grandfather helped found the Savage Club and was the original of Mr Pickwick. His father, George Grossmith the elder, was the famous Gilbert and Sullivan singer and wrote the immortal *Diary of a Nobody* with his brother Weedon in 1894. Our man, George Grossmith Junior, was born in 1874 and died in 1935. The *Dictionary of National Biography* says of him that 'he originated the "dude" comedy, at the Gaiety Theatre 1901–1913.' He made his name in parts like Lord Percy Pimpleton, the Honourable Augustus Fitzpoop and Bertie Boyd.

After the First War he went into management and presented *Oh, Boy!* by the famous team of Wodehouse, Bolton and Kern at the Kingsway Theatre in 1919. From then till 1927 he and Wodehouse worked together closely and they met again in Hollywood in 1930, where Wodehouse's first job was to write scripts for a picture starring Grossmith. Their theatrical ventures included *The Golden Moth* (1921), *Sally* (1922), *The Cabaret Girl* (1922), *The Beauty Prize* (1923), *Oh, Kay!* and *The Three Musketeers*. Wodehouse was therefore in constant contact with the man who had created the dude on the musical stage.

I don't claim that Grossmith was the only source of Bertie, but there are one or two unusual coincidences. Wodehouse said that Lord Mildmay was like Bertie. He also said that he knew lots of people like that before the First War. Lord Mildmay and the Cazalet brothers provided Wodehouse with the third source of Bertie; somewhere in Edwardian London there was one man, perhaps there were many, who gave Wodehouse the idea, but I think the important shift in the early 1920s that turned Bertie from a stage dude into the believable character we know so well came from George Grossmith. It is he who introduced the dude to the musical comedy stage, who worked closely with Wodehouse at exactly the right time (1919–24), and who fits exactly that statement of Wodehouse's: 'In writing a novel, I always imagine I am writing for a cast of actors.'

What of the man without whom Bertie is as nothing – Reginald Jeeves? There were many like Jeeves in the early part of this century and they held an honoured and respected place. The phrase 'gentleman's gentleman' was not satirical or ironic. A butler or steward might be responsible for a dozen, even a hundred servants but a personal attendant was in some respects a butler's superior. A butler was tied to a house, a manservant was tied to a man. He took status by his master's rank, he behaved in public with the dignity that his master's status deserved. In *Something Fresh* Wodehouse described the upper servants at Blandings using the titles of the employers of their fellows in full but referring to their own by nickname or Christian name. The underlying motive was an attachment that was recognized and respected.

The Pelicans had extraordinary manservants. George, 'Swears' Wells's man, threw himself into the river when the Pelican treasurer of the club's floating bar fell overboard. George surfaced after seconds amid cheers from the admiring Pelicans. 'It's all right, Guv'nor. I've got it!' was George's cry as he swam back to the launch proudly bearing the bag of money the unfortunate treasurer had taken with him. The rescue of the treasurer was the members' affair. His business was to rescue Swears's money.

Captain Fred Russell's man was idle, indolent and couldn't cook. Russell ('Brer Rabbit') had a ready answer to queries why he kept this miserable servant. 'That man' he claimed proudly, 'could cash a cheque in the middle of the Sahara desert.'

We know that Jeeves took his name from a cricketer Wodehouse watched at Cheltenham before the First War. We also know that J. M. Barrie had a remarkable manservant in the 1920s who caused some adverse comment amongst his master's friends, as Jeeves did in Bertie's family. Barrie's man was Frank Thurston; a quiet sardonic man who protected Barrie during the last years of his life, Thurston achieved a reputation for omniscience. His habit of completing or correcting the quotations of his master's literary friends aroused some surprise, as did his knowledge of French, Spanish, Greek and Latin. He must have been one of the few people to have put Margot Asquith in her place, and she went in awe of him.

Bertie describes often the way Jeeves would 'shimmer for a moment and then vanish' or 'although I could swear that he had not moved, Jeeves had vanished from the room'. Denis Mackail's biography of Barrie says of Thurston:

> Could one be quite certain – though one didn't like to mention it – that he hadn't gone out of the dining room by one door and re-entered, which was a physical impossibility, by the other?

and he describes the uncomfortable awe one feels in the presence of such a man.

Did he really despise one or was it merely that he knew everything at a glance – including one's weaknesses and faults?

Richard Usborne rightly points out that Jeeves was created long before Thurston joined Barrie, and that Wodehouse did not visit Barrie at his Adelphi flat. But I suggest that Jeeves, like Bertie, was based on an unknown and 'grew' as his master grew, with facets of other men. Denis Mackail, who publicized Thurston's genius to the world, was a friend of Wodehouse's in the early 1920s and remembered long evenings of talk with Wodehouse. We know they talked of plots and dialogue and swopped ideas. Could it not, would it not be natural for Mackail to talk of Barrie, whose biography he was engaged on at the time and whose valet bore a strong resemblance to Jeeves? Wodehouse had met Barrie when he played cricket for *Punch* against Barrie's team back in 1903, and Barrie and his entourage seem almost a compulsory topic for discussion with Mackail.

I do not claim that Jeeves was founded on Thurston – the dates simply do not allow it. But I do think that Mackail and Wodehouse must have discussed Barrie's omniscient servant and that some of it crept into the writing of Jeeves.

There is another name to consider – Eugene Robinson, Wodehouse's butler in 1921. Many Wodehouse enthusiasts deny his importance because the first Jeeves story appeared in 1917, four years before Robinson appeared. I'm not so sure.

Robinson appears in *Bring on the Girls*, the delightful volume of theatrical reminiscences written jointly by Wodehouse and Bolton in 1953.

Plum was back in London, living in a house in Onslow Square, next door to the one that had been the home of William Makepeace Thackeray. When Guy went to see him, the door was opened by a butler. Plum explained this wasn't swank. 'It's business,' he said. 'This chap is an author's model.'

'A what?'

'Come, come, you've heard of artist's models. Audrey Munson was one, if you remember. Well, he's an author's model. I'm writing some stories about a butler. At least, he's not a butler, he's a valet, but the two species are almost identical. I study this bird and make copious notes. Do you like the name Jeeves?'

'Is that what he's called?'

'No, that's the name of the man in my stories. This one is Robinson . . .'

The next few pages describe how Bolton is asked to test Robinson's frighteningly efficient mind and conclude with Robinson rescuing Wodehouse and Bolton from a kidnapping charge when they meet the wrong child off the boat train.

It is very light, very tongue-in-cheek – but I wonder. In the back of my mind are those passages in *Performing Flea* when Wodehouse describes Hollywood or Monte Carlo to Townend saying that he doesn't think he'll get any material out of them. Yet immediately after he left them we find Mr Mulliner telling stories of derring-do in the studio and Bingo Little and Freddie Widgeon facing disaster as their last ten francs vanish at the Casino. I remember the questions to Townend for *Sam the Sudden*: what was Sam wearing? what would he see? what would he smell? I remember his saying that he visualized his characters as living actors.

I suggest that Wodehouse might have done exactly what he said he did and realized that if Jeeves was going to be a major character, then some homework would be in order. It's not proven but the dates for Eugene Robinson are firm enough and *The Inimitable Jeeves* and its successors reflect just that touch of improvement which Robinson might have produced – and the first story of *The Inimitable Jeeves* was being written about the time Guy Bolton rang the door bell that night in Onslow Square.

I don't know what happened to Robinson afterwards, although there are not many Eugene Robinsons in Somerset House. Perhaps he was the Eugene Spencer Robinson of Manor Gardens, Warminster, who died in 1965 or the Eugene

William Robinson of 8 Melton Street, NW1, who died in 1939. He may not have been the only source for Jeeves but, together with Mackail's accounts of Frank Thurston, he played an important part in the 'growth' of Jeeves in the first few years of the 1920s. With the Cazalets, Lord Mildmay and George Grossmith he helped create one of the best-loved partnerships in fiction.

CHAPTER XX

HAMPSHIRE AND SUSSEX

ARLY in 1903 Wodehouse was living at 23 Walpole Street
in Chelsea, where he was visited by Herbert Westbrook,
who arrived with a letter of introduction. We saw in chapter IV
how they became friends and Westbrook, who was a teacher at
a prep school in Hampshire, invited Wodehouse down there.
The school, Emsworth House, stood in the village of
Emsworth, which lies on the small River Ems that forms the
border between Sussex and Hampshire. It is on the coast about
halfway between Chichester and Portsmouth.

The owner of the school was Baldwin King-Hall, with
whom Wodehouse became friends and to whom he later
dedicated a book. Wodehouse spent some months at the
school, living in a small room over the stables, returning to
London in August 1903 when he became a full-time assistant
on the 'By the Way' column of *The Globe*. In January the
following year he returned to Emsworth and rented a house
called 'Threepwood' down the lane from Emsworth House.
He appears to have used Threepwood for his permanent
address for the next three years while writing his daily column
and fitting in the theatrical work that started to come his way.

In 1907 Wodehouse and Westbrook, who had now joined
him on *The Globe*, moved to London but in 1910 Wodehouse
was back in Emsworth again and this time he bought
Threepwood for £200. From 1910 to 1913 he seems to have
commuted between Emsworth, London and New York,
although Emsworth seems to have been his base. In 1914, in
New York, he married and spent the next few years there, and

178

Threepwood appears to have been sold. The Wodehouses continued to visit King-Hall at Emsworth House but it was not until 1928 that they came to the area again, when they rented Rogate Lodge for the summer. That is the sum of his residence in the two counties, but he used them in his books for sixty years.

I think there are three reasons why he used these two counties so much. The first is a practical one. He said on more than one occasion that he had made a mistake putting Blandings in Shropshire. As his plots developed, it became clear that this was too far from London. You can't 'pop' up to London or down to Blandings – it's a good day's journey; Kent, Hampshire and Surrey offer far more scope for dramatic arrivals and departures.

The second reason is that Emsworth had a special place in Wodehouse's life. It was his first stamping ground where he started to work in his own way rather than at the behest of others. It was the place he lived at the time David Cecil speaks of, when impressions went deeper and stayed. Thirdly, his sojourn at Emsworth and his visits to Baldwin King-Hall later, meant that he knew the area well and was reminded of it on those countless journeys to and from America, all of which involved travelling through Hampshire to Southampton.

Place-names from Emsworth and nearby occur frequently in the novels. The most famous are the dramatis personae of *Something Fresh*, written in America in 1914. It was the first Blandings novel and the first novel of Wodehouse's taken by *The Saturday Evening Post*. Bob Davis, the American editor of *Munsey's Magazine*, advised Wodehouse to write about the things he knew best – and we were given the first Blandings story.

Freddie Threepwood takes his name – the family name – from Wodehouse's cottage; the title of the earldom is Emsworth itself, the village in which the cottage stands. Freddie's cousin, Lord Stockheath, takes his title from the village of Stockheath two miles northwest of Emsworth, while Lord Emsworth's heir, Lord Bosham, takes his name from the famous sailing centre three miles to the east. Lady Anne

Warblington, Lord Emsworth's sister, gets her married name from the small hamlet that lies a mile due west of Emsworth and a distant relative, the Bishop of Godalming, is given an appropriately distant title from thirty miles away – although it is still within our scope since it is the last place of any size you pass through when, like Wodehouse, you travel from London to Emsworth. Even Lord Emsworth's first name is traceable to the Clarence Pier at Southsea nearby.

Colonel Mant and Beach needed some work to establish their sources, and the information came from the invaluable Kelly's Directories. The 1902 edition for Hampshire lists the Emsworth residents and one name stands out. It belongs to four brothers who clearly ran Emsworth – one owned the butcher's shop, another the bakery, and a third combined the offices of chief of the fire-brigade, tax-collector and postman. They were Richard, William, Frederick and John Mant, and the gallant colonel joined his relatives in the little Hampshire village. Beach was easy. The name has been changed now, but when Wodehouse lived there his house 'Threepwood' stood in Beach Road.

The identification of the family means that we can approach another puzzle with some confidence. Where did the name 'Blandings' come from? There is no place name of that spelling in the United Kingdom. Blandford Forum is as near Market Blandings as one can get, but that is far away in Dorset. If Wodehouse took eight names from in and around Emsworth, wouldn't he also have used a local source for the castle those eight inhabit? I therefore nominate for the original of Blandings the village of Blendworth, the point on the A3 road where you turn off for Emsworth.

The first Emsworth reference comes in *Mike*. It is a straightforward 'Wodehouse allusion', a reference to people he knew who would smile to see their names appearing. *Mike* was published in *The Captain* as a serial in 1907/8 and started a nine-day wonder as schoolboys all over England adopted the eccentric turn of speech of the urbane Rupert/Ronald Psmith. In chapter 4, Mike Jackson is asked by the captain of cricket which school he had been at before. His reply is a tribute to

Wodehouse's friends at Emsworth House School:

> 'A private school in Hampshire,' said Mike. 'King-Hall's
> at a place called Emsworth.'
> 'Get much cricket there?'
> 'Yes, a good lot. One of the masters, a chap called
> Westbrook, was an awfully good slow bowler.'

From *Mike* onwards, Hampshire place names occur frequently. In *A Gentleman of Leisure* Jimmy Pitt pretends to
have stolen the Duchess of Havant's diamonds; Havant is a
mile from Emsworth. In *The Prince and Betty* the name of the
island that shields Emsworth from the open sea is given to Lord
Arthur Hayling. The Countess of Southborne appears in *The
Man Upstairs* in 1914 and the Duchess of Hampshire and Lady
Millicent Southborne crop up in *Meet Mr Mulliner*. The
Hampshire connection then thins slightly but from Wodehouse's stay at Rogate Lodge in 1928, we have a revival of local
names led by Bertie, Lord Roegate in *Lord Emsworth and
Others* (1937).

Wodehouse drew many of his houses from this small section
of Hampshire and started with Emsworth House itself. This is
the setting for *The Little Nugget* of 1913 and Wodehouse used
the routine of the school and the stables in which he himself
stayed as important factors in the plot. I went down to
Emsworth to see what remains of the village Wodehouse knew
eighty years ago. From maps in the Westminster library I knew
where Emsworth House had been and I hoped that if I started
in the right place, the rest might follow as it did at Dulwich.

The River Ems comes down through the village and runs out
into the bay, so sheltered that it is nearly a lagoon, protected
from the south by Hayling Island. In the centre of Emsworth I
turned west and drove slowly along the main road to Havant. I
knew where Emsworth House ought to have been and,
immediately after passing Record Road on the right, I came to
it. The main building has gone now and an Old People's Home
occupies the site but at the back, where the gardens meet the
northern wall, are the traces of the stables where Wodehouse

lived and which were the setting for the final capture of the Little Nugget.

Somewhere nearby had to be Wodehouse's cottage 'Threepwood'. All I had to go on was Jasen's reference that it was 'down the lane'. Two roads run from the main road either side of Emsworth House; I drove along the main road, turned right down to a T-junction where a council estate now stands, right and right again and came back to the main road up Record Road.

As I passed the 1920s houses of the far end and came back towards the main road to the older houses built in the 1890s, I saw it on the right – 'Threepwood' inscribed over the door of a red-roofed house.

The 'Threepwood' sign was a new one and had been put up only months before to restore the house to its original name! Apart from providing the family name of one of Wodehouse's best loved series, it was also the mise-en-scène for the Ukridge story 'A Bit of Luck for Mabel' published in 1940. It opens with Ukridge (based on Herbert Westbrook) sitting in the narrator's cottage and telling how he nearly married money. The atmosphere and description of the cottage are those of Threepwood and I am sure that the story or something like it was told by Westbrook one night to Wodehouse as they sat there in 'Threepwood' all those years ago.

I had always suspected that Bertie Wooster's midnight bicycle ride in *Right Ho, Jeeves* was based on some equally epic ride that Wodehouse had made. My suspicions were confirmed by Beverley Nichols's *Are They the Same at Home?* where he tells of the Wodehouse family arriving at Southampton from New York on their way to London and Wodehouse's sudden decision on the platform to visit his old friend King-Hall at Emsworth. Having spent a couple of days there, he bought a bicycle and cycled the sixty-five miles to London. Not the behaviour one expects of a middle-aged gentleman like Wodehouse but certainly sufficient to provide the basis of the superb description of Bertie Wooster's anguish and misery.

I wondered idly what had happened when Wodehouse arrived unexpectedly at Emsworth all those years ago, and I asked a young couple walking along Record Road if they knew of anybody who had lived there a long time. They directed me to No. 23, where I introduced myself to Mrs Dobbs. I explained what I was doing and asked if she had ever seen or met Wodehouse.

'Seen him? He used to stay here!'

Mrs Dobbs remembered him well. He was a well-known figure in the village during her youth and she recalls him going for long walks on his own. (Everybody who knew him noticed the same thing – those long walks to take exercise and work out his plots.) Mrs Dobbs's mother was a friend of the matron at Emsworth House and would take in visitors when Emsworth House had no room. She could not remember him buying a bicycle to go to London but she recalls him arriving without notice, staying the night and, when she took him his breakfast, already sitting up in bed, working hard and surrounded by paper.

Mrs Dobbs told me something of Emsworth itself and confirmed other suspicions I had of the part the village played in his books. I knew that Emsworth had been famous for the oysters that grew in the lagoon sheltered by Hayling Island. Some time in the 1890s there was a typhoid scare and the Emsworth oysters came under suspicion; the trade withered and never recovered. Mrs Dobbs also told me that one great event in local folklore, presumably during the prosperous oyster period, was the throwing of the local policeman into the harbour. As soon as she mentioned the incident, a whole series of references came into my mind. A small seaside town, a policeman thrown into the harbour – that's 'Something to Worry About' from *The Man Upstairs* of 1914. Millbourne is the name of the village there but the description is that of Emsworth, even to the demise of the oyster-beds.

Wodehouse used the incident more than once. The unfortunate Constable Butt of *Mike* was the first member of the constabulary immersed to help a Wodehouse plot along. Constable Cobb of *The Man Upstairs* was threatened with the same fate but escaped it. He was luckier than Constable Potter in *Uncle Dynamite* or Constable Simms of *The Girl in Blue*. I don't know the name of that unfortunate member of the Force who suffered such indignity long ago in Emsworth but his memory is still with us.

Wodehouse's use of Emsworth also provides the answer to the famous puzzle of the distance of Blandings from London that arose in *Something Fresh*. Lord Emsworth, visiting Mr Peters in London and bored to tears by his discourse on scarabs, wished he was back at Blandings 'seventy miles away'. We will not find Blandings in or near Emsworth; all that happened was that Wodehouse used so many sources from the Emsworth area for his first Blandings story that he used its distance from London as well. Only later, when his books were published in both England and America, did he start to disguise his sources more carefully.

Blandings is not near Emsworth but Wodehouse did know some of the stately homes in the area. His uncle, Captain Walter Pollexfen Deane, lived in the village and, shy as he was, Wodehouse must have had some social obligations. The incident when he made the butler laugh and dash from the room when the Wodehouse trousers shot up over his tie took place near Emsworth and he certainly used at least one great house nearby in his novels.

The local stately home for Emsworth is Stansted Park, an imposing building about two miles due north of Emsworth. It has a long drive flanked by rhododendrons, beautiful grounds, and sits in the woods that spread along the coastal hills. In *The Little Nugget* Wodehouse called it, not Stansted, but 'Sanstead House' and made it the building in which the action takes place. The routine of the school is that of Emsworth House but Wodehouse needed the isolation of Stansted Park for the plot.

In *A Damsel in Distress* (1919) the action takes place in Belpher Castle in Hampshire. The local village of Belpher is described:

Ten years before, Belpher had been a flourishing centre of the South of England oyster trade. It is situated by the shore, where Hayling Island, lying athwart the mouth of the bay, forms the waters into a sort of brackish lagoon, in much the same way as Fire Island shuts off the Great South Bay of Long Island from the waves of the Atlantic . . .

The rest of the passage describes how the typhoid scare killed off the oyster trade. We are back at Emsworth again, and Belpher Castle is Stansted Park. For his American readers Wodehouse described the village and its situation by using its exact equivalent in America – where he was living at the time he wrote it, at Bellport in the Great South Bay off Long Island.

'Norworth Court' of *The Prince and Betty* bears a remarkable resemblance to Southleigh Park near Emsworth – *Nor*worth/*South*leigh – and in *The Girl on the Boat* the main action takes place at 'Windles' near Windlehurst, Hampshire. It is twenty miles from Southampton, one can feel the sea breezes and, a slip for Wodehouse but a valuable clue for us, a mile down the road is a signpost pointing to Havant and Cosham. We are back at Emsworth again, probably at Southleigh Park, now a research establishment for an electronics firm. If we look for an alternative 'Windles' with a lake fifty yards from the house and a ruin between the two where an amiable bulldog can maroon dyspeptic American businessmen, then Southwick Park a few miles away will satisfy the requirement as well. Other disguised places include 'Dryden Park, Midford', which sounds very like Drayton House, Midhurst (*My Man Jeeves*), and 'Heron's Hill, Sussex' which strongly resembles Heron's Ghyll in Sussex.

Except for Blandings, houses weren't important in Wodehouse's stories but localities were, and when he needed a house the right distance from London, sufficiently isolated to produce the 'desert island' effect that his novels required, then the Hampshire/Sussex border is the right place.

When Bertie and Jeeves set off on another adventure, they will drive down the Portsmouth Road and 'once clear of Guildford' Bertie will relax and start that conversation to clear his mind (and the reader's) on the complexities of the situation.

Emsworth itself and Stansted Park are identified beyond doubt; the remainder are memories of his early days there, refreshed by all those journeys up and down to Southampton to catch the boat to America. There's a pleasant postscript. At page 156 of *The Little Nugget*, Mr Arnold Abney has to leave 'Sanstead House' for a night to get one of his ex-pupils out of trouble. The pupil is the 'Earl of Buxton' and the worried parent is the 'Duke of Bessborough'. Wodehouse couldn't write that now. When he knew Stansted Park, it belonged to Mr Wilder. Its owner now is Lord Bessborough.

CHAPTER XXI

NEW YORK AND
LONG ISLAND

IT is difficult to say how many times Wodehouse travelled to America; I don't think even he could have given the total. A rough summary looks like this:

1904	3 weeks in New York.
1909	7 months at the Hotel Earle, New York.
1910–14	Several visits: 'I sort of shuttled to and fro across the Atlantic.'
1914	August. Married in New York and went to live at Bellport, Long Island. Stage work around New York. Moved to Great Neck, Long Island.
1918	To London, returning to Great Neck.
1919	January. To London.
1919	June. Back to Great Neck.
1920	To London.
1921	To New York for three weeks.
1922	To New York.
1922	August. Return to London.
1923	To Great Neck, then in May to Easthampton, Long Island.
1924	To London.

And so it goes on with frequent trips across the Atlantic till 1939 and Wodehouse's internment, his return to New York in 1947 and his final home in Remsenburg, Long Island, whither he moved in 1952.

From his first visit in 1904 till his marriage in 1914, he made his home in New York at the Hotel Earle in Greenwich Village, which he remembers fondly in his preface to the 1972 edition of *The Small Bachelor*. The young man or woman from the mid-West looking for the Bohemian life appears in his books often, and he met them when he shared rooms with other young writers in that small hotel.

As late as 1965 in *Galahad at Blandings* he described them as only he could:

> Of the two young men sharing a cell in one of New York's popular police stations Tipton Plimsoll, the tall thin one, was the first to recover, if only gradually, from the effect of the potations which had led to his sojourn in the coop. The other, Wilfred Allsop, pint-size and fragile and rather like the poet Shelley in appearance, was still asleep.

Wodehouse describes how the events of the night before had brought the two together:

> The party in the Greenwich Village studio. Quite a good party, with sculptors, avant garde playwrights and other local fauna dotted around, busy with their Bohemian revels. There had occurred that morning on the New York Stock Exchange one of those slumps or crashes which periodically spoil the day for Stock Exchanges, but it had not touched the lives of residents in the Washington Square neighbourhood, where intellect reigns and little interest is taken in the fluctuations of the money market.

In *Ring for Jeeves* he tells us of Mrs Spottsworth:

> Hers had been one of those Horatio Alger careers which are so encouraging to girls who hope to get on in the world, showing as they do that you never know what prizes Fate may be storing up for you around the corner. Born Rosalinda Banks, of the Chilicothe Ohio Bankses, with no assets beyond a lovely face, a superb figure and a mild talent for vers libre, she had come to Greenwich Village to seek her fortune and had found it first crack out of the box. At a studio party in Macdougall Alley she had met and fascinated Clifton

Bessemer, the Pulp Paper magnate, and in almost no time at all had become his wife.

Those extracts were written forty and fifty years respectively after Wodehouse had attended a Greenwich Village party but his extraordinary memory served him well.

In the early books, the settings follow his movements closely. *A Gentleman of Leisure* starts in New York and its main characters are New Yorkers experiencing life in Wodehouse's first English stately home – Dreever Castle in Shropshire. Immediately afterwards, when Wodehouse was 'shuttling to and fro across the Atlantic', *Psmith, Journalist* reversed the process and put Psmith, his most English character, amongst the New York gangs. *The Little Nugget* brought the same gangs over to England, to Emsworth in Hampshire.

In September 1914 Wodehouse was married in the Little Church Around the Corner on 29th Street in New York. Out of sentiment or because it was good material, Wodehouse set nearly all his American marriages there thereafter. He and his wife went to live at Bellport, Long Island, which is protected from the Atlantic by Fire Island in the same way Emsworth in Hampshire is protected by Hayling Island – a similarity that Wodehouse used to describe the village of 'Belpher' in *Damsel in Distress*.

Soon after Wodehouse arrived in Bellport, he set to work on *Uneasy Money*, which is set not in Bellport but 'Brookport', Long Island. In every other respect it is the same, even to the names of the small towns grouped around it. The Wodehouses moved back to New York for the winter and we get *Piccadilly Jim*, which is set in New York, and in the same year *The Man with Two Left Feet* came out with its mixture of stories set in London and New York. The Wodehouses returned to England in 1918 and we have *A Damsel in Distress*, which continues the series of American heroes fighting for their girl in an English stately home.

The coincidences continue. The Wodehouses go back to America and stay in a hotel – *Indiscretions of Archie* is set in a

New York hotel. They move to Long Island and so do Ginger Kemp and Sally when they find their happy ending in *The Adventures of Sally* – in exactly the same spot the Wodehouses were living.

There is a pause for a few years till *The Small Bachelor* (1927) takes us back to Greenwich Village and a further gap till *The Luck of the Bodkins* (1935) appeared as the final word on trans-Atlantic crossings. *The Girl on the Boat* had made us aware of such blood-curdling events as the passengers' concert, but the saga of the Atlantic leviathans will never be told better than in *The Luck of the Bodkins*. With all those crossings behind him, Wodehouse was not the man to waste good material.

For the next fifteen years, with the exception of *Laughing Gas* and the other Hollywood stories, the American references grow rarer. Wodehouse was well enough known to set his stories where he liked and the American public enjoyed his Blandings and Drones Club stories as much as his English readers did. New York was the place young heroes came from to win their bride in England and where girls had wealthy fathers who would be furious if they knew their daughters wanted to marry an Englishman.

In 1947 the Wodehouses crossed the Atlantic for the last time. They lived in New York and Wodehouse started working in the theatre again. In 1952, they moved out to Long Island to Remsenburg, near their old friends the Boltons. 'Bensonburg' not Remsenburg is the name he gave to the Long Island village where the heroines lived in *French Leave*, published four years later. The small chicken farm the three girls run is a common feature of the area.

From 1953 onwards, place names from Long Island occur often, including the Tuttle family who take their name from Tuttle Bay, the nearest beach to Remsenburg. Long Island's greatest claim to fame must be as the home of the best-loved golf-course in the world. In *Portrait of a Master* Wodehouse says:

I loved Great Neck in those days [1918]. There were an awful lot of actors there . . . I used to play golf with them at the Sound View Golf Club. That's the place where I wrote about the Oldest Member and all my golfing stories . . .

Like Freddie Threepwood in *Plum Pie*, Wodehouse realized that America was to be his final home, and in that book he records the fate of the golf-course he had made so famous. It adds nothing to the plot, it is a 'Wodehouse allusion' which one or two of his old friends might recognize:

Freddie's bijou residence in Great Neck was near what had been the Sound View golf course till the developers took it over . . .

New York and Long Island never became as famous as Blandings or the Drones Club but they gave a background of reality to his novels. From *A Gentleman of Leisure* to *Plum Pie* sixty years later, they provided just the contrasts he wanted to mix his Anglo-American characters and environments.

꧁ ꧂

CHAPTER XXII

LONDON HOUSES

THERE are two Londons in Wodehouse's novels. One is the slightly seedy, cheap-and-cheerful London of the early books with its main axis running east–west from Fleet Street to Chelsea. The later, more gracious, city has its centre in Mayfair and runs north–south with its western boundary at Kensington and its eastern border around Leicester Square.

Both are well drawn and both are accurate, although the earlier London is the more closely described. From about 1922 we are in the 'second' London, and now Wodehouse's young men are the Berties and Bingos and Freddies of the Drones Club. Although they are amongst his best creations, their London is drawn second-hand as he imagined they saw it. Gally Threepwood and Lord Ickenham allow Wodehouse to indulge in nostalgia in their stories of derring-do on Mafeking Night but they are the exception.

If Wodehouse heroes are poor they live in scruffy little streets off the King's Road in Chelsea; if they are well-to-do like Bertie Wooster, they live in Mayfair. Respectable aunts live in Knightsbridge, Kensington or on Wimbledon Common like Ukridge's Aunt Julia. Wodehouse's own addresses, as far as I know them, were:

1900	Markham Square, Chelsea
1901	Walpole Street, Chelsea
1910	Flat in London (address unknown)
1911–12	In London, address unknown
1913	Prince of Wales Mansions, Battersea
1914	London – address unknown

1919	Walton Street, Knightsbridge
1920	Walton Street
1921	King St, St James's
1922	No. 4 Onslow Square
1923	King St, St James's
1924	23 Gilbert St, Mayfair
1925	Gilbert St again
1927	17 Norfolk Street, Mayfair (now Dunraven St)
1928–30	Norfolk St
1931	Mews flat, Mayfair (short period)
1932	Dorchester Hotel
1933	Norfolk St
1934	Seamore Ct, Mayfair and Dorchester Hotel
1934–37	Occasional mentions of Norfolk St
1939	Mews flat 'off Berkeley Square'

Nearly every one of them appears in his books somewhere.

His first London home was Markham Square in 1900, when he came from Shropshire to work in the Hong Kong and Shanghai Bank. He loathed his lodgings there and moved to Walpole Street, a pleasant road that runs from the King's Road to Burton's Court and the Chelsea Royal Hospital. Walpole Street features largely in *Not George Washington*, written jointly with Herbert Westbrook. He even uses the same number as his own house, No. 23, and writes of the difficulty the young author (drawn on himself) has in trying to stop his landlady and her daughter from wasting his good writing time after tea by talking of the better days they had seen.

23 Walpole Street, Chelsea, ought to be one of those houses proudly bearing a blue plaque. Wodehouse lived there in the early 1900s, Denis Mackail lived there in the 1920s (Wodehouse visited him there and told him of his, Wodehouse's, earlier tenure) and Mackail was followed by Mrs Maxtone-Grahame, the author of *Mrs Miniver*. A good record for any house.

Markham Square, which Wodehouse disliked so much, doesn't appear under its own name in *Not George Washington*. He expresses his dislike of his first digs very strongly but, because he had left it shortly before, he evaded the issue and used the nearest name to it in the area. Instead of reading of Markham Square we therefore hear of Manresa Road, which starts with the same syllable and is only two hundred yards away. Not until *Ukridge* was published in 1924 does Wodehouse say his piece about the Chelsea square he disliked so much.

> My first intimation that he had been trying to hurry matters on came when he and I were walking along the King's Road one evening and he drew me into Markham Square, a dismal backwater where he had once had rooms.
> 'What's the idea?' I asked, for I disliked the place.
> 'Teddy Weeks lives here,' said Ukridge. 'In my old rooms.'

It is the only time we read of Markham Square – I wonder if Wodehouse remembered his dislike of it in later years. He may have done so since his grandson was living at the same address in 1963.

Arundell Street is the opening scene of *Something Fresh*, the first Blandings Castle story. Wodehouse described it exactly as it was, a small backwater, a cul-de-sac forty yards long where Leicester Square runs into Piccadilly Circus. On one side was a small hotel, the Previtali, facing a similar establishment, the Mathis, on the other side. The far end was occupied by lodgings of which the hero, Ashe Marson (a struggling writer of course), has one while the heroine has another. There are six pages of description of that little spot off Leicester Square and they are accurate even to the names of the hotels.

How did he know it so well? In the introduction to *Performing Flea* Townend relates how Wodehouse used the anecdote Townend had given him and turned it into *Love among the Chickens*. He gave Townend a share of the proceeds and, on the strength of the money, Townend took digs in Arundell Street, where Wodehouse visited him. In 1924, when Wodehouse wanted a suitable address for Ukridge, his mind must have gone back to the friend who first gave him the idea (*Ukridge* is dedicated to Townend) and, with one of the associations of ideas we saw in chapter IV, Ukridge is firmly installed in 'Arundel Street, Leicester Square'.

Markham Square, Walpole Street and Arundell Street set the pattern for London houses for the next sixty years – that depending on the sort of address he wanted, Wodehouse would pick a house or address in London that either he or one of his friends had lived in.

In *Not George Washington*, Julian Eversleigh, the joint hero, based on the joint author Herbert Westbrook, has digs in the top floor over the baker's shop at the corner of Rupert Court and Rupert Street, off Leicester Square. In 1907 the shop on that corner was indeed Forscutt's the muffin bakers, and its passing was mourned by the old actor Maxwell Fawcett in *The Adventures of Sally*.

In 1913 Wodehouse worked with Charles Bovill on a revue and was invited by him to stay at his flat at 94 Prince of Wales Mansions, Battersea. A couple of years later (two years is the norm for fact to become fiction with Wodehouse: one year for drafting, one year for writing, rewriting and publication) in *The Man with Two Left Feet* we read:

> Battersea may have its tough citizens but they do not live in Battersea Park Road. Battersea Park Road's speciality is Brain, not Crime. Authors, musicians, newspapermen, actors and artists are the inhabitants of these mansions. A child could control them. They assault and batter nothing but pianos; they steal nothing but ideas; they murder nobody except Chopin and Beethoven.

In *Bill the Conqueror* (1924) Bill West and Judson Coker take up residence at 9 Marmont Mansions, Prince of Wales Road, Battersea, and Jerry Vail, the hero of *Pigs Have Wings* (1952), lives along the same road. The last mention is in *Ice in the Bedroom*, where Leila Yorke tells of her early married life in Prince of Wales Mansions, Battersea.

A good question in any Wodehouse quiz would be – where is Lord Emsworth's town house? The correct answer is: 'In the London house Wodehouse lived in longer than any other – 17

Norfolk Street, Mayfair.' In *Summer Lightning* Ronnie Fish invites Sue Brown to tea and decides to take her to the family's town house. At the doorway they meet Lady Constance, Ronnie loses his head, introduces Sue as the wealthy Miss Schoonmaker, and we are off on another Blandings story of impersonations and young love. That was Norfolk Street and Wodehouse used the same name twice on the page to show it wasn't a mistake. *Summer Lightning* was published in 1929, two years after Wodehouse had taken No. 17 Norfolk Street (now Dunraven Street); it is up in the top left-hand corner of Mayfair off Grosvenor Square and was Wodehouse's address from 1927 until some time in the late 1930s.

Norfolk Street gave him a close acquaintance with that part of London that lies around Berkeley and Grosvenor Squares and he used them often. Green Street, which crosses Norfolk Street, is mentioned at least four times in his novels and 'Bloxham Mansions' in Park Lane, the home of Stanwood Cobbold, Horace Pendlebury-Davenport and Oofy Prosser, looks suspiciously like Grosvenor House just around the corner from Norfolk Street.

When he came to London for a few months in 1923 and took a service flat in King St, St James's, he saved the address for Freddie Threepwood to use in *Blandings Castle* and for Gally Threepwood to use after that. And when he wasn't using his own addresses, he used those of his friends and relations.

Lady Lakenheath, aunt of Ukridge's Milly, is the relict of Sir Rupert Lakenheath, who retired in 1906 after being Governor of various 'insanitary parts of the British Empire'. In *Love among the Chickens* and in *Ukridge* eighteen years later she lives in Thurloe Square, South Kensington, as does Mrs Winnington-Bates, the imperious lady we never meet in *Sam the Sudden*. Wodehouse's uncle, Captain Pollexfen Deane CMG, never achieved the rank of Governor, but he was in the Colonial Civil Service and his relict, Wodehouse's Aunt Juliette, lived in Thurloe Square during the years in question (1906–21).

Jill Mariner of *Jill the Reckless* lived in 'Ovingdon Square, Knightsbridge'. 22 Ovington Square, Knightsbridge, was the

196

home of the little Bowes-Lyon girls with whom he used to have tea and whose mother lived there when *Jill the Reckless* was written. Onslow Square where Ukridge's Mabel lived in 'A Bit of Luck for Mabel' a story from *Eggs, Beans and Crumpets* (1940), was where Wodehouse himself lived in 1922, and the address given to Mustard Pott in *Uncle Fred in the Springtime* at 6 Wilbraham Place, Sloane Square, is only two doors away from the address of a cousin, Sir Edward Frederick Wodehouse, KCB, KCVO.

Aunt Dahlia's address clinches the argument. It crops up in *The Code of the Woosters* (1938) and *Jeeves and the Feudal Spirit* (1954) and is quite specific. When Bertie arrives at Totleigh and realizes that Sir Watkyn Bassett knows exactly why he has come, viz. to steal the famous cow-creamer, he sends a telegram expressing his doubts and fears to 'Mrs Travers, 47 Charles Street, Berkeley Square, London'. That was the address of Wodehouse's friend and colleague Ian Hay, whom he had invited to stay at Hunstanton and with whom he had gone on a golfing holiday in Scotland.

In *Bachelors Anonymous* Ivor Llewellyn (8 Ennistone Gardens) and Sally Fitch (Fountain Court, Park Lane) were given the addresses of Wodehouse's grand-daughter and of Mrs Thelma Cazalet-Keir, his son-in-law's sister (and the editor of *Homage to P. G. Wodehouse*). In *The Girl in Blue* the address in Chelsea Square given to Willoughby Scrope, the lawyer, was the current address of Wodehouse's grandson, also a member of the legal profession.

The legal firm of Nichols, Nichols and Nichols first appears in *Uneasy Money* in 1916 and bobs up at intervals till *Bachelors Anonymous* in 1973. There they are located at 27 Bedford Row, where they must be fairly near Scrope, Ashby Pemberton, their legal colleagues of *The Girl in Blue*. Bedford Row crops up many times in the novels but there is a gap of twenty years before these last two references appear. The reason they come to life again is that they were written just about the time that 17 Bedford Row became the offices of Wodehouse's English literary agents, A. P. Watt.

Denis Mackail says that in 1939 the Wodehouses, who had

given up their house in Norfolk Street, took a mews flat 'off Berkeley Square'. Was this the hallowed spot known as 'Halsey Court' – the home of Chimp Twist, Jeff Miller, Jerry Shoesmith, Sam Bagshott and Johnny Halliday? We are given various directions for it. It is 'around the corner from Barribault's', it is 'off Bond Street'. We know it is a small, seedy cul-de-sac more suited to Aldgate than Mayfair, but there has never been a Halsey Court in Mayfair. There is a Halsey Street in Chelsea, just off Walton Street where Wodehouse lived in 1919 and 1920, but this is too far away.

If we follow the directions in *Money in the Bank*, there is only one place it can be. Jeff Miller walked from Lincoln's Inn Fields to Halsey Court, Mayfair, and we read that he 'crossed Berkeley Square and arrived at Halsey Court. He passed through the court's narrow entrance and turned to the right. This brought him to Halsey Chambers, on the third floor front of which he lived' – and to a motherly welcome from Ma Balsam, who looks after this famous domicile throughout its appearances in the novels.

If you walk from Lincoln's Inn Fields to Berkeley Square and cross the Square, you arrive not at 'Halsey Court' but at Hay's Mews. Remembering Wodehouse's accuracy of description, Hay's Mews will fit very well, especially if it was where he lived himself when he took that mews flat in 1939.

Hay's Mews has come up in the world now. It is smart, it is expensive, it has been developed, but it still has traces of the seediness Wodehouse drew. Its southern end faces directly on to 47 Charles Street, the home of Ian Hay, which Wodehouse used for Aunt Dahlia's London address, and it fits every allusion and direction Wodehouse gave for Halsey Court. It was precisely as he described – a small backwater where a young man could live cheaply in central London.

If Hay's Mews is Halsey Court, where is Barribault's Hotel? It is 'around the corner' from Halsey Court, but which corner? Barribault's took over pride of place as 'the' Wodehouse hotel fairly late – I think the first mention of it is in the 1940s, when it appears as the successor to Mario's as the place for young lovers to meet, to be seen dining with the wrong girl or to celebrate. Mario's by all the directions given for it should be the old Trocadero in Shaftesbury Avenue. The Ivy, over which the real Mario presided, was far too small and select. It would be nice to name Romano's as the original but the novels distinguish clearly between the two. The Trocadero fits all the clues for Mario's.

Barribault's is grand and very expensive. It is one of the great London hotels built before 1939. We must look for it among:

The Dorchester   The Connaught
Grosvenor House   Brown's
The Hyde Park Hotel   The Mayfair
Claridge's   The Berkeley
The Ritz

The Savoy and the Ritz can be struck out right away; they are in the right league but their topography excludes them. They are not in Mayfair and Wodehouse was always accurate. We are left with the Dorchester, Grosvenor House, the Hyde Park, Claridges, Brown's, the Connaught and the Mayfair.

They all have possibilities. The Dorchester and Grosvenor House on Park Lane sound right and have the right feel, but the Dorchester is referred to at least once as being a separate establishment from Barribault's. Brown's is in Dover Street, the home of the Drones Club and in real life the old home of the Bath Club, one facet of which Wodehouse used to draw the Drones. A nice idea but with insufficient supporting evidence. The Mayfair in Berkeley Street has echoes of Bertie Wooster, and the Connaught in Carlos Place off Grosvenor Square would fit as well.

I have visited them all and one claimant appeared clear and unquestioned. It is only mentioned twice in the novels although it was the nearest to Wodehouse's London house. We are given clear instructions for it – although it is *not* in Clarges Street off Piccadilly as is stated in *Ice in the Bedroom*. There is not, nor has been, a hotel of any size in Clarges Street this century. It can't be Clarges Street but it can be a slip of the typewriter. Barribault's on my reckoning is Claridge's, and the error of Clarges Street/Claridges is one that dozens of tourists make every day.

In *Spring Fever* (1948) Terry Cobbold and Stanwood Cobbold meet in Berkeley Square.

> An hour's aimless rambling through London's sunlit streets had taken Terry to Berkeley Square, and she had paused to survey it and to think with regret how they had ruined this pleasant oasis with their beastly Air Ministries and blocks of flats, when she was aware of a bowed figure clumping slowly towards her on leaden feet. It was Stanwood in person, and so dejected was his aspect that all thought of being cold left her.

They wander on together and 'turn into Duke Street' and 'Barribault's Hotel loomed up' before them. Two pages later as Terry sees her fiancé walking into Barribault's with Stanwood's fiancée on his arm, 'Duke Street' swims about her.

A map of Mayfair is at Plate 2. At the top is Grosvenor Square. At the top centre Duke Street meets Brook Street and in Brook Street you will find Claridge's. Just to the right of Duke Street is Gilbert Street, where the Wodehouses lived in 1924, and some five hundred yards to the left is Dunraven Street (ex-Norfolk Street), where he lived longer than anywhere else in London. Claridge's fits Barribault's very well and still inspires that awe and respect that afflicted so many of Wodehouse's shy heroes. It is the only hotel in that corner of Mayfair – Claridge's it must be.

One address is missing and it is the one I would have been happiest to find – the abode of Bertie Wooster. In *The Inimitable Jeeves* of 1923 he lives at 6A Crichton Mansions, Berkeley Street. In *Thank You, Jeeves* of 1934, his address is Berkeley Mansions. Berkeley Mansions stood in Mount Street till 1966 and would fit very well. Berkeley Street is another eminently appropriate address but there has never been a Crichton Mansions there. Was it a Wodehouse allusion perhaps, Jeeves being Bertie's Admirable Crichton? Wodehouse met Barrie in 1902, the year *The Admirable Crichton* came out, and this may be the connection. But this is all I have – I have read the lists of residents of both streets back to 1910 and there are no names I recognized.

I live in hope. If I can find a factual basis for most of the London addresses Wodehouse used from his own first lodgings in 1900 to his grandchildren's addresses in the 1970s, then one day I'll find Bertie's flat as well – and the reason Wodehouse used it.

CHAPTER XXIII

⋅◄§§►⋅

THE WODEHOUSE TRIANGLE:
SHROPSHIRE, GLOUCESTERSHIRE,
WORCESTERSHIRE AND
WILTSHIRE

THE 'Wodehouse Triangle' is the term I coined for that area of England bounded by the River Severn to the west, the Holyhead Road to the east and the London–Bath road to the south. These four counties were Wodehouse's spiritual home. He used Hampshire and Sussex for their propinquity to London, he enjoyed writing of London and its suburbs, but the counties that lie beside the Severn were where he spent his childhood. It was here that his uncles and aunts lived, and it was up and down these counties that he travelled during his school holidays until his father retired, came home from Hong Kong and, after that short sojourn in Dulwich, moved his family into The Old House at Stableford in Shropshire.

Somewhere in this part of England is the home of Aunt Dahlia, of Sir Watkyn Bassett and Lord Emsworth. Somewhere on the banks of the Severn is the 'Angler's Rest' where Mr Mulliner regales his audience with stories of fire and flood in Hollywood, London or anywhere else that has caught the imagination of his creator. A surprising number of co-incidences came to light by following the same method as before: which areas did Wodehouse know, how did he know them, and where did he use them in his books?

Our starting point is Wiltshire, the southernmost county of the group. The 'Wodehouse centre' is Cheney Court. You will find it by driving along the road from Chippenham to Bath and turning right into the small village of Box. Pass under a railway bridge and fifty yards further on, on the left-hand side, is a fine

Jacobean house. This is Cheney Court. It was to this house that Mrs Deane, Wodehouse's maternal grandmother, and her four daughters moved after the death of the Rev. John Deane in 1887 and Wodehouse stayed here often during his school holidays. The *Dulwich Record* shows that this was his permanent address until his parents returned from Hong Kong. An aged grandmother and four maiden aunts are not the ideal company for a ten-year-old boy and I think this is reflected in the ménage he drew in *The Mating Season*. In that novel the young landowner Esmond Haddock has five aunts living on the premises, and Wodehouse named them Miss Charlotte Deverill, Miss Emmeline Deverill, Miss Myrtle Deverill, Miss Harriet Deverill and Dame Daphne Wink-worth, née Miss Daphne Deverill. This is a 'double memory' or association of ideas of Cheney Court as he remembered it and the five Wiltshire villages that lie nearby – Brixton Deverill, Monkton Deverill, Kingston Deverill, Longbridge Deverill, and Hill Deverill.

'The Pride of the Woosters Is Wounded' is one of the short stories in *The Inimitable Jeeves* and is important for us as the occasion when Wodehouse 'slipped' and wrote of Bertie and Bingo Little meeting in what is clearly meant to be the Drones, although he gave us the real name – Buck's Club. The plot revolves around Bingo's love for Honoria Glossop, and Bertie finds himself having to push Honoria's young brother off a bridge so that Bingo can rescue him. It all takes place 'at the Glossops' place at Ditteridge'. The only Ditteridge in England lies four hundred yards from Cheney Court.

Phipps, the burglarious butler of *The Old Reliable*, was induced to start his career of crime by reading 'Three Dead At Midways Manor'. Kay Derrick, the heroine of *Sam the Sudden*, was the daughter of Colonel Derrick of 'Midways Hall, Wiltshire'. The only house in England by that name lies about six miles south of Cheney Court and Wodehouse's memory misled him slightly. Midway Manor is famous as being the home of not Colonel, but General Shrapnel, and the gateposts of the manor still record the names of the battles in which his invention was used.

Gloucestershire has little for us at this stage, but somewhere there is the home of Sir Watkyn Bassett, Totleigh Towers. Wodehouse got the name Totleigh from his holidays with Uncle Philip down at Bratton Fleming in Devonshire, but I think we can look for Totleigh Towers' owner amongst the Gloucestershire villages of Winterbourne Bassett, Berwick Bassett and Wootton Bassett, through which Wodehouse travelled as a schoolboy.

Worcestershire is the heart of Wodehouse country. It is the home of Aunt Dahlia, the Earl of Droitwich, the Earl of Powick and other Wodehouse notables. It shares with Devonshire the first place for providing Wodehousean place-names, so it is often difficult to distinguish between the real and the fictional. From a letter to *The Times* in January 1979 it is clear I was not the only one who had noticed the appointment of a new vicar to the parish of Upton Snodsbury with Broughton Hackett and Naunton Beauchamp and Grafton Flyford with North Piddle and Flyford Flavell. A collection of names as good as anything Wodehouse invented, and a useful start to the question, where is Brinkley Court? It is from Brinkley Court that Aunt Dahlia leads her reluctant entourage on blackmailing expeditions, prize-givings and election campaigns, and the whole world knows that her address is Brinkley Court, Market Snodsbury, Worcs.

To find Wodehouse's connection with the county, place your finger on the River Severn at Tewkesbury and run it north to Upton-upon-Severn. Just north of that is Hanley Castle. That's where Uncle Edward Isaac was the vicar, and over to the left is Malvern where various other aunts and relations lived. Go back to the Severn and run your finger north to Worcester itself; just before the city you will see Powick. That's where Wodehouse's paternal grandmother lived, the widow of the Waterloo veteran.

We know that Wodehouse and his brothers used to spend some of their holidays at Powick and that he used to visit Hanley Castle. We also know that in the 1920s he used to visit Droitwich, where he stayed at the Château Impney Hotel. So, in chronological order, Powick, Hanley Castle and Droitwich are all places he knew, and it is clear that he remembered them.

If you start at Hanley Castle and look east across the Severn, you will find Bredon Hill and the first of the Worcestershire references. Wodehouse's second book, *A Prefect's Uncle*, was published in 1903. It is a school story and the name of the school was Beckford. You'll find Beckford just south of Bredon Hill. In *Mike*, where we first meet Psmith, Mike Jackson's father takes him away from Wrykyn (which we will find in Shropshire) and sends him to a school called 'Sedleigh' in another county. We read that the first outing of the archaeological society is to look at the 'Roman Camp at Elmbury Hill, two miles from the school'. In that case we should look very hard, not at 'Sedleigh' but Sedgebarrow, just to the east of Bredon Hill, which is two miles from the Roman camp at Elmley, not 'Elmbury'.

Money for Nothing is the book which we know Wodehouse based on Hunstanton Hall in east Norfolk, although he spent two pages setting it firmly 'where the grey stone of Gloucestershire gives place to Worcestershire's old red brick'. This is the line from Bredon Hill to Hanley Castle. We are told that Rudge Hall is seven miles from Worcester and eighteen from Birmingham. This is undeniably Droitwich, and Wodehouse was staying there when he wrote that section of the book. We also learn that Rudge Hall is twenty miles from 'Healthward Ho! at Lowick', the establishment run for flabby businessmen by our old friend Chimp Twist. It needs little imagination to connect 'Healthward Ho! at Lowick' with Ham Hill at Powick, Wodehouse's grandmother's house, where he stayed often as a boy.

As I read through the guide-books on Worcestershire, I noticed that all the references to Powick made the same point. Whether they were official publications or gossipy memoirs, Powick means (or meant) one thing to every good Worcastrian – the county lunatic asylum. This means we can start working out the location of the town Wodehouse used so often – East Wobsley/Wibley/Weobley, a sort of Clapham Junction through which all Wodehouse's characters seem to pass.

Mike Jackson's train goes through it in *Mike* (1909); George

Mulliner lives there in *Meet Mr Mulliner* (1927); John Carroll dines there in *Money for Nothing* (1928); it is where Bertie and Boko Fittleworth attend fancy-dress balls in *Joy in the Morning* (1947). The name comes from Herefordshire twenty miles to the west but Wodehouse grabbed it and brought it east to the banks of the Severn. In *Meet Mr Mulliner* George Mulliner has to change at Ippleton to get the train back home to East Wobsley. At Ippleton he can see the county asylum through the trees – and we are back at Powick, where Wodehouse's grandmother lived and where he would have caught the train to travel the ten miles down the river to Hanley Castle. If Ippleton is indeed Powick, then Hanley Castle would fit very well for East Wobsley – as well, perhaps, as it does for Market Snodsbury itself, the home of Aunt Dahlia.

Ham Hill, the house Wodehouse knew at Powick, is a Victorian shooting lodge, set amongst deep woods with a superb view across the valley to Worcester. It is delightful but far too small to be Brinkley Court. Upton Snodsbury must be considered for its name but Hanley Castle is still the best candidate. We know from the Isaac family that Wodehouse knew Hanley Castle well and that, as nephew of the local vicar, he knew the local landowners, the Lechmeres of Severn End, which lies across the main road from the village. Severn End is a delightful red-brick building, it fits the descriptions we have of Brinkley, it is in the right place for Bertie Wooster to set off on his disastrous bicycle ride 'towards Pershore'. It is also exactly the right distance from Upton-upon-Severn, which had a street called River Row where Bertie can try his hand at electioneering.

'Langley End' of *If I Were You*, the home of 'Lord Droitwich', sounds very like Severn End, and the village of Hanley Castle shares with Aunt Dahlia's Market Snodsbury the advantage of having its own Grammar School. Market Snodsbury as drawn by Wodehouse seems too small for the privilege but the Grammar School is indeed there, only twenty yards from the Hanley Castle Vicarage that Wodehouse knew. On balance, Severn End, the gracious home of the Lechmeres, seems as near Aunt Dahlia's Brinkley Court as we will get and the local town, Upton-upon-Severn, can easily be transposed into Market Snodsbury. The train of thought is: 'Upton-upon-Severn – too near. Upton Snodsbury – right sound but it's a real name. Upton on its own is no good. Snodsbury on its own – not enough. What did I do with Blandings? Market Blandings. Right, let's call it Market Snodsbury.' It's not conclusive, but if ever Wodehouse had a real house in mind, then Severn End fits very well for Brinkley and Upton-upon-Severn/Hanley Castle fit every reference we have for Market Snodsbury.

Droitwich, upstream, is where Wodehouse used to retire from the London social life he disliked so much. He used to stay at the Château Impney Hotel and visit the salt baths, writing his notes for his next novel at the shallow end of the baths. He used it as a name for one of his earls and quoted its distance from Worcester and Birmingham to identify Rudge Hall in *Money for Nothing*.

I drove through Droitwich in my search for Blandings and called at the Château Impney Hotel to see whether it was of interest. There was always the chance that, like Dulwich, if I went where Wodehouse went, something would catch my eye that had caught his. It did – the hotel itself took my attention, as it must catch everybody's who sees it. Wodehouse used it to describe the home of Sir Buckstone Abbott in *Summer Moonshine*:

Whatever may be said in favour of the Victorians, it is pretty well generally admitted that few of them were to be trusted within reach of a trowel and a pile of bricks. Sir Wellington least of any. He was as virulent an amateur architect as ever grew a whisker. Watching the holocaust in his nightshirt, for he had had to nip rather smartly out of a burning bedroom, he forgot the cold wind blowing about his ankles in the thought that here was his chance to do a big job and do it well. He embarked upon it at the earliest possible moment, regardless of expense.

What Sir Buckstone was now looking at, accordingly, was a vast edifice constructed of glazed red brick, in some respects resembling a French château but, on the whole perhaps, having more the appearance of those model dwellings in which a certain number of working-class families are assured of a certain number of cubic feet of air. It had a huge leaden roof, tapering to a point and topped by a weathervane, and from one side of it, like some unpleasant growth, there protruded a large conservatory. There were also a dome and some minarets.

Victorian villagers gazing up at it had named it Abbott's Folly, and they had been about right.

Château Impney (Plate 11) was built by the famous salt processor John Corbett for his French wife in 1869 who, if rumour is correct, refused to live in it. There are some who claim that Hadlow Castle in Kent is *the* ugliest building in England but Château Impney must run it pretty close. When Wodehouse wanted to describe an architectural monstrosity like Walsingford Hall in *Summer Moonshine* or Ashby Hall in *Company for Henry*, Château Impney seems a very good source.

After Droitwich we cross the border into Shropshire, the home of so many Wodehouse heroes and heroines. When Wodehouse's father retired from the Hong Kong Civil Service on health grounds in 1895, he took a house in Dulwich for a few months, then moved his family to The Old House at Stableford in Shropshire. The boys were still at boarding school but came home to Stableford for the holidays and Wodehouse knew the area from the age of fourteen to twenty-one. His parents moved to Cheltenham in 1902 and although he can only have known it for those short seven years, Wodehouse kept his affection for Shropshire all his life. It creeps into dozens of his novels from the first, *The Pothunters*, in 1902 to the last more than seventy years later.

Shropshire is a difficult county to describe; it doesn't have a ready-made reputation like Devonshire, Yorkshire or Kent. It is oblong in shape with the Severn running up the right-hand edge, across the top and down the left-hand side. To the east of the river are the green pasturelands of the north Midlands, to the west a series of wooded valleys running down to the mountains of the Welsh border.

The section we must look at lies around Bridgnorth in the east of the county. From Bridgnorth a road, the A454, runs east to Wolverhampton. Two miles from Bridgnorth, you will find Worfield and due north of that is Stableford – and for Stableford you need a very large-scale map indeed.

Stableford is a hamlet into which four roads run and which mix themselves in such confusion that it is easier to park one's car and walk. There are about twenty houses in the village, into one of which the family moved in 1895. It is still there, and the photograph of The Old House was taken from the croquet lawn Wodehouse's father laid out (Plate 8).

In his first half dozen books, all school stories, Wodehouse based his plots on Dulwich but used the topography around Stableford. In *The Pothunters* Barrett cannot decide whether to go along the 'Stapleton Road' to the west to look for birds' eggs or to go east along the 'Badgwick Road'. He goes east and soon comes to the famous 'Badgwick Dingle'. If you walk out of The Old House at Stableford and turn east, you come not to 'Badgwick Dingle' but to Badger Dingle.

Tales of St Austin's picks up just about every village name within walking distance of Stableford. The main town is 'Stapleton' itself, the village of 'Worbury' lies three miles away (this is Worfield, which is indeed three miles away) and 'Rutton' is out of bounds. So it ought to be, since Roughton lies just beyond Worfield. In *The Gold Bat* we hear of 'Chesterton, a small hamlet two miles away'. That's exactly what it is. In *The Head of Kay's* the school is called 'Eckleton', after Ackleton, which lies half a mile east of Stableford, and in *Mike* we hear of Worfield again, this time under its real name. If you look closely at the map, you will see the origin of Wodehouse's most famous school – Wrykyn – whose alumni we meet for sixty years. Having exhausted all the names in his immediate vicinity, Wodehouse noticed that the small hamlet on the A454 road south of Stableford was called Wykyn. Off to the north is the famous hill The Wrekin, and Stableford is halfway between them, thus we have Wrykyn – a mixture of the two names. Easy when one works it out.

Mike is best known as the book that introduced Psmith. Rupert Psmith (who changed his name to Ronald when Wodehouse found he had put him in the same book as Rupert Baxter) was based on Rupert D'Oyly Carte. There is no detective work here; Wodehouse was quite happy to admit the fact. In the preface to *The World of Psmith* he wrote:

> The character of Psmith . . . is the only thing in my literary career which was handed to me on a plate with watercress around it. Rupert D'Oyly Carte was long, slender, always beautifully dressed and very dignified. He habitually addressed his fellow Wykehamists as 'Comrade' and if one of the masters chanced to inquire as to his health, would reply 'I grow thinnah and thinnah.'

We owe a debt of gratitude to Rupert D'Oyly Carte, born 1876, died 1948, and to the cousin of Wodehouse's who had been at Winchester with him and who told Wodehouse about him. Carte was the son of the famous Gilbert and Sullivan impresario and became chairman of the D'Oyly Carte Company and the Savoy Hotel. His alter ego, Psmith, was the first Wodehouse hero to achieve fame; in the 1920s Wodehouse's fame was as the creator of Psmith; Lord Emsworth and Jeeves still had their renown to come.

When Mike Jackson meets Psmith at Sedleigh, he is delighted to find they both come from Shropshire. Mike is welcomed by Mr Outwood as coming from 'Crofton in Shropshire near Brindleford' (this is Corfeton near Bridgnorth in Shropshire) and Mr Outwood goes on to speak of the famous 'Cluniac monastery of St Ambrose at Brindleford'. This is the Cluniac monastery that lies seven miles from Bridgnorth, and Psmith claims to live at Corfby Hall (this is Corfeton Hall near Bridgnorth), which he says lies near 'Much Middlefold'.

'Much Middlefold' is the Shropshire equivalent of 'East Weobsley' in Worcestershire; everybody who is anybody seems to live there. In 1903, Gethryn in *A Prefect's Uncle* wonders whether to take the Much Middlefold road; three years later in *Love among the Chickens* Jeremy Garnet claims it as his birthplace; while Ashe Marson, the hero of *Something Fresh*, makes the same claim in 1915. Lord Pershore of *My Man Jeeves* lives there and Sally Nichols is overcome by the beauty of it in *The Adventures of Sally*; she also refers to the house there as 'Monk Crofton', another variation of the Crofton/Corfeton theme Wodehouse used so often. As late as 1973, Sally Fitch also claimed it as her birthplace in *Bachelors Anonymous*.

Wodehouse used Bridgnorth and Stableford often and Much Middlefold is obviously a disguise; the clue is probably in the train of thought that took The Wrekin and Wykyn and turned them into Wrykyn. Further, Sally Fitch, Jeremy Garnet and Ashe Marson all claim to have been born in the vicarage at Much Middlefold. Working on these two factors, I suggest that since Much Wenlock lies north of Bridgnorth and Middleton Priors and Middleton Scriven lie to the south, Much Middleford is Stableford again, in the middle, and the vicarage is Wodehouse's memories of all the clerical uncles with whom he spent those early years while his parents were in Hong Kong.

Although most of the names of the Blandings saga stem from Hampshire, two at least came from Shropshire. The Blandings housekeeper is Mrs Twemlow and you will find Twemlow names all over the county; two at least are within a mile of Stableford. The other name is of the man without whom Blandings is incomplete – Rupert Baxter.

How would we describe the super-efficient master of Blandings' affairs? Without emotion, ruthless? A modern Malvolio? A twentieth-century Puritan? If you were, as Wodehouse was, a schoolboy living in the Severn valley, there is a local hero whose name you were bound to know. As a nephew of four vicars it was almost impossible for him not to know it; a name that would come to epitomize certain characteristics in his mind. It was the name of a famous Puritan preacher whose hymns are still sung today and whose home on the slopes of The Wrekin is shown to the public. He was born at Rowton near Stableford, he preached up and down the Severn Valley, he organized resistance in Shropshire against King Charles in the Civil War. It wasn't Rupert Baxter – it was Richard Baxter.

CHAPTER XXIV

※§§※

BLANDINGS

THE work on Aubrey Upjohn, those walks around Dulwich till I found the sphinxes, the London addresses of Wodehouse and his friends, all led to one conclusion – that it was unlikely that Blandings was *not* based on fact. With the evidence they provide there had to be an original for Blandings somewhere.

We were introduced to Blandings in 1915 in *Something Fresh*. We paid a sad farewell to it in 1977 when the draft and notes were published of the book Wodehouse was working on when he died. They were given the appropriate title *Sunset at Blandings*. That makes sixty years of writing about this fabled spot and is probably a record of some sort. Blandings has joined that group of place-names that have become synonymous with a style of writing; like Dotheboys Hall, 221B Baker Street, Brideshead or the Close at Barchester, it needs no explanation. It has become one of the great Arcadies of fiction.

Geoffrey Jaggard recognized its pre-eminence in his *Blandings the Blest* in 1968:

It may be fanciful, and is certainly not worth pursuing, yet it is the Castle, static and silent though it be, which perpetually plays a leading part. Gardeners, butlers, chatelaines, even Earls and their Countesses, all are expendable. It watches them come and go. Its ordered domestic routine is as smooth under a Hermione or Julia as under a Constance. It has watched its younger sons despatched to South Africa or North America with as much impassivity as it has observed an 18th-century earl performing a neat gavotte, or a 16th-century one dealing adequately with a band of marauding Welsh caterans. It accepts, generation after generation, Tudor monarchs, Georgian statesmen or Texas millionaires as its guests, and has been nurse and guardian to all the members of a prolific family for many centuries. Far more than a mere setting, it has a dramatic role, and a puissant role, in its own right.

Jaggard makes the point that although Wodehouse takes his Blandings characters to London and even America, this is only an extension of their real lives, which are lived in Shropshire. To be complete they must return to 'the epicentre which is that noble pile which stands immemorially at the head of the pleasant Vale of Blandings.'

Wodehouse placed Blandings in Shropshire. From it you can see The Wrekin and the Welsh mountains. It stands on rising ground and dominates the country around. It has a lake, a boat house, a Greek temple overlooking the lake, rose gardens, a Dutch garden, spreading parkland, splendid stables and terraces. It was built as a castle in the middle of the fifteenth century and over the years has been altered to become a comfortable and gracious residence.

There are differing opinions as to when Blandings first appeared. Although it was not named till 1915, my own view is that its predecessor was Dreever Castle of *A Gentleman of Leisure* in 1910. It was Wodehouse's thirteenth book, and reflects the double influence of the New York he had just come to know and the stately English homes he had known as a boy. It was the first Wodehouse novel to bring American heroes to England, and provides an excellent contrast between the corruption of law-enforcement in New York and the dreamy splendour of the English countryside.

In the days before the Welshman began to expend his surplus energy in playing Rugby football he was accustomed, whenever the monotony of his everyday life began to oppress him, to collect a few friends and make raids across the border into England, to the huge discomfort of the dwellers on the other side. It was to cope with this habit that Dreever Castle, in Shropshire, came into existence. It met a long-felt want. In time of trouble it became a haven of refuge. From all sides people poured into it, emerging cautiously when the marauders had disappeared. In the whole history of the castle there is but one instance recorded of a bandit attempting to take the place by storm, and the attack was an emphatic failure.

On receipt of a ladleful of molten lead, aimed to a nicety by one John the Chaplain – evidently one of those sporting parsons – this warrior retired, done to a turn, to his mountain fastnesses and is never heard of again.

In later years we are given the pastoral approach:

Blandings Castle slept in the sunshine. Dancing little ripples of heat-mist played across its smooth lawns and stone-flagged terraces. The air was full of the lulling drone of insects. It was that gracious hour of a summer afternoon, midway between luncheon and tea, when Nature seems to unbutton its waistcoat and put its feet up.

(Summer Lightning)

Wodehouse said once that he found descriptions of people or places very difficult, but he kept up the same high level of poetry and humour throughout his long life. In the same way that his descriptions of Bertie Wooster's train of thought arouse admiration among psychiatrists, so whenever he describes Blandings he seems to be able to produce new heights of imagery that make us laugh at the same time as they impress on our minds exactly the reaction Wodehouse wants.

A constant factor in this study is that while characters may be based on more than one person – Bertie Wooster is an example – buildings tend to be more definite. Hunstanton Hall, Fairlawn in Kent, Threepwood in Hampshire are all identifiable once we know where to start. Blandings is different. Like Bertie Wooster it is too big, too important to come from one source.

There are hundreds of castles in England and Wales; Blandings could be any one of them. It might not even be a castle at all; it might be one of the innumerable Manors, Courts, Halls or Places that are still such a feature of the English countryside. An ominous introduction to *Burke's Landed Gentry* reads:

Until 1914, the English countryside had, at an average of every two miles, a great house to lead and protect those who lived in the shadow of its estate.

I took heart from a cartoon in *Punch* of some twenty years ago. The cartoon, by Fougasse, shows a man and a woman striding determinedly towards a telephone box. The caption reads: 'To save time, you go through A to M and I'll do N to Z.' I was in the same position. I was sure there was a Blandings somewhere: all I had to do was to eliminate the places it wasn't and see what was left.

I started with the assumptions that:

(a) Blandings did exist.

(b) It was probably within the 'Wodehouse triangle' near the River Severn.

(c) It was a building or buildings he had known between the ages of seven and twenty-five (1888–1906).

(d) It needn't be a castle but must look enough like one to put the idea in Wodehouse's head.

(e) It doesn't have a moat.

The last factor proved invaluable. Time and again I pondered over some splendid building but the presence of a moat saved me from fruitless investigation. It is possible that Blandings does have a moat and that Wodehouse simply ignored it, but it is highly improbable. When he knew a house with a moat like Hunstanton, he used it to the full – if you're a humorous writer moats are good material. We never hear of a Blandings moat. We are told firmly of necklaces thrown out of windows to fall on the grass; Rupert Baxter jumps out of the windows into rose-beds; Pilbeam and young lovers swarm up and down drainpipes. There is no whisper of a moat.

The process of elimination was greatly helped, oddly enough, by the factor that has proved the undoing of so many great houses like Blandings. More and more owners of stately homes have been forced to open them to the public, and this has resulted in more guidebooks being published. *The Guide to Houses Open to the Public* cost only a pound but saved me months of work. Although it didn't tell me which were or might be Blandings, it showed me plenty that couldn't be.

There is no point in detailing all the splendid buildings that Blandings is not. It owes nothing to those beautiful buildings in Kent that he would have known around his daughter's home at Fairlawn. Leeds Castle, Hever, Bodiam, Scotney, Penshurst and Knole are delightful but they are not Blandings. As I looked further afield, another factor became important. Blandings doesn't have a moat and neither does it have round towers. It has at least one tower from which its fortunate inhabitants can look out over the Shropshire countryside. What I decided was that it did not have the big, round towers one sees at Windsor or Bodiam. If the towers weren't round they must be square, and I built up a mental picture which turned out to be exactly the same as the splendid drawing by Ionicus in *Sunset at Blandings*. The picture (at Plate 10) didn't come out till after I had found the real Blandings, but it was the image I was trying to fit to reality.

Hunstanton haunted me. It couldn't be Blandings because Wodehouse had written two Blandings stories before he went to Hunstanton; when he saw it he started using it at once. Yet if he could transpose Hunstanton so easily to Worcestershire, then he might have transposed Blandings as well. He said once: 'I placed Blandings in Shropshire because I was so happy there as a child.' A strict interpretation of that is that Blandings wasn't in Shropshire. In any event, in *Wodehouse at Work* Usborne states that:

In shape and size and messuages Wodehouse's Blandings Castle owes a great deal to his boyhood memory of Corsham, the stately home of the Methuens near Bath. The young

Pelham, spending holidays with a clergyman uncle nearby, was taken to Corsham to skate on the lake and the image of the great house remained on the retina of his inward eye.

That sent me racing down to Wiltshire to have a close look at Corsham Court. It is a splendid building in late Elizabethan or Jacobean style. It has a garden, a lake, a yew walk and an earl. But it is not Blandings. It is not a castle and it lies only a few yards from the centre of Corsham itself. The sense of isolation, of a place apart from the world, is simply not there. The Court is now shared by Lord Methuen and an Art school and the grounds and house are open to the public. It is not Blandings, yet walking round the gardens and park produced an odd sense of *déjà vu*.

A favourite stroll for the people of Corsham is to walk from the main street, past the front of the Court and on across the park to the lake which lies about a third of a mile from the house. Standing at the lakeside, one gets an unusual view of the house. Although there cannot be more than twenty feet difference in height, the Court seems to loom over the countryside, dominating everything in sight. It is a strange effect, difficult to appreciate except from the edge of the lake – and this was how Wodehouse described Blandings sometimes. This was how it looked to unhappy young lovers as they took their worries into the far corners of the estate and looked back at the castle lowering threateningly against a stormy sky.

There is a picture of Corsham Court at Plate 12. On the left of the picture running back towards the stables is a high yew walk. On the right of the picture, the grounds run down to the lake while the gardens lie behind the house. There is a secluded rose-garden and a small folly at the end of the main lawn. There is a fine cedar tree near the house ideal for Gally Threepwood to set his deckchair under, or affix his hammock to. The gardens are very promising.

But, as I continued my search among other candidates, I discovered that dozens of them have yew-walks, that a fine cedar tree near the house is the norm, and that we are a nation of rose-growers. Further, Corsham Court is not a castle and its proximity to Corsham itself prevents it being the main source of Blandings. In an interview with the *Observer* in October 1971, Wodehouse said: 'Blandings was a sort of mixture of places I remembered.' I am happy to accept Corsham Court as one of them. As a memory of a great house looming over the countryside, it will do very well.

Something Fresh, the first Blandings novel, came out in 1915 when Wodehouse was thirty-three. From what we know of his early adult life, he spent most of his time after he left the bank in London, Emsworth or New York. He may have been to other places; he played cricket for the *Punch* team in country-house matches in 1903. But those words of Bob Davis's he never forgot – 'Write about things you know' – mean that we should look at the part of England he knew best, the counties that border the Severn.

Oddly, I was unable to discover a complete guidebook to any county; even the splendid Victoria County Histories lack some particular. But I found that if I read two or more good guides on each county, then all the houses I wanted were mentioned. A further check of pictures or photographs of likely candidates could then be made elsewhere.

For Hampshire the result was negative. Plenty of beautiful seventeenth- or eighteenth-century houses but nothing like Blandings, even though all the family names came from that small village on the Hampshire coast. I carried on through the Southern counties, then moved north and west to the Midlands and the River Severn. I concentrated on where I knew Wodehouse had been, and from various illustrated guides I was able to exclude Bowood, Great Chalfield, Lacock Abbey, Longleat, Wardour Castle and Wilton in Wiltshire. In Worcestershire I was able to dispose of Hanbury Hall, Spetchley, Birtemorton and others, but had to look more closely at Croome Court, Severn End, Hagley Hall and Hartlebury Castle. In Herefordshire possibilities were Madresfield, Eastnor Castle and Croft Castle.

In Shropshire there are dozens of candidates. There are thirty-one castles and twice as many later buildings that looked hopeful.

By a slow process of elimination I reduced the list to manageable proportions by concentrating on the appearance of the building and the layout of the estate. The building had to look enough like a castle for Wodehouse to describe it as one, and the estate had to have the features in it that he described. Corsham Court's gardens made it a candidate, but although it has a park and a lake, they are not as we know them at Blandings.

These two limitations meant that I was unable to rely on guidebooks no matter how well illustrated they were. The pictures, naturally enough, tried to make the subject look as impressive as possible. There were frontages that looked like Buckingham Palace but were only fifty feet across, there were vistas to horizons that looked superb but were only a hundred yards long.

After two years (not as impressive as it sounds – twenty minutes in the British Museum at lunchtime was the daily ration) I came down to a short list:

Cholmondely Castle, Cheshire
Chirk Castle, Denbighshire
Powis Castle, Montgomeryshire
Rowton Castle, Shropshire
Onslow Hall, Shropshire
Attingham Hall, Shropshire
Longner Hall, Shropshire
Condover, Shropshire
Acton Burnell Hall, Shropshire
Willey Park, Shropshire
Aldenham Park, Shropshire
Morville, Shropshire
Chillington, Shropshire
Patshull Hall, Shropshire
Apley Park, Shropshire
Croft Castle, Herefordshire
Eastnor Castle, Herefordshire
Weston Park, Staffordshire
Witley Court, Worcestershire
Ragley Hall, Worcestershire

Croome D'Abitot, Worcestershire
Madresfield, Worcestershire
Thornbury Castle, Gloucestershire
Sudeley Castle, Gloucestershire
Berkeley Castle, Gloucestershire
Corsham Court, Wiltshire

I had pored over photographs of every one, but Corsham had shown me that pictures were not enough; they could show which houses I could exclude, but only by visiting them was I going to be able to decide which could be Blandings. The view from the lake was what Wodehouse remembered from Corsham. I had to try the same method with the others; only by walking where he had walked would I be able to see what he saw.

I set off from London on a wet Friday night in October. My plan was to start at the northern end and work my way south, an idea that went fairly well, although I had not appreciated how few bridges there are over the Severn. I spent a lot of time retracing my route to look at candidates on the other bank.

Midnight on Friday found me sleeping in some discomfort in the back of my car on the road outside Cholmondely Castle in Cheshire, and at six o'clock in the morning I drove slowly up the drive, turned the car round on the gravel in front of the castle and drove quickly out again.

This proved to be the pattern with nearly all the houses I visited. The photographs and guidebooks had given me an idea of what each place looked like, but I had to see how big it was and how it sat in its surroundings.

Chlomondely Castle isn't Blandings. It is the wrong shape and the grounds are not as Wodehouse described them. Chirk Castle, over in Denbighshire, isn't Blandings either. It stands on a hill, strong and defiant with great round towers, but it does not fit any more than Powis Castle which looks over the Severn. Powis has famous terraced gardens, and a distant Wodehouse relation married into the family, but one look was sufficient to dismiss it from the list.

Rowton Castle on the road back to Shrewsbury is pleasant but is far too small. It is a country mansion with Gothic additions. Attingham, just southwest of Shrewsbury, has a fine park and one of the most splendid porticoes in the country carried up to the roof on tall columns, but isn't Blandings either. And so it went on. Condover is claimed to be the finest Elizabethan house in the county. It is, but it isn't what we are looking for, although I walked its grounds for twenty minutes to check every view and angle of the house.

Acton Burnell was next – the home of the Smythes. Some people think it fits the Blandings topography very well, and we must remember that Psmith looked on the name Smythe as a cowardly evasion. It is a heavy classical building, it has a lake in its grounds with a ruined castle beside it, but it isn't Blandings. Willey Park near Ironbridge has an enormous landscaped park. The house was built by Wyatt in 1815 and has two lakes below the steep slope on which the house stands. It is certainly the most isolated mansion I saw in my travels but it doesn't fit in any particular.

After Willey Park I drove towards Bridgnorth. It was in this part of Shropshire that Wodehouse had lived and I felt that here, if anywhere, there would be something I would recognize. Bridgnorth lies on the Severn with one side of the town rising sharply from the river. Stableford, where the Wodehouses lived, is three miles to the northeast. In a circle around Bridgnorth lie a wealth of candidates: Morville and Aldenham to the west, Quatford Castle and Dudmaston Hall to the south, Stanley Hall and Apley Park to the north. To the east, near Stableford itself, lie Davenport House, Patshull Hall, Chillington and Weston Park.

Somewhere amongst these splendid estates had to be something. In *Bring on the Girls* Wodehouse explains to Guy Bolton how he came to know some of them:

> 'The only thing I didn't like in my formative or Stableford period was the social stuff. Owners of big estates round about would keep inviting me for the weekend.'
>
> '*You?*'
>
> 'I don't wonder you're surprised. Even today I'm about as pronounced an oaf who ever went around with his lower jaw

drooping and a glassy look in his eye, but you have literally no conception what I was like in my early twenties . . .

'Picture to yourself a Trappist monk with large feet and a tendency to upset tables with priceless china on them, and you will have the young Wodehouse. The solution to the mystery of my mixing with the County is that my brother Armine was very popular. He played the piano like a Gershwin and could converse pleasantly on any subject you cared to bring up . . .'

Two of the houses that Wodehouse knew near Stableford have gone: Badger Hall, described as 'Badgwick Hall' in the early school stories, has been demolished, as has Tong Castle. The British Museum has pictures of both and neither is Blandings, although Tong Castle rivals Château Impney in its ugliness. It was demolished in 1956 and seems to have been a Shropshire imitation of the Brighton Pavilion.

Morville and Aldenham are interesting. They lie to the west of Bridgnorth, over the river from Stableford, and I think they may have been in Wodehouse's mind when he described Matchingham Hall, the home of Sir Gregory Parsloe. When Maudie Montrose/Digby/Stubbs goes to reproach Sir Gregory in *Pigs Have Wings*:

The car slowed down and slid to a halt beside massive iron gates flanked by stone posts with heraldic animals on top of them. Beyond the gates were opulent grounds and at the end of the long driveway a home of England so stately that Maudie drew her breath in with a quick 'Coo!' of awe. Tubby, it was plain, had struck it rich and come a long way since the old Criterion days when he used to plead with her to chalk the price of his modest refreshment up on the slate, explaining that credit was the life-blood of Commerce without which the marts of trade would have no elasticity.

Aldenham Park's gates are famous, and they and the house are exactly as Maudie described them. They are the only ones that fit the description within twenty miles of Stableford and the local church is called St Gregory's!

Stanley Park, north of Bridgnorth, is as historic as its name suggests, but it is too small, and Apley Park across the river isn't Blandings either. It has a superb setting and I made a mental note that it was the best candidate I had seen so far, although it was smaller than I had imagined Blandings to be. From Apley Park I went to Stableford to see The Old House where Wodehouse had been so happy (see Plate 8) and on to Patshull and Chillington. Both are large, both have lakes, but neither fits the descriptions we have. So I went on to Weston Park – and found Blandings.

Weston Park is, like Blandings, the home of an earl – the Earl of Bradford. His house is a gracious red-brick building in the classical style. It is not a castle, but Weston Park is certainly one of the places we are looking for.

Corsham Court has the silhouette of a great house against the skyline that Wodehouse remembered. If you wish to see the Blandings terraces looking out over a sunlit park, the lake with the Grecian temple, the boathouse and The Wrekin on the horizon – then go to Weston Park. It was an extraordinary sensation, like meeting an old friend unexpectedly or seeing a film of a book one knows well. As I stood on the gravel outside the front door of Weston Park I had no doubts whatever that this was the scene Wodehouse had described so often.

This wasn't Blandings Castle but it was the view from Blandings. The terraces were in the right place, the lake was where it ought to be, the gardens were right. A plan of the Weston estate can be superimposed on the sketch by Ionicus and leave only a few blurred edges (see Plate 13).

I started to tick off the factors that supported my theory. Immediately to my left were the rhododendrons that shield the house from cars as they go down the drive (Sue Brown and Ronnie Fish in *Summer Lightning*); the stables whence the cars come were around the corner behind me. The terraces fronting the house separate it from the park by a stone balustrade as at Blandings, and Shifnal, the local market town, is five miles away.

From Shifnal the approach through the park is exactly as

Wodehouse describes it, along a pleasant drive through the deer park and the trees, the house appearing on the left and the drive swinging right before it bends left again to pass the front door and continue into the stable yard. Shifnal is therefore Market Blandings. Although Market Blandings is stated to be only two miles from Blandings in the later novels, in the first novel *Something Fresh* George Emerson has to walk five miles back to the castle carrying food for Aline Peters. Wodehouse used the real distance because he had no reason not to. Only later did he adapt the facts to fit his plots. In size of population and location Shifnal fits Market Blandings perfectly, and also solves the great railway mystery: how does one travel from London to Blandings?

All the arguments and discussions over the trains one catches from Paddington have omitted one factor – that Wodehouse himself travelled regularly from Shropshire to London. Stableford lies halfway between Bridgnorth and Shifnal and he could have travelled from either station. If he went from Bridgnorth he had to change trains, whereas from Shifnal there is a direct line – and this is a vital factor in the Blandings journeys.

In *Sunset at Blandings* Colonel Cobb set out a fascinating set of deductions to find Blandings, based on the times of the trains given in the novels. He concluded that Buildwas, some miles to the west, fitted the timing best. Although Buildwas fits on the times given, Colonel Cobb didn't know that Wodehouse *had* travelled from Stableford regularly and Shifnal gives the faster, direct, service to London.

Amongst the facts I discovered about the families in Somerset House was their habit of having clergymen relatives in strategic parts of England. A Wodehouse married the Rev. Mr Isaac of Hanley Castle and *his* brother was vicar of Albrighton. Albrighton lies between Stableford and Weston Park, and if you imagine the Wodehouses at Stableford would not have known their brother-in-law's brother, you have a very odd idea of family feeling among the Victorians. The vicar would have been the perfect sponsor to introduce the Wodehouses to Weston Park. It may sound rather like Jane

Austen but, as a Colonial Judge, Wodehouse's father certainly would have been on the visiting list of the great houses in the area. Wodehouse's youth was nearer to Jane Austen than it is to us and, remembering Wodehouse's own account of his visits to the local magnates, it seems impossible that he did *not* know Weston Park.

Another factor is that, despite the many arguments that Blandings lies west of the Severn, there has always been one strong hint that it lies to the east. Can any Wodehouse enthusiast forget the name of the local newspaper that recorded the triumphs of the Empress of Blandings? It is *The Bridgnorth, Shifnal and Albrighton Argus* and pulls Blandings well over to the east of the Severn and to the area of Weston Park.

Weston Park also solves – as nowhere else in twenty miles does – the problem of Blandings Parva. This is a small hamlet that Wodehouse described as standing at the gate of Blandings and it seems to vanish or appear according to the whim of the moment. At Weston Park the same thing happens to the village of Weston-under-Lizard.

Watling Street, the A5 trunk road, runs east–west along the northern edge of the Weston Park estate. The house is south of the road and the normal approach to it is through the park. If you are coming from Shifnal in the west, you drive along the A5, turn into the gates and drive through the park, parallel to the main road you have just left. This is the route described in the novels. But, if you want to, you can proceed further along the main road until you reach the village of Weston-under-Lizard and then turn sharp right and enter the estate from the back through the kitchen gardens. If you are a guest at Weston you might never see the village at all; it is behind the house, stables, etc. and you would have no reason to see it, since you would normally come to and leave Weston Park by the drive through the park. But, if you lived locally as Wodehouse did, you would know of the village and its relationship to the great house.

In *Leave It to Psmith* the house party goes off to 'Bridgeford' (Bridgnorth) to help Lord Emsworth unveil a statue. Miss Peavey returns by train to Blandings. If you lived at Weston Park, then you could make exactly the journey she made by travelling north on the branch line from Bridgnorth, changing and then coming to Shifnal.

The last reason is the best. We know that Wodehouse loved his time at Stableford. Within twenty miles of Stableford there is no estate with the same layout as Weston Park – and Weston Park fits every description we have of the Blandings estate and lies only seven miles from Wodehouse's home. It is Blandings, but only the estate. I still had a castle to find.

I drove south through Shropshire to Worcestershire, into Wales and back into England and Gloucestershire. I saw Quatford Castle, Arley Castle, the grandeur of Witley Court, Westwood House, Madresfield, Croome D'Abitot and the Gothic grandeur of Eastnor Castle, but none of them was Blandings. I went further south to see Thornbury Castle and Berkeley. Thornbury is a ruin now but I had high hopes of Berkeley. I knew that it dominated the countryside around, that it has been inhabited by the same family longer than any other castle in England, but it is not Blandings. I spent some time there convincing myself, but it fits in no particular.

After six hundred miles I was beginning to fear that my theories were wrong. I had visited Malvern and Hanley Castle and four other places in the west where relations of the Wodehouses had lived, and after Berkeley all I had left were a few houses in the Cotswolds and Sudeley Castle. I came back through Cheltenham to Toddington, a splendid Victorian edifice, now a school like so many of those I had looked at, and drove to Winchcombe to look at Sudeley Castle – and at Sudeley I found my castle.

It was the same feeling as I had at Weston Park. The impression of looking at something wrong became the realization that I was looking at the right thing the wrong way round. It was Blandings Castle but, like Ionicus, I had imagined the towers to be on the left. They aren't, they are on the right, because Sudeley is Blandings Castle as surely as Weston Park is the Blandings estate.

Sudeley Castle is now the home of the Dent-Brocklehursts

who bought it in 1837. The main structure was built in 1441, became the home of Katherine Parr and was visited by Queen Elizabeth I three times. It was a Royalist centre during the Civil War and fell into disuse till the Dent family bought and restored it in the nineteenth century.

Why is it Blandings? There are several reasons, although they are not as immediately apparent as those that apply to Weston Park.

How did Wodehouse know the area? Although I had looked at the childhood/boyhood period closely, which led me to concentrate on Cheney Court, Hanley Castle and Stableford, I had set my timescale when Wodehouse would have known Blandings between 1887 and 1906. In 1902 Wodehouse's parents moved from Stableford to Cheltenham, and we know Wodehouse visited them there because he got the name Jeeves while watching a Warwickshire cricketer of that name play at Cheltenham before the First War. Indeed Cheltenham could properly be considered his home during that period. He may have had digs in London and spent much of his time with the King-Halls at Emsworth, but any twenty-one-year-old will normally assume that 'home' is his parents' house. Cheltenham is only five miles away – we have propinquity at least.

Secondly, I have always been puzzled by the description of Dreever Castle in *A Gentleman of Leisure*. This, to my mind, was the original Blandings Castle and like Blandings it is set in Shropshire. As Jimmy Pitt and Molly McEachern walk towards it, they reach a point when they look down the hill towards the castle. That's unusual – normally you look up at a castle, not down on it. They were normally built on high ground for defence. There are few where you can look down on them, and Sudeley is one.

The shape of the castle is unusual. Those towers that are such a feature (see Plate 14), how many castles in this part of England have them? Most have the strong round towers or follow the old pattern of a single strong keep surrounded by a curtain wall with towers along it. Sudeley was built in 1441 (which is the period Wodehouse gives us for Blandings) and this is late in the castle era; the Lancastrians kept a very close eye on their possible rivals, and licences to fortify were issued sparingly. Sudeley was built late and this probably accounts for its unusual shape. Is there any other 'quadrangular' castle with square towers nestling beneath a hill as Sudeley does?

We read often of the castle being in 'the Vale of Blandings'. In one novel it stands firmly 'at the south end of the Vale'. You don't find 'Vales' in Shropshire. They occur further south in Gloucestershire and Worcestershire – around Sudeley. Sudeley stands at the south end of the Vale of Evesham and nearby are the Vale of Berkeley, the Vale of Gloucester, the Vale of the White Horse and the Vale of Pewsey. They are all to be found where the Cotswolds run down to the west and are a clear indication that at least one source for Blandings came from well south of Shropshire.

The nearness of Sudeley to Cheltenham also solves the other half of the great railway question. We saw how Shifnal and Weston Park met the need to travel from London to Blandings without changing trains – which the other route up the Severn Valley does not do. The second mystery has always been that in two books the first stop from London is Swindon, while in other books it is Oxford. These statements are incompatible on the Blandings-must-be-in-Shropshire theory, but they fit very well indeed if, as Wodehouse said, Blandings was a mixture of places he remembered. It is Oxford and the northern line for Wodehouse's real journeys to Stableford (and Weston Park/ Blandings). It is Swindon and the southern route for his visits to his parents at Cheltenham and Sudeley/Blandings.

It is possible that Wodehouse knew Sudeley before his parents moved to Cheltenham; he might have known it when he stayed with the Isaacs at Hanley Castle. Sudeley and Hanley Castle are in two different counties, but it's less than fifteen miles between them across the valley.

The final clue took a long time to find. The castle is the right shape and the right size, the 'Vale' pulled Blandings south of Shropshire in the same way that the *Bridgnorth, Shifnal and Albrighton Argus* pulled it east of the Severn. The railway puzzle is solved by Sudeley but we need something else. At the back of my mind was the memory of a name that didn't fit, a vital Wodehouse 'slip'. I found it eventually in the second Blandings book, *Leave It to Psmith* (1923), where Joe Keeble tries to persuade Lady Constance to keep her necklace in the bank:

> 'Well you know, there's no sense in taking risks.'
> 'Don't be absurd. What risks can there be?'
> 'There was a burglary over at Winstone Court, not ten miles from here, only a day or so ago.'

There's only one place called Winstone in England and Joe Keeble was right. It's not ten miles from Sudeley/Blandings; it's nine and a half miles. In case Wodehouse's finger slipped on his typewriter, I checked Winson – and that's only ten miles from Sudeley as well.

The annoying thing is that once I found them they were obvious – for the most prosaic of reasons. When Wodehouse went to Dulwich, Cheney Court, Wiltshire was his address (with the grandmother and aunts). When his father returned to England and they went to live at Stableford, then Shropshire became his home and from 1902 his home was Cheltenham. In each case, the Blandings source – Corsham Court, Weston Park and Sudeley – was the nearest 'big house'. We know he went to Corsham Court to skate on the lake, it is more than probable that he visited Weston Park in his brother's wake, and Sudeley is a pleasant afternoon's walk from Cheltenham if you are a keen walker as Wodehouse was.

Somewhere there should be another Blandings to provide us with the interior. Where is the slippery oak staircase? Where is the famous gallery? The staircase with that vital bend in it could well be a childhood memory of Cheney Court, which has just such a staircase for Wodehouse and his brothers to fight their way up and down. Hunstanton had a similar staircase and a well-known collection of pictures and curiosities, but Wodehouse didn't go to Hunstanton till after two Blandings novels had been written. Perhaps somewhere there is another house hiding its secrets, but Blandings is exactly what Wodehouse said it was – a mixture of places he remembered.

The three great houses, Corsham, Weston Park and Sudeley, still stand as impressive and as beautiful as when he knew them. Their claims to be Blandings are obvious and prosaic, once we found them. Weston Park and Sudeley fit every description of Blandings we are given, and if you superimpose Sudeley Castle on the Weston estate, you get a copy of the sketch by Ionicus.

That's no proof in itself. The proof is that at Weston and Sudeley I found Blandings when I didn't expect to. They were unexpected but they were obvious. They are the heart of the Wodehouse world – they made Blandings.

EPILOGUE

❦

THERE was a time when people behaved as Wodehouse drew them, there were people who acted as Ukridge did. There was a time when every peer of the realm seemed to be marrying chorus-girls or Americans (there were at least three American wives in the stately homes around Stableford when Wodehouse lived there). He knew the time and the people and preserved them for us in dozens of delightful books. It was the high summer of Edwardian England and it was a pleasant time for more people than social historians would have us believe.

There are still many gaps. Somewhere on the Thames above Reading is a house Wodehouse knew and used often in his novels. Somewhere in England there are people who knew him and who heard brave tales of rejection slips, of Covent Garden Balls and of borrowed frock-coats for those formal calls on aunts in South Kensington. During the course of my writing this book both Perceval Graves and Guy Bolton have died, each with memories of those distant days. They enjoyed their youth in a happier, sunny world and Wodehouse knew it too and drew it for us.

We can still walk down Croxted Road in Dulwich, go through the little gate under the railway bridge and watch the Dulwich team doing their stuff. We can still walk through the woods above Emsworth and admire the grace of Stansted House. If you follow the trail I did, try and end it at Weston Park. This, if anywhere, is the centre of the world Wodehouse drew – the smiling beautiful countryside he loved so much and called Blandings.

APPENDIX

❧❦

The Oldest Member's Home Course

Walter S. White

THOUGH disguised by many aliases and transatlantic crossings, the Oldest Member's home course had a real existence at the Sound View Golf Club in Great Neck, Long Island, New York. In his *P. G. Wodehouse: Portrait Of A Master* David A. Jasen quotes Wodehouse, 'That's the place where I wrote about the Oldest Member and all my golfing stories.' Wodehouse played at Sound View from 1918 to 1921 and probably, on occasion, later, but 'all' presumably means the 20 stories in *The Clicking Of Cuthbert* and *The Heart Of A Goof*, as he sold his house in Great Neck in 1921. The course disappeared in the late 1940s, taken over by developers, as noted in 'Life With Freddie' in *Plum Pie*.

The course cannot be reconstructed from the stories alone because there are too many gaps and inconsistencies. But a search carried on, intermittently, over many months provided the tools for such a reconstruction. Completed, it shows the extent to which Wodehouse followed a line of least resistance by simply describing real golf holes at Sound View when he needed backdrops for his stories, thus fully supporting the thesis that Norman Murphy has so convincingly presented in his *In Search of Blandings*. Furthermore, by providing a basis for comparison, this reconstruction also lets one recognize

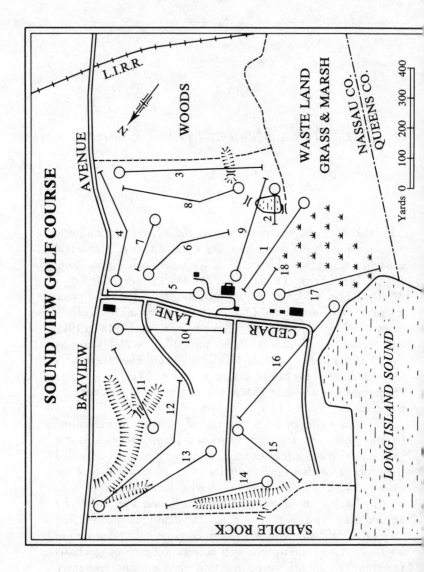

SOUND VIEW GOLF COURSE

Wodehouse's stagecraft when he invents a variation to suit a plot or enhance the drama of some action.

The clubhouse and boundaries of part of the course are shown on two old maps reprinted in a 1975 pamphlet entitled *This Is Great Neck*, which also contains a photograph of the clubhouse, unfortunately the side opposite from the Oldest Member's terrace. The topography and cultural features of the area are shown on the US Geological Survey map (2,000'/inch) of the Sea Cliff quadrangle. A Long Island collector of golf memorabilia kindly gave me a photocopy of a pre-1931 scorecard. (The name of the course was changed in 1931.) It lists the yardages for all the holes. Finally I was fortunate in locating Joseph DeMane, who had caddied and played at Sound View from 1929 to 1942. His enthusiasm in sharing his detailed recollections of the course has been a delight as well as a tremendous help.

The account presented here has a map compiled by fitting holes of the lengths given by the score card to the topographic and cultural features of the area, using the general layout and supplementary descriptions provided by Joseph DeMane. Before I had the latter in hand I had only been able to plot five holes correctly using the stories alone. As it turns out, the layout and hole lengths are such that one has very little leeway to vary the placement of holes, so the map should be more than adequate for literary research.

The capsule descriptions of the holes include distances and pars from the score card, lay of the land from the topographic map, and special features of the holes from Joseph DeMane.

Brief descriptions of the holes at Sound View Golf Course:
No. 1.   355 yds, par 4. Down hill to island green in marsh. (This island green does not figure in any of the stories, and it may represent a post-Wodehouse lengthening of the hole.)
No. 2.   130 yds, par 3. The Lake Hole needs no introduction.
No. 3.   485 yds, par 5. Up hill, blind second shot over brow. Gully 50–100 yards from tee, crossed by footbridge.

No. 4. 385 yds, par 4. Dogleg right, following curve of Bayview Avenue. Bunkers across fairway near bend.

No. 5. 310 yds, par 4.

No. 6. Also 310 yds, par 4. Dogleg left around trees. Drive downhill, then up to elevated green. No bunker on left at bend.

No. 7. 175 yds, par 3. Elevated green, deep trap in front.

No. 8. 415 yds, par 4. Down hill, then up. No traps.

No. 9. 338 yds, par 4. Drive over pond, then up hill to elevated green just below clubhouse terrace. Footbridge on path around pond.

No. 10. 367 yds, par 4. Up over brow of hill.

No. 11. 307 yds, par 4. Gully across fairway near a green that has bunkers to right and front.

No. 12. 525 yds, par 5. Dogleg right, gully in front of green.

No. 13. 356 yds, par 4. Up hill, blind second shot. Bunkers across fairway.

No. 14. 376 yds, par 4. Down hill. Fairway sloped to right into gully.

No. 15. 277 yds, par 4. Up hill to elevated green.

No. 16. 490 yds, par 5. Slight downhill. Dropoff to bay, right of green.

No. 17. 344 yds, par 4. Drive over marsh, then up hill.

No. 18. 105 yds, par 3. Straight up hill. Very undulating green. Trap across front, another behind.

The order of the holes in the 1930s, when Joseph DeMane played, is the same as that on the score card, but the first and second nines are interchanged compared with their order in almost all the golf stories (early 1920s). The second hole of the stories, the celebrated Lake Hole, is the 11th hole of the 1930s, and so forth. I have numbered the holes so that they show the sequence of the stories (Order A) rather than the sequence as it was in the 1930s (Order B).

On at least four occasions, the Oldest Member refers to changes made between the time a story took place and the time of his narration, but these asides are not consistent with one another and appear to be mere corroborative detail. Only in 'Excelsior' (1948 – dates after titles are of the first magazine publication as given in Jasen's *Portrait*) does the interchange of the 9th and 18th holes follow the sequence of Order A to Order B. In 'The Magic Plus Fours' (1922), 'There's Always Golf' (1936) and 'Rodney Has A Relapse' (1949) the change is in the opposite direction, from Order B to Order A. Wodehouse may well have been aware of the change in the mid or late 1920s, but though he did use the later sequence, Order B, in some of the later stories ('Scratch Man', 1940; 'Tangled Hearts', 1948) he used the earlier sequence in others ('Letter Of The Law', 1936) as well as 'There's Always Golf' and 'Rodney Has A Relapse', just mentioned.

Individuals familiar with the golf stories will find many old friends here: the immortal short second; the Lake Hole (the lake can be visited today in Pond Park, a small private park); the long third up over the brow of the hill; the dogleg fourth and twelfth (the former with its bunkers across the fairway); the fourteenth, the Ravine Hole. One can easily follow the unscrupulous Bingham's shot from the first tee to the 17th fairway en route to his boat by the 16th green as he sets out on 'The Long Hole'. The waste land beyond the first green, traversed by Jukes, is still there. (The rest of their routes to Times Square can be followed just as easily as all the place names in the US version of the story, unlike those in the UK version, are real and come in proper sequence.) Ravines (gullies) that spell disaster in so many of the stories are all present and accounted for, as are the footbridges, though the only place where a bridge remains today is over the outlet of the lake, where Harold Pickering dunked Sidney McMurdo in 'Scratch Man'.

More interesting, in some ways, than the features that Wodehouse described faithfully from originals in their proper places at Sound View, are others that he changed for the purposes of some of the stories, changes that can now be identified. This scene-shifting occurs most commonly at the hole where the story ends. 'The Magic Plus Fours', 'Scratch Man', and 'Tangled Hearts' all end at the lake, moved to the second nine to make room for nine or more holes before the climax. (Wodehouse obtained the same result in 'Rough Stuff' without altering the course by having the round start at the tenth hole.) Where the plot calls for an eighteenth fairway long enough for some mayhem ('Chester Forgets Himself' and 'There's Always Golf') or a slosh at the tee much too powerful to be appropriate for a short par-3 ('Farewell To Legs'), the 18th becomes a par-4. In 'Rodney Fails To Qualify', Wodehouse keeps the essential features of the par-3 seventh, but sets the stage for his watery finish by piping in a river to surround the green. Another invented prop is the Sahara-like bunker on the left of the fairway around the bend of the sixth hole, where the Oldest Member suggested William Bates might propose to Jane. Norman Murphy speculates that Wodehouse's inspiration for this bunker may have been an enormous one that is on the sixth hole at Addington, where Wodehouse datelined his preface to 'The Heart Of A Goof'; like the sixth at Sound View, it is a dogleg left, though the bunker is on the right.

Some features that do not fit Sound View do not appear to have been altered to satisfy the needs of a plot or action. Two concrete examples from stories clearly based, overall, on Sound View may be mentioned. 'Chester Forgets Himself' (1923) contains the only complete hole-by-hole log for 18 holes. ('Ordeal By Golf' 1919, which describes eleven holes, all of which fit Sound View, is a close second in completeness.) All but the last three holes of 'Chester' fit the pre-1931 score card. In the story these have pars of 4, 3 and 4 respectively and par for the course is 71. On the score card pars for these holes are 5, 4 and 3, and par for the course is 72. The 17th hole as shown on the map is so perfectly placed for Bingham's drive in 'The Long Hole' (1921) that the 1930s position is almost certainly correct for Wodehouse's day as well. As suggested earlier, the climax of 'Chester' requires a par-4 18th hole, so it looks as though Wodehouse simply interchanged the pars on the last two holes without worrying about their placement. This does not explain why the par-5 16th of the card is a par-4 in the story. Possibly the hole really was lengthened sometime in the late 1920s but, if not, there is no ready explanation for a shortening; the length does not affect the plot.

'The Letter Of The Law' provides a second example of

enigmatic departures from the Sound View model. Five of the eight holes described in the story fit Sound View, but three do not: the 12th hole of the story is a par-4 (drive plus mashie shot), the 376-yard 14th is called 'short' and the 277-yard 15th is twice called 'long'. Perhaps by 1936 some of the details of the course were fading in Wodehouse's mind and he was simply improvising; the intangibleness of 'short' and 'long' rather supports this interpretation.

Of the 31 stories in *The Golf Omnibus* six say nothing about individual golf holes. In 18 stories the golf holes that are depicted generally fit the Sound View course, though the quality of the fit varies from story to story. All eleven holes described in 'Ordeal By Golf' fit, as do 15 of the 18 in 'Chester Forgets Himself', whereas in three, 'Keeping In With Vosper', 'Scratch Man' and 'Tangled Hearts', the only tie is the Lake Hole. The seven remaining stories do not fit Sound View: 'Sundered Hearts', 'The Clicking Of Cuthbert', 'The Heel of Achilles', 'High Stakes', 'Farewell To Legs', 'Feet Of Clay' and 'Sleepy Time'. In most of these only one or two holes are mentioned, not enough even to suggest, much less pinpoint, some other course. 'High Stakes' (1925) touches on six holes and, with a bit of stretching, the specifications could fit the East Course of the Maidstone Club at East Hampton, Long Island, where Wodehouse summered in 1923. Whether or not the remaining stories have wholly fanciful settings would be difficult to prove, considering the number of courses Wodehouse must have played in the wanderings of his golfing years. Perhaps the sharp dropoff, after 1927, in both the frequency of the golf stories and the Oldest Member's attention to detail occurred because the Sound View Course lost its immediacy as it receded from Wodehouse's present into his past.

A WODEHOUSE CHRONOLOGY

Date of USA publication and title, where different, given in square brackets. Dates for short stories and articles refer to first appearance in a book.

1881   Born No. 1, Vale Place, Epsom Rd, Guildford, Surrey. Accompanies parents to Hong Kong.

1883   Placed in charge of Miss Roper in Bath along with his two brothers.

1886   Parents return to England for the Great Exposition. Wodehouse and brothers sent to Dame School in Croydon, Surrey, run by the Misses Prince. (Holidays for next nine years spent with relatives in Devon, Worcestershire and Wiltshire.)

1889   Three brothers sent to Elizabeth College, Guernsey.

1891   Eldest brother Peveril stays at Elizabeth College, Armine sent to Dulwich, Pelham sent to Malvern House, Kearnsey, Kent.

1894   Wodehouse joins Armine at Dulwich.

1895   Wodehouse parents return from Hong Kong and take a house – No. 62, Croxted Road, Dulwich. At end of year Wodehouse parents move to Stableford in Shropshire.

1899   Wodehouse in First XI, First XV and co-editor of *The Alleynian*. Wodehouse leaves Dulwich and joins Hong Kong and Shanghai Bank. Has lodgings in Markham Square, Chelsea. First article published in Feb. 1900 in

Public School Magazine.

1902   Moves to Walpole Street, Chelsea. Leaves the Bank and joins *The Globe* as member of 'By the Way' column. *The Pothunters* published.

1903   Meets Herbert Westbrook. Stays at Emsworth House School in Hampshire. Pub. A *Prefect's Uncle* and *Tales of St Austin's*.

1904   Rents Threepwood in Emsworth. Visits New York. Pub. *The Gold Bat* and *William Tell Told Again*. Writes lyrics for musical *Sergeant Brue*.

1905   First article published in *The Strand*. Pub. *The Head of Kay's*.

1906   Writes lyrics for *The Beauty of Bath* for Seymour Hicks. Pub. *Love among the Chickens*, first adult novel [USA 1909].

1907   Takes flat in London. Pub. *The White Feather* and *Not George Washington* in conjunction with Westbrook. Writes lyrics for *The Gay Gordons* and *The Bandit's Daughter*. Engaged to write lyrics for the Gaiety Theatre.

1908   Pub. *The Globe By the Way Book*. Shares flat in London with Westbrook. Writes 'The Luck Stone' with Bill Townend for *Chums*.

1909   Pub. *The Swoop* and *Mike* (introducing Psmith). Goes to New York and stays at Hotel Earle.

1910   Returns to England. Buys Threepwood at Emsworth. Pub. *A Gentleman of Leisure* [USA *The Intrusion of Jimmy* 1910] and *Psmith in the City*.

1911   Living at Threepwood and visits New York twice. Writes two plays, *A Gentleman of Leisure* and *After the Show*.

1912   Pub. *The Prince and Betty*. [USA *The Prince and Betty* published earlier in the year and some characters extracted to use in the UK version. Remaining characters and plot used in *Psmith Journalist*.]

1913   Pub. *The Little Nugget* [USA 1914] and the play *Brother Alfred*. Sells Threepwood. Moves to 94 Prince of Wales Mansions, Battersea. Visits New York.

1914   Writes lyrics for *Nuts and Wine*. Joins *Vanity Fair* magazine in New York. Marries and moves to Bellport, Long Island. Pub. *The Man Upstairs*.

1915   Pub. *Something Fresh* (first Blandings novel) [USA *Something New 1915*]. Meets Guy Bolton in December and joins him and Jerome Kern as musical comedy team.

1916   Writes lyrics for *Pom Pom* and *Miss Springtime*. Lives in New York in winter, moving out to Long Island for the summer.

1917   Pub. *Uneasy Money* [USA 1916] and *The Man with Two Left Feet* [USA 1933]. Continues writing lyrics for musicals, Bolton writing the book and Kern the music. Involved in rehearsals and pre-New York tryouts up and down East Coast. Bolton and Wodehouse produce book and lyrics for six New York shows in ten months: *Have a Heart, Oh Boy!, Leave It to Jane, Kitty Darlin', The Riviera Girl* and *Miss 1917*.

1918   Pub. *Piccadilly Jim* [USA 1917]. Writes lyrics for *Oh Lady! Lady!, See You Later, The Girl behind the Gun, The Canary* and *Oh, My Dear!*. Moves to Great Neck, Long Island. Visits Palm Beach. To London, rents 16 Walton St.

1919   Back to New York. Pub. *My Man Jeeves, A Damsel in Distress* [USA 1919]. Lyrics for *The Rose of China*. Back to Walton St, London, returns to New York.

1920   Pub. *The Coming of Bill* [USA *Their Mutual Child* 1919]. Lyrics for *Sally*. Back to England, to London and Felixstowe.

1921   Pub. *Jill the Reckless* [USA *The Little Warrior* 1920] and *Indiscretions of Archie* [USA 1921]. Lyrics for *The Blue Mazurka* and *The Golden Moth*. To New York, back to England, stays with King-Hall at Emsworth, then to King St, St James's, London.

1922   Pub. *The Clicking of Cuthbert* [USA *Golf without Tears* 1924] *The Girl on the Boat* [USA *Three Men and a Maid* 1922] and *The Adventures of Sally* [USA

Mostly Sally 1923]. To New York with George Grossmith, to Palm Beach, to New York, back to England to 4 Onslow Square. To Dinard. Lyrics for *Pat (The Gibson Girl)* and *The Cabaret Girl.*

1923   Pub. *The Inimitable Jeeves* [USA *Jeeves* 1923] and *Leave It to Psmith* [USA 1924]. Lyrics for *The Beauty Prize* with George Grossmith. Living at Southampton and East Hampton, Long Island. To London, King Street, and back to New York.

1924   Pub. *Ukridge* [USA *He Rather Enjoyed It* 1926] and *Bill The Conqueror* [USA 1925]. Lyrics for *Sitting Pretty.* Living at Great Neck, New York. To Paris, to Harrogate, takes 23 Gilbert St, Mayfair.

1925   Pub. *Carry On, Jeeves* [USA 1927] and *Sam The Sudden* [USA *Sam In the Suburbs* 1925]. Still at 23 Gilbert Street, then to New York.

1926   Pub. *The Heart of a Goof* [USA *Divots* 1927]. Book and lyrics for *Hearts and Diamonds* and *Oh, Kay!* and script for *The Play's The Thing.* To London, to Hunstanton and New York.

1927   Pub. *The Small Bachelor* [USA 1927] and *Meet Mr Mulliner* [USA 1928]. From New York to London, to Droitwich, rents 17 Norfolk St, Mayfair. To Droitwich again, to Hunstanton, to New York. Script for *Her Cardboard Lover* and *Good Morning, Bill.* Book and lyrics for *The Nightingale* and the lyric for 'Bill' in *Showboat.*

1928   Pub. *Money For Nothing* [USA 1928]. Lyrics for *Rosalie* and *The Three Musketeers.* Script for *A Damsel in Distress* with Ian Hay. Leaves New York for London, to Droitwich, to Norfolk St, London, takes Rogate Lodge in Sussex, to Droitwich to Château Impney Hotel, to Scotland with Ian Hay.

1929   Pub. *Mr Mulliner Speaking* [USA 1930] and *Summer Lightning* [USA *Fish Preferred* 1939]. Script for *Candlelight.* Script for *Baa Baa Black Sheep* with Ian Hay. Living at Norfolk St, visits Southsea, to Hunstanton for Christmas.

1930   Pub. *Very Good, Jeeves* [USA 1930]. Script for *Leave It to Psmith* with Ian Hay. Leaves London for Hollywood.

1931   Pub. *Big Money* [USA 1931] and *If I Were You* [USA 1931]. Leaves Hollywood for London (mews flat).

1932   Pub. *Louder and Funnier, Doctor Sally* and *Hot Water* [USA 1932]. To Auribeau, Alpes-Maritime, S. France. Visits London in December for marriage of his step-daughter Leonora to Peter Cazalet.

1933   Pub. *Mulliner Nights* [USA 1933] and *Heavy Weather* [USA 1933]. From France to Norfolk St, London, to Hunstanton for the summer.

1934   Pub. *Thank You, Jeeves* [USA 1934] and *Right Ho, Jeeves* [USA *Brinkley Manor* 1934]. Norfolk St to Cannes, to London – Seamore Close and The Dorchester. To Paris and Le Touquet.

1935   Pub. *Blandings Castle* [USA 1935] and *The Luck of the Bodkins* [USA 1936]. Script for *The Inside Stand*. Living at Low Wood, Le Touquet.

1936   Pub. *Young Men in Spats* [USA 1936] and *Laughing Gas* [USA 1936]. To Hollywood for a second time.

1937   Pub. *Lord Emsworth and Others* [USA *Crime Wave at Blandings* 1937]. From Hollywood to Le Touquet.

1938   Pub. *Summer Moonshine* [USA 1937] and *The Code of the Woosters* [USA 1938]. Mainly at Le Touquet, visits London, Norfolk St.

1939   Pub. *Uncle Fred in the Springtime* [USA 1939] Living at Le Touquet. Presented with D. Litt. by Oxford University.

1940   Pub. *Eggs, Beans and Crumpets* [USA 1940] and *Quick Service* [USA 1940]. Interned by Germans.

1941   Wodehouse released under Geneva Convention agreements for civilian internees when aged 60. At request of American broadcasting company, broadcasts to America describing his internment. Broadcasts satirical of German military camp procedures, but Germans realize tremendous propaganda advantage and allow broadcasts to continue. Against written protests of

BBC, British Government launches official attack against Wodehouse for 'broadcasting for the Germans'.

1942   Wodehouse allowed to stay in hotels in Berlin but not allowed to leave the country.

1943   Wodehouse allowed to leave for Paris.

1944   Wodehouse learns of reaction to his broadcasts, and asks that an inquiry be made by British Government. Home Office send investigator who concludes eventually that no offence has been committed. Despite this, Wodehouse is advised that feeling is against him and that he should not return to England for the time being. Stepdaughter Leonora dies in England.

1945   Moves from Paris to Barbizon.

1946   Pub. *Money in the Bank* [USA 1942].

1947   Pub. *Joy in the Morning* [USA 1946] and *Full Moon* [USA 1946]. Scripts for *Arthur* and *Game of Hearts* with his old friend Guy Bolton. Moves to New York.

1948   Pub. *Spring Fever* [USA 1948] and *Uncle Dynamite* [USA 1948]. Script for *Don't Listen Ladies* with Guy Bolton.

1949   Pub. *The Mating Season* [USA 1949]. Still living in New York.

1950   Pub. *Nothing Serious* [USA 1951] and writes script for *House on the Cliff*. Tours with the company.

1951   Pub. *The Old Reliable* [USA 1951] and writes script for *Kilroy Was Here*.

1952   Pub. *Barmy in Wonderland* [USA *Angel Cake* 1952] and *Pigs Have Wings* [USA 1952]. Moves to Remsenburg, Long Island.

1953   Pub. *Ring For Jeeves* [USA *The Return of Jeeves* 1954] and *Performing Flea* [USA *Author! Author!* 1962].

1954   Pub. *Bring On the Girls* [USA 1953] and *Jeeves and the Feudal Spirit* [USA *Bertie Wooster Sees It Through* 1955]. Script for *Come On, Jeeves* with Guy Bolton.

1956   Pub. *French Leave* [USA 1959].

1957   Pub. *Over Seventy* [USA *America, I Like You* 1956] and *Something Fishy* [USA *The Butler Did It* 1957].

1958   Pub. *Cocktail Time* [USA 1958].
1959   Pub. *A Few Quick Ones* [USA 1959].
1960   Pub. *Jeeves in the Offing* [USA *How Right You Are, Jeeves* 1960].
1961   Pub. *Ice in the Bedroom* [USA *The Ice in the Bedroom* 1961].
1962   Pub. *Service with a Smile* [USA 1961].
1963   Pub. *Stiff Upper Lip, Jeeves* [USA 1963].
1964   Pub. *Frozen Assets* [USA *Biffen's Millions* 1964].
1965   Pub. *Galahad at Blandings* [USA *The Brinkmanship of Galahad Threepwood* 1965].
1966   Pub. *Plum Pie* [USA 1967].
1967   Pub. *Company for Henry* [USA *The Purloined Paperweight* 1967].
1968   Pub. *Do Butlers Burgle Banks?* [USA 1968].
1969   Pub. *A Pelican at Blandings* [USA *No Nudes is Good Nudes* 1970].
1970   Pub. *The Girl in Blue* [USA 1971].
1971   Pub. *Much Obliged, Jeeves* [USA *Jeeves and the Tie that Binds* 1971].
1972   Pub. *Pearls, Girls and Monty Bodkin* [USA *The Plot That Thickened* 1973].
1973   Pub. *Bachelors Anonymous* [USA 1974].
1974   Pub. *Aunts Aren't Gentlemen* [USA *The Catnappers* 1975].
1975   Died, leaving first draft *Sunset at Blandings*, pub. 1977.

BIBLIOGRAPHY

Binstead, A. M. ('Pitcher'), *Pitcher in Paradise*, Sands & Co., 1903.

Binstead, A. M., and Wells, E., *A Pink'Un and A Pelican*, Sands & Co., 1898.

Booth, J. B., *'Master' and Men*, Werner Laurie, 1927. *Old Pink'Un Days*, Richards Press, 1924. *Palmy Days*, Richards Press, 1951. *Pink Parade*, Thornton Butterworth, 1933. *Sporting Times*, Werner Laurie, 1938.

Boyd, F. M., *A Pelican's Tale*, Herbert Jenkins, 1919.

Burke's Peerage, Baronetage and Knightage, 1911.

Cazalet-Keir T., (Ed.), *Homage to P. G. Wodehouse*, Barrie & Jenkins, 1973.

Cecil, Lord D., *Early Victorian Novelists*, Constable & Co., 1957.

Cochran, C. B., *Showman Looks On*, Dent, 1945.

Deghy, G., *Paradise in The Strand*, Richards Press, 1958.

Edwards, O. D., *P. G. Wodehouse*, Martin Brian & O'Keefe, 1977.

French, R. B. D., *P. G. Wodehouse*, Oliver & Boyd, 1966.

Graves, C., *The Bad Old Days*, Faber & Faber, 1951.

Hall, R. A., *The Comic Style of P. G. Wodehouse*, Archon Books, 1974.

Jaggard, G., *Blandings The Blest*, Macdonald & Co., 1968. *Wooster's World*, Macdonald & Co., 1967.

Jasen, D., *A Bibliography and Reader's Guide to the First Editions of P. G. Wodehouse*, Barrie & Jenkins, 1971.

Jasen, D., *P. G. Wodehouse: A Portrait of a Master*, Garnstone Press, 1975.

Mackail, D., *Life with Topsy*, Heinemann, 1942.

Nichols, B., *Are They the Same At Home?*, Cape, 1933.

Pain, B., *Humorous Stories*, Werner Laurie, 1930.

Sutherland, D., *The Yellow Earl*, Cassell, 1965.

Usborne, R., *Wodehouse at Work*, Herbert Jenkins, 1961.
Wodehouse at Work to the End, Barrie & Jenkins, 1976.

Wells, E., *Chestnuts by Swears*, Sands & Co., 1903.

Wind, H. W., *The World of P. G. Wodehouse*, Hutchinson, 1981.

INDEX

251

INDEX

INDEX

INDEX

254

INDEX

INDEX

INDEX